English nationalism, Brexit and the Anglosphere

MANCHESTER
1824

Manchester University Press

New Perspectives on the Right

Series editor
Richard Hayton

The study of conservative politics, broadly defined, is of enduring scholarly interest and importance, and is also of great significance beyond the academy. In spite of this, for a variety of reasons the study of conservatism and conservative politics was traditionally regarded as something of a poor relation in comparison to the intellectual interest in 'the Left'. In the British context this changed with the emergence of Thatcherism, which prompted a greater critical focus on the Conservative Party and its ideology, and a revitalisation of Conservative historiography. *New Perspectives on the Right* aims to build on this legacy by establishing a series identity for work in this field. It will publish the best and most innovative titles drawn from the fields of sociology, history, cultural studies and political science and hopes to stimulate debate and interest across disciplinary boundaries. *New Perspectives* is not limited in its historical coverage or geographical scope, but is united by its concern to critically interrogate and better understand the history, development, intellectual basis and impact of the Right. Nor is the series restricted by its methodological approach: it will encourage original research from a plurality of perspectives. Consequently, the series will act as a voice and forum for work by scholars engaging with the politics of the right in new and imaginative ways.

Reconstructing conservatism? The Conservative Party in opposition, 1997–2010
Richard Hayton

Conservative orators: From Baldwin to Cameron
Edited by Richard Hayton and Andrew S. Crines

The right and the recession
Edward Ashbee

The territorial Conservative Party: Devolution and party change in Scotland and Wales
Alan Convery

David Cameron and Conservative renewal: The limits of modernisation?
Edited by Gillian Peele and John Francis

Rethinking right-wing women: Gender and the Conservative Party, 1880s to the present
Edited by Clarisse Berthezène and Julie Gottlieb

English nationalism, Brexit and the Anglosphere

Wider still and wider

Ben Wellings

Manchester University Press

Published by Manchester University Press
Altrincham Street, Manchester M1 7JA
www.manchesteruniversitypress.co.uk

British Library Cataloguing-in-Publication Data
A catalogue record for this book is available from the British Library

ISBN   978 1 5261 1772 4   hardback
ISBN   978 1 5261 1773 1   paperback

First published 2019

Typeset by Newgen Publishing UK
Printed in Great Britain
by TJ International Ltd, Padstow

To my father and my father-in-law

Contents

Acknowledgements

I can honestly say that this book was a pleasure to write. It had its origins in an honours course on English nationalism and Euroscepticism back in 2011. I am grateful to Helen Baxendale (now a Rhodes Scholar at Oxford University) for introducing me to the topic of the Anglosphere through her well-informed essay on this topic. Thanks also go to Oliver Hartwich at the New Zealand Initiative. Oliver's invitation to debate Daniel Hannan in Auckland in 2012 was another important boost to my interest in this topic and its links with Euroscepticism.

The invitation from Pauline Schnapper and Mark Bevir to present a paper at the Centre of British Studies at the University of California, Berkeley in 2013 gave the idea behind this book further impetus. Ontario provided the next setting for a further elaboration of the arguments in this book in 2014, so my thanks go to the 'Toronto Three': Arthur Aughey, Michael Kenny and Krishan Kumar. The 'Huddersfield Two' – Chris Gifford and Andy Mycock – also played significant roles in helping me think about the relationship between English nationalism, Euroscepticism and the Anglosphere. So too did leading lights of the 'M4 School' of Euroscepticism studies, Ben Leruth, Nick Startin and Simon Usherwood, along with those French Anglophiles, Karine Tounier-Sol and Angès Alexandre-Collier and the English Francophile, Matthew Graves. Anglosphericals, notably Andrew Gamble, Srdjan Vucetic and Kathy Smits have also been supportive and collegial at crucial moments, whilst the Future of England Survey researchers' findings have been appreciated from afar.

I began writing this book in earnest in July 2016 and a period of research leave in the first half of 2018 was crucial in helping it to see the broad, sunlit uplands of publication. Colleagues at Monash University have been both encouraging and supportive of this research topic and indeed of my employment at Monash after July 2013. Thanks go to Tom Chodor, Alice Davies, Natalie Doyle, Nick Economou, Sherin Fernando, Rae Frances, Tommy Fung, Zareh Ghazarian, Peter Howard, Julie Kalman, Katrina Lee-Koo, Pete Lentini, Ben MacQueen, Paul Muldoon, Narelle Marigliotta, Roseanne Misajon, Marko Pavlyshyn, Swati Parashar, Maria Rost Rublee, Paul Strangio, Jacqui True and Pascaline Winand. I am very glad to count former ANU colleagues as continuing colleagues: Annmarie Elijah, John Hart, Kim Huynh, Helen Keane, Jacquie Lo, Maria Maley, Daniel Stoljar, Emma Vines, Ryan Walter, David West, as well as Bruce Wilson at RMIT University. Richard Hayton has been hugely supportive of this topic throughout.

Friends are just as important as colleagues when writing a book. The World Cup WhatsApp chat group of Paul, Ivan and Keith helped me feel connected to England when progression from the group stages threatened to turn the world upside down. Research trips to England would not be the same without the deep understanding of the English psyche provided by Kirk, Claire and Claire, Simon and other patrons of the Five Bells o' Stanbridge, a great pub located at that crossroads of history, south-west Bedfordshire. Tim and Kim were great Victory companions, along with Uma and David; and one day I will get down the front for a Jim Drury and the Renegades gig. Nausica and Iury – two English-speaking people doing their bit to uphold the current world order from Lecce – and Jean-Charles and Sarah doing the same in different ways from Brussels, helped keep my optimistic European spirit of the 1990s alive.

Imogen and Paul got married in 2015 and my nephew Alex came, like Global Britain, into the world a year later. Thanks go to Rini and Ray in Vancouver for introducing me to the Canadian version of 1812. My mother, Joyce, and mother-in-law, Esther, and my dad's partner, Sue, have been incredibly supportive in different ways since I have known them. This book straddled a move from Canberra to 'Marvellous Melbourne' for Shanti, Adi and Ria: it has been an absolute pleasure to see how Shanti's career has flourished and how Adi and Ria have thrived in their new environment since relocating in the middle of 2013.

This book is dedicated to two people. The first is my father-in-law Jojok – a generous and compassionate polymath from Java who spent much of his life amongst the English-speaking peoples and could muster Americans, Australians, English and Canadians in his own immediate family. His untimely death in June 2018 robbed us of a wonderful person. I hope I can emulate his spirit of generosity one day. It is also dedicated to my own father, Nick. Living life to the full on a Brighton–Dieppe axis, my dad has an incredible capacity to enjoy life, whatever circumstances might prevail. An involved father long before Baby Bjorns were fashionable, his strong intellect has been an inspiration to me as I have moved through life. I owe him thanks for that and for taking me to see QPR beat Liverpool 2–0 at Loftus Road in 1977. The rest, as they say, is history.

Part I

Discovering England

1

Introduction: English nationalism, Euroscepticism and the Anglosphere

Dare to dream that the dawn is breaking on an independent United Kingdom ...
Let June 23 go down in our history as our independence day! (Nigel Farage, cited in
Withnall, 2016)

It is hard to understate the historic significance of the vote to leave the European
Union (EU) that emerged from the rain on the morning of 24 June 2016. It was
the greatest policy failure leading to a geo-strategic reorientation since the Suez
Crisis of 1956 and potentially the greatest loss of markets since independence in the
Indian subcontinent in 1947, if not the Thirteen Colonies in 1783. But Suez left few
traces on the electorate or domestic British politics and was conducted in the 'black
box' of foreign relations. In contrast, the decision to leave the European Union was
enacted by the electorate who, in so doing, challenged the sovereignty of Parliament
that some Brexiteers claimed they were trying to save. Moreover, this was a campaign and outcome dominated by England. Examining this event as a 'moment' of
English nationalism opens up fruitful ways of understanding both the vote to leave
the European Union and the nature of English nationalism itself.

In parts of the world where national memory is conditioned by resistance to
British imperialism the idea of the English seeking and winning their independence
is disconcertingly absurd. In almost every part of the world – from the Americas, to
Asia, Africa, the Middle East and even within the United Kingdom (UK) itself – the
English (not the Scots, Welsh and least of all the Irish) are the chief malefactors in
many national narratives that end in independent nationhood for formerly subject
peoples. Until recently, the English were a people from whom you sought independence, not a people seeking to regain their own nationhood by rising up against the
inequities of foreign rule.

Yet this is how Brexit was portrayed in Nigel Farage's victory speech at 4 a.m. on
24 June 2016: with the important caveat that Farage was ostensibly speaking for
the United Kingdom, not for England. But the disparity in support for leaving the
European Union in the four nations of the United Kingdom raised the question of
which nation might be seeking its independence and from what or whom? A newly
politicised English identity was not just a salient feature of the 2016 referendum but

also of the ten years leading up to it. In this way politicised Englishness became an important element in explaining the decision to hold the Brexit referendum and its eventual outcome.

Raising questions of where sovereignty lay and who exactly was in charge in the United Kingdom was only one of the political dilemmas that were opened by the attempt to resolve three others. In seeming to resolve one grand dilemma – the United Kingdom's membership of the European Union – the referendum deepened two more inter-related problems: England's relationship to the United Kingdom and Britain's relationship to the world. The way that the decision to leave the European Union was arrived at opened up questions about what kind of country the United Kingdom had become. The outcome of the referendum vote was the result of diverse causes: the political effects of wealth disparities, the use of xenophobia to mobilise parts of the Leave vote and the difficulties of political communication in a democratic system that was adapting slowly to the disruptive effects of misinformation borne by new media. The national divisions that the 2016 referendum exposed are often noted. Yet little sustained attention has been given to the place of nationalism as an ideology (rather than shorthand for xenophobia) in explaining Brexit. This book attempts to make such an explanation.

This book builds on research that highlights the peculiar Englishness of Euroscepticism and the Englishness of Brexit (Wellings, 2012; Henderson et al., 2017). Some analysis downplays the particularity of Brexit in favour of broader, underlying strains and tensions in Western democracies, noting the 'long-standing suspicions' of the European project as a sub-text to Brexit (Flinders, 2018: 185–188). These shorter-term explanations are important, but we must not throw the English baby out with the comparative bathwater. Analysing the UK's 'awkwardness' through the lens of an emergent politicisation of English nationhood and longer continuities in the construction of English nationalism allows for a medium-term explanation of Brexit, as well as allowing us to gain valuable insights into English nationalism. Doing so therefore allows us to open up new fields of explanation for this major event in British and European political history. In this sense, Brexit is understood as an extended event, not solely the referendum campaign of 2016. The analysis that follows considers the politics of nationalist mobilisation in the years preceding the decision to leave the European Union and the inter-relationship between an elite project to alter the UK's relationship with the EU and popular grievances. The famously 'awkward' relationship between the UK and the EU cannot be understood separately from the increasingly awkward set of relationships between the nations of the United Kingdom themselves (Wellings, 2015). In this light – with an interpretation of English nationalism at its centre – Brexit becomes explicable as the result of an important but contingent alliance between a politicised Englishness and an elite project that aimed at withdrawing the United Kingdom from the European Union. It was this cross-sectional alliance that shifted politicised Englishness into an English nationalism defined by a political desire to separate the UK from the EU.

In order to respond to and manage popular grievance that was increasingly voiced in the language of this politicised Englishness, a political strategy formed that was shaped by this emergent nationalism. An elite project to get Britain out of the EU and reposition it in a globalising world was able to ally with a recently politicised Englishness mobilised by the issue of the United Kingdom's membership of the European Union and the free movement of labour that membership entailed. By so doing, it delivered a slim but significant majority to take the UK out of the EU in the referendum of 2016. The contingent alliance between elites and masses was not the only aspect of the creation of this 'national' moment. Past and future were joined in a critique of present political arrangements. Britain's imperial past allowed Brexiteers to imagine a global future for the United Kingdom. The 'Anglosphere' was part of this particular national imagination that appeared to offer a solution to the dilemma of exit from the EU. As a named ideology it emerged at the same time as England began to emerge as a de facto political community in the asymmetric-ally devolved United Kingdom. England found itself at the centre of a three-level game bought about through the politics of Brexit. The three levels of this dilemma were, first of all, how to get the UK out of the EU whilst, secondly, keeping the UK together on English terms and, thirdly, how to reintegrate a post-EU UK into the 'wider world' as a means to lessen the rupture of withdrawal from the EU and miti-gate the possibility of a break-up.

By reframing Brexit through the lens of English nationalism, this book offers a medium-range explanation for the origins and outcome of the campaign to secure the United Kingdom's departure from the European Union and the part played by 'the Anglosphere' in it. It also helps explain the nature of contemporary English nationalism as an emergent political project, and not just a 'stand alone' entity or 'Little England', but backed by other countries to help fill the diplomatic and trading space left by the UK's departure from the EU. Grounded in the growing lit-erature on the politics of English nationalism and nationhood, this book examines the important – yet under-researched – inter-relationships between three ideas and ideologies in British politics: English nationalism, Euroscepticism and the Anglosphere. There may be good reasons to hesitate in calling each of these political ideas an ideology. However, if we do so based on a broad understanding of ideology as an interconnected set of ideas which form a perspective on the world that have implications for action-oriented political behaviour (Leach, 2002: 1), we can begin to appreciate how each relates to and informs the other which in turn helps us com-prehend Brexit – and to comprehend it as a major moment in the history of English nationalism.

The current manifestations of these three political ideas are closely linked to con-temporary politics and in that sense are relatively novel. The first recorded use of the term 'Eurosceptic' was in the British press in 1985 (Vasilopoulou, 2018: 23). Thatcher's 'Bruges Speech' in 1988, although tame by Brexiteers' standards, gave this putative resistance to particular directions in European integration some political coherence. Whether or not there was such a thing as English nationalism was a moot point after New Labour's electoral win (and the Conservatives' poor showing in Scotland and Wales) in 1997. Nevertheless, a politicised Englishness emerged just after the re-emergence of Euroscepticism as a parliamentary force in the 1990s and – as we shall see – there were important links between these two phenomena. The last element in this ideational trinity, the Anglosphere, developed as a project on the disgruntled right of the political spectrum in the English-speaking democracies at the high point of the influence of the 'Third Way' in 1999–2000.

Notwithstanding the novelty of these political phenomena, they all rest on much older ideas and traditions in English politics and thus have significant continuities with the past. Importantly, this gives each of them legitimacy as a response to the political dilemmas outlined above and provides reassuring continuity in times of political dislocation. But these ideologies are not only a response to these great dilemmas: in their own ways they helped cause those dilemmas too. This is because the understanding of sovereignty in these ideologies differs markedly from the understanding of sovereignty required to legitimise European integration. Sovereignty is a crucial element in any nationalism and it holds a special place in the long development of English political practice and national consciousness (Black, 2018). Sovereignty is a major constitutive element of Eurosceptic thought that seeks alternative models of European integration or an alternative to European integration altogether. Anglosphere thought nurtures the constitutional development of sovereignty in England as part of its collective historical narrative and suggests that alternatives to European integration are to be found in a renewed set of international relationships based on the civilisational commonalities stemming from this English past.

This book examines these important inter-relationships between English nationalism, Euroscepticism and the Anglosphere. Building on important analyses of English nationalism from Tom Nairn to the more recent (and differing) accounts of this phenomenon written by Krishan Kumar, Arthur Aughey and Michael Kenny, it explains the nature of what Nick Startin and Simon Usherwood have referred to as the 'pervasive, embedded and persistent' nature of Euroscepticism (Startin and Usherwood, 2013: 10). It does so in this case in the United Kingdom, by linking it with an analysis of nationalism in England and shows that what we might call 'Euroscepticism' is far more embedded and persistent than even these authors' enquiry into the general EU-wide phenomenon suggests.

This re-energised English worldview was located at the intersection of three political inter-relationships: between English nationalism and Euroscepticism; between Euroscepticism and the Anglosphere; and between the Anglosphere and English nationalism. The memory of England's historical development that underpins the dominant articulation of British sovereignty inclines the English worldview away from the EU and out towards the 'English-speaking peoples', recently rehabilitated and reconceptualised for a global era as 'the Anglosphere'. The strain that these competing conceptions of England and Britain placed on national traditions were expressed in the arguments whether to 'Remain' in or 'Leave' the European Union up to and after the historic vote to take the UK out of the EU held on 23 June 2016.

Thus, far from being inwardly focused and parochial, when understood as a contingent alliance between electorate and elites, contemporary English nationalism is a globally connected phenomenon, which is deeply engaged with the wider world. To be sure, nationalism in England displayed what we might call a 'defensive posture' towards European – and even British – levels of governance and those policies that we associate with globalisation in the decade after the Global Financial Crisis. The debate during the Brexit referendum campaign was certainly tainted by xenophobia, symbolised the murder of the Labour and pro-Remain MP Jo Cox during the referendum campaign and in the rise in hate crimes: the Home Office reported a 41 per cent rise in racist or religious abuse in the month after the vote (cited in the *EU Observer*, 2016). But this does not necessarily make it parochial. Instead of the Brexit vote being caused by a deepening parochialism, it was an awkward but decisive alliance between sections of the electorate disaffected by the effects of neoliberal globalisation and elites attempting to expose Britain to more of the same. The arguments of the official Leave campaign sought to stress Britain's global links as an alternative to a European vocation for the United Kingdom. From this historically informed perspective, English nationalism was one of the least parochial on the planet. This global orientation is crucial in explaining the link between English nationalism, Euroscepticism and the Anglosphere that shaped Britain's European policy from the 1960s right up to the Brexit referendum in 2016 and the politics of withdrawal thereafter.

Stating the argument

This book mounts an argument that resistance to European integration and the drive to withdraw the UK from the EU was constitutive of the contemporary manifestation of English nationalism. Euroscepticism revitalised English nationalism as a defence of British sovereignty. In doing so, it created the conditions for a contingent alliance between supporters of an elite project to withdraw from the EU and realign the UK with its 'true friends' in the Anglosphere and sections of the electorate expressing popular grievances through a recently politicised Englishness.

English nationhood is expressed in a variety of ways and is informed by a variety of ideological traditions (Kenny, 2014). However, the single most important concept shaping English nationalism as a political ideology is the historically derived notion of sovereignty at the heart of the British political tradition. Whilst this appears most obviously to be about politics, it is about that elusive concept 'culture' too. Nationalism politicises culture and the alignment or misalignment of 'national values' and everyday experiences with the political structures of governance is a major motor of nationalist mobilisation. To understand English nationalism as a pervasive, persistent and embedded phenomenon and as a structuring force in British politics, one needs to comprehend the relationship between the political and the historical in articulations of England that coalesce as presentations of 'English political culture' and the relationship of that version of England to structures of governance. So whilst some of the drivers of contemporary English nationalism – that which Richard Wyn Jones and colleagues characterised as 'devo-anxiety', Euroscepticism, immigration (Wyn Jones et al., 2013) – violate general principles of nationalism (that the state and nation should be congruent and that the nation should be governed by 'its own people'), the worldview that shapes these demands and makes them appear legitimate is based on an English understanding of sovereignty that is presented as being both political and cultural.

What makes this English worldview politically appealing when faced with major dilemmas of statecraft is a heady brew of initial success – symbolised by the Glorious Revolution of 1688 and the subsequent Whig interpretation not just of English history but of British politics – and the expansion, imitation and endurance of that system; the latter symbolised by England and Britain's 'finest hour' in 1940 (what followed was by implication not as good). In all of this lay an important relationship between history and memory: in creating a narrative that legitimised the operation and existence of government and governance within the United Kingdom and the British Empire, this version of the past shaped and informed the contemporary politics of nationalism in England.

The narrative thread that links English nationalism, Euroscepticism and the Anglosphere is founded on three pillars: first of all, England's constitutional development; secondly, the expansion and contraction of first the 'Atlantic' Empire and then the truly 'British' Empire; and, thirdly, the memory of twentieth-century conflict in preserving English sovereignty and global liberty. The emergence of the English constitution in the seventeenth century laid important foundations for the expansion of English trade that, in turn, laid the foundations of the 'first' empire in the 'Atlantic world' (including the archipelago that today comprises the United Kingdom and Ireland). Despite the loss of the American colonies by 1783, further expansion in Asia, Oceania and Africa, in addition to the consolidation of Canada, led the 'second' British Empire to its greatest territorial extent and, in the settler colonies and Dominions, to the imitation and adaptation of the English constitution as forms of government and governance. The endurance of the United Kingdom throughout the twentieth century – in 1917–18, most dramatically in 1940, but even in 1983 after the Able Baker scare – appeared to give the notion of sovereignty at the heart of English constitutionalism a providential lease of life, anointing it with another form of success – endurance. However at the beginning of the twenty-first century the endurance of this sovereignty was challenged not militarily, but by the perceived threats from an encroaching European Union and a secessionist Scottish nationalism. Between 2011 and 2019, the British Government ran the risk of 'losing' not only the EU but Scotland too. But this prospective major loss of markets was simultaneously compensated by the tantalising prospect of the return to a 'global Britain', a champion of free trade, a 'world island' in Andrew Gamble's phrase (Gamble, 2003: 34); something like a bigger and colder version of Singapore.

Faced with these political challenges, 'England' unwittingly re-emerged as a political community, with defenders of English sovereignty articulating narratives that mobilised fellow nationals in its defence. But politics could never allow such an emergence to be a straightforward process of 'national awakening' as nineteenth-century ideologues depicted the process. Focusing on sovereignty as the core concept in English nationalism certainly illuminates an understanding of English nationhood, but it blurs its boundaries too. This is a crucial point if we are to understand English nationalism in the past and today. England's sovereignty has for many centuries extended beyond the borders of England itself. Justifying the extension of English sovereignty from early modern times, through the two empires and within the United Kingdom itself produced legitimising narratives to explain the English and their form of governance to themselves and others. Despite challenges from national and class-based movements, those legitimising narratives that were produced to counter such movements won internal legitimacy owing to their endurance over time. Although esoteric in their purely constitutional form, these predominantly conservative (and Conservative) explanations for what we might call the 'national tradition' in English politics, created a worldview that was markedly different from the secessionist nationalisms in other parts of the United Kingdom. It is one that differed notably from the ideal type of nationalist movements that sought to throw off foreign rule. English nationalists do not seek to make the state and nation congruent: instead they instinctively defend British sovereignty – its existence, operation and memory. In its formative stages, English national narratives sought to justify foreign rule (their own) rather than critique it. Importantly, it is this expansive 'national tradition' that conditions English responses to the dilemmas of nationhood and national belonging presented in contemporary British politics.

English nationalism: expressing and occluding England

In its secessionist or autonomist guises, nationalism is a political goal to be attained, or a political problem to be managed, via statecraft. It is also an ideology that legitimises the daily existence of a state or justifies the creation of a new one. Both these elements of nationalism operate in the United Kingdom. The multi-national composition of the United Kingdom meant that managing autonomist and secessionist nationalism assumed an important role in British politics once home rule was proposed as an answer to the 'Irish Question' between 1885 and 1914. Although diminishing in salience after the Government of Ireland Act (1920),

secessionist and autonomist nationalism returned on the geographic peripheries of
the United Kingdom in the 1970s and after. But following devolution a new national
question gradually forced its way onto the political agenda: the 'English Question'.
However, this national question did not at first seem to share the same autonomist
or secessionist goals of the nationalisms of the periphery. Furthermore, by the turn
of the twenty-first century the dilemma of what to do with England could not be
seen in isolation from other national questions that situated the United Kingdom
in Europe and the rest of the world. Whereas devolution and the push for Scottish
independence were inadvertently posing the 'English question' in the UK, the
United Kingdom's difficult part in the process of European integration was posing
the 'British Question' in Europe. Moreover uncertainty about Britain's place in the
European Union by extension posed further questions about the United Kingdom's
relations with the rest of the world. In this evolving domestic and geo-political situation, structured by the embedding of 'globalisation' since the 1990s, older ties with
what were referred to as 'traditional allies' or simply 'the Anglosphere' were renewed
and reformulated and suggested as an answer to Britain's 'European Question'.

As an ideology, nationalism can be divided into two broad types: autonomist-
secessionist and integrationist (with irredentist nationalism sitting between the
two main forms). Although both variants ultimately seek to integrate an existing
or formative national community, autonomist-secessionist nationalists seek to
delegitimise existing political borders and the extension and operation of sovereignty within those borders. Their response to the dilemma of where to draw political boundaries is to suggest that a reorganisation of geo-political space around
their nation is the form of governance best suited to the material and psychological
needs of the group of citizens that they seek to represent through independent
statehood. In their view, new borders are more legitimate than the pre-existing ones.
Integrationist nationalists seek to reinforce existing state structures and forms of
governance by legitimising those structures as already the best suited to the material
and psychological needs of the citizenry. Both types of nationalists create and sustain nations and ideas about nationhood in their attempt to legitimise the political goals – disintegration or unity – that they seek to bring about. It is this contest
about political legitimacy that shapes the content of particular nationalisms: the
myths, memories and goals that animate and sustain nationalists and resonate with
a broader citizenry as part of a political struggle.

Thus nationalism is born of political contestation, and particular nationalisms
co-constitute themselves with reference to significant political others. But nationalist narratives cannot be created from nothing even if they can be articulated within
different political and cultural traditions that give them different emphases and
narratives upon which to draw. The past sets boundaries on the present and what
claims are legitimate to make within political traditions and which will resonate
within given constituencies in the existing or putative political community. For
this reason, it is important to consider the historical development of any particular

nationalism in relation to other important national narratives and existing power relations that secessionist or integrationist nationalists seek to alter or sustain. In the case of nationalism in England, it is important to comprehend the series of 'national questions' that intruded on Westminster politics and how these shaped dominant understandings of English nationhood.

The first of the 'national questions' in British politics arose after the politics of the 'long eighteenth century' had created a sense of Britishness in support of the pluri-national United Kingdom (Colley, 1992; Newman, 1987). The so-called 'Irish Question' emerged in the wake of agitation for an independent Ireland after 1848. The response from the Liberal Party was 'home rule in the round', three successive attempts to introduce 'home rule' between 1885 and 1914 that ultimately helped make defence of the Union one of the defining features of the Conservative Party.

This political process was not related to the United Kingdom alone. The 'devolution' of responsible government mirrored a process that started in the colonies following a rebellion in Quebec in 1837 and the issuing of the Durham Report three years later. 'National questions' that asked what was the best way to organise the Empire and the growing assertiveness and self-confidence of colonial elites were resolved by according those settler colonies the almost-independent status of Dominions between 1867 and 1935. These colonial nationalisms were deeply informed by an integrationist imperialism that in turn fed back into understandings of nationhood in the United Kingdom, including England (Wellings, 2002). Conversely, secessionist nationalisms within the Dominions were contained or defeated by pan-imperial military efforts, notably that of the Afrikaners in South Africa in 1899–1902. Legitimising the extension of British sovereignty throughout the Empire became an important element for nationalists in all of these emergent nationalisms, England included.

When the first serious crack in the British Empire came, it was in Ireland. Irish independence was a drawn-out affair, ranging from uprising and civil war between 1916 and 1923, the Government of Ireland Act of 1920 that made Ireland a Free State in the British Empire, to full independence by 1949. By the time of Irish independence, decolonisation and the end of Empire had begun in earnest. National questions sprung up throughout Britain's Asian, African and Caribbean colonies. When these questions had been resolved by granting independence, the political dilemma of how to respond to secessionist nationalism returned to British politics in Northern Ireland. Scottish and Welsh nationalisms also emerged as political forces in the 1970s, posing their own 'national questions'. Through the debates about devolution in the 1990s, Scottish nationalism became the 'motor' of nationalist politics in the UK, taking over the mantle from Northern Ireland after the stabilisation of power-sharing governments in 2007 until the Brexit vote in 2016.

It is important to note the assumptions built into these 'national questions': England was assumed to be an unproblematic and invisible element in the framing of political dilemmas. In this way, it was elided with rule from Westminster and with the idea of 'Britain' itself. Three broadly consistent explanations for this elision have been offered. Tom Nairn provided an account of what he termed 'the English enigma' in the 1970s, noting that 'some vital elements in the modern political principle of political nationality are diminished, or lacking in England' (Nairn: 2003 [1977]: 285). For Nairn, the historically precocious nature of the development of English national consciousness – 'God's firstborn' in Liah Greenfeld's evocative phrase (Greenfeld, 1992: 27) – was channelled into and ultimately subsumed by the British state and expressed through the monarchy. This historic outcome ensured the continuation of the 'absolutism of Parliament' after the long seventeenth century and 'prevented the emergence in Britain of the doctrine of popular sovereignty as the true source of power' (Nairn: 2003 [1977]: 290).

This explanation of political quiescence was given an imperial dimension by both Benedict Anderson and Krishan Kumar. Anderson – a New Left stable mate of Nairn's – augmented Nairn's explanation with the concept of 'official nationalism'. This variety of nationalism emerged in the mid-nineteenth century in response to the challenge to pluri-national empires by autonomist-secessionist nationalists. This challenge forced those in power to adopt and adapt nationalist ideas about legitimacy for their own empires. The 'fundamental legitimacy for most of these dynasties', argued Anderson, 'had nothing to do with nationalness'. Anderson noted that in these pluri-national empires:

> Romanovs ruled over Tartars and Letts, Germans and Armenians, Russians and Finns. Habsburgs were perched high over Magyars and Croats, Slovaks and Italians, Ukrainians and Austro-Germans. Hanoverians presided over Bengalis and Québecois, as well as Scots and Irish, English and Welsh. On the continent, furthermore, members of the same dynastic families often ruled in different, sometimes rivalrous states. What nationality should be assigned to Bourbons ruling in France and Spain, Hohenzollerns in Prussia and Romania, Wittelsbachs in Bavaria and Greece? (Anderson, 1991: 83)

Yet the nationalist challenge to the legitimacy of these dynastic pluri-national empire-states forced imperial officials and supportive citizenry to legitimise empires in language and symbols that looked more and more like the types of mythic tropes that nationalists themselves drew upon: history, governance, common language or lingua franca.

Traces of this explanation about the diversion of an early form of English national consciousness into an official nationalism, whose function was to legitimise the British state and its Empire, can be found in Krishan Kumar's account of the making of English national identity. Building on comparative analyses, Kumar argued that imperialism did not so much inform expressions of English nationhood but instead inhibited it. It was Britain's imperial mission that prevented anything resembling the nationalisms emerging in Continental Europe from forming in England during the nineteenth century. Kumar's notion of 'missionary nationalism' concedes that empires, 'though in principle opposed to claims of nationality, may be carriers of a certain kind of national identity which gives to the dominant groups a special sense of themselves and their destiny' (Kumar, 2003: 34). For Kumar, being at the heart of an imperial mission led to a diminution of expressions of strident nationhood for fear of upsetting the imperial applecart and causing nationalist reactions from peripheral groups. 'Such people', suggested Kumar, 'will be careful not to stress their ethnic identity; rather they will stress the political, cultural or religious mission to which they have been called' (Kumar, 2003: 34). This meant that Britain's imperial mission both restrained and inhibited expressions of English national identity. Thus where we might (theoretically) expect to find examples of 'national identity' and its attendant myths and memories, we instead find muted and conflated expressions of nationhood that informed – and were in turn informed by – wider imagined political communities and different, if cognisant, ideologies.

None of this was the source of a political dilemma in England until the very end of the twentieth century. Devolution in the UK – a response to the 'national questions' of the 1990s – resulted in an asymmetric constitutional resettlement (House of Lords Constitution Committee, 2016). In this situation, as Arthur Aughey noted, England's constitutional place experienced a series of 'ironic inversions'. During the period when nationalism was becoming the principal means of legitimising the organisation of geo-political space, England's constitution and the ideas of nationhood that were so closely linked to it were, in Ernest Barker's phrase, a 'self-evident fact' that did not require explanation let alone theorisation (cited in Aughey, 2016: 351). But after devolution this 'self-evident' nature became reconceptualised as 'absence' and was therefore now a problem in a polity that was reorganising political space along national lines. What was once the source of England's political confidence was now a source of insecurity and resentment. Perceptions of absence diminished in the latter part of the 2000s to be replaced by 'resentment' when a politicised Englishness emerged as a significant element of British (and European) politics (Mann and Fenton, 2017: 136). This emergence of politicised Englishness that Aughey called 'the disordering of English self understanding' (Aughey, 2016: 353), pushed another 'national question' – this time England's own – slowly but surely up the political agenda. This phenomenon created three inter-related political dilemmas: the English question, the British question and the European question.

English Euroscepticism: pervasive, embedded and persistent

Speaking in Berlin in November 2014, John Major sought to explain the growth in support for parties or candidates advocating withdrawal from the European Union witnessed in the 2014 elections to the European Parliament: 'We have never been a comfortable partner', he explained – a statement that would have caused little surprise amongst his German audience. More surprisingly, he singled out the 'we' in this statement as one nation in particular: 'In England', he added, 'which is 85% of the population of the United Kingdom, opposition has reached a critical mass and now, for the first time, there is a serious possibility that our electorate could vote to leave the EU. I put the chance of exit at just under 50%' (Major, 2014).

In claiming that the English were never comfortable partners in the process of European integration (a claim more accurate at the level of politics rather than government and a sentiment that varied in intensity over time), Major drew attention to England's contribution to what Startin and Usherwood conceptualised to be the 'pervasive, embedded and persistent' nature of Euroscepticism, as noted above (2013: 10). This comparative research added important avenues of analysis into the study of Euroscepticism initially concerning its nature – embedded and persistent – and later its organisation – transnational and pan-European (Fitzgibbon, Leruth and Startin, 2017: 11). This research raised questions about the exact cause and nature of such embedded persistence. The argument in this book is that resistance to European integration revitalised English nationalism as a defence of British sovereignty whilst the Englishness of this worldview inclined Britain away from the EU and towards the Anglosphere. Politicians framing this dilemma via the dominant traditions in English nationalism, sought to re-energise links with 'traditional allies' and mobilise popular support for withdrawal from the EU via imagining the United Kingdom at the centre of a web of like-minded, English-speaking nations who collectively offered an alternative to Britain's place in Europe.

Making Euroscepticism a core concern of European Studies is itself a recent phenomenon (Brack and Startin, 2015: 239). The study of European integration is famously partisan in its personnel (Varsari, 2010). The relationship between academia and EU funding is deep and strong: we might even say persistent and embedded. This had some appreciable effect on research into European integration. In the field of European integration history, what Wolfram Kaiser identified as 'the federalist hurrah historiography and the conventional diplomatic history of interstate negotiations', resulted in the field being in his view 'conceptually underdeveloped' (Kaiser, 2010: 45). Paul Taylor suggested that we should turn our attention to the means by which European integration may unravel. Noting that any theory of integration required two elements – as a system defined against certain criteria that was different from an existing one and a sense of a dynamic process within the current system able to produce a new one – Taylor suggested that European disintegration ought to be a major concern to scholars and practitioners alike (Taylor, 2008: 92). Brexit gave greater urgency to this need for a theory of European *dis*integration as well as European integration (Lequesne, 2018: 290). A theoretical appreciation of nationalism combined with one of Euroscepticism will leave us well placed to understand this countervailing tendency in general and help to explain Brexit in particular.

Writing in 2012, Cas Mudde identified two main schools of thought about emerging research on Euroscepticism: the so-called 'Sussex' and 'North Carolina' schools (Mudde, 2012: 193). The Sussex School was constituted by the pioneering research of Aleks Szczerbiak and Paul Taggart and their two-volume edited collection, which was published under the title of *Opposing Europe* in 2008 (Szczerbiak and Taggart, 2008a and 2008b). This research focused on the categorisation and definitions of various political parties and movements that in one way or another opposed the policies or principle of European integration. Most enduring was their binary typology of opposition to European integration as 'hard' and 'soft' Euroscepticism, where 'hard' Euroscepticism referred to principled opposition to the political project of European integration and 'soft' Euroscepticism to opposition to the trajectory of European integration or planned extension of EU competencies (Szczerbiak and Taggart, 2018: 13). In other words, 'soft' Eurosceptics engaged in 'policy contestation' at the EU level, whereas 'hard' Eurosceptics engaged in 'polity contestation' (Trenz, 2018: 293).

The 'North Carolina' school pursued a slightly different approach in terms of methodology and focus. Based on research conducted by Liesbet Hooghe and Gary Marks, this school emphasised that the wellspring of Euroscepticism as a pan-European phenomenon was the issue of party management. Most importantly, Hooghe and Marks popularised a chronological break in the study of European integration by arguing that a 'permissive consensus' towards this process had broken down after the debate about political and monetary union around the negotiation and signing of the Treaty of Maastricht in 1991–93. This was replaced thereafter by a 'constraining dissensus' that meant that room for political manoeuvre was greatly reduced by the growth of popular scepticism towards the European project (Hooghe and Marks, 2009: 1).

We might now add a third school to this list. Importantly for the argument mounted in this book, it is one that opens up avenues of enquiry sympathetic to the place of nationalism and nationhood as explanatory factors in resistance to European integration. Although tempting to call this the 'M4 School' after the motorway linking the universities of Surrey and Bath, where much of the coordinating activity originated, it would be better to link this school with the idea underpinning its approach to Euroscepticism, that of embedded persistence. Other scholars took the implications of such embedded persistence further. Cécile Leconte suggested that the pre- and post-Maastricht dividing line was drawn too sharply (Leconte, 2010: 166). Claudia Schrag Sternberg adopted a similar position, but focused on contestation over legitimacy rather than Euroscepticism as such (with Euroscepticism as a by-product of this contestation). Schrag Sternberg's concerns accorded with those of Craig Parsons: that certain political ideas win out over others and that contestation of the European project has been a persistent and embedded feature of European integration from its start (Parsons 2003; Schrag Sternberg, 2013).

These analyses ally with a constructivist understudying of European integration that should alert us to the importance of the discursive creation and contestation of the idea of Europe (Trenz and de Wilde, 2012: 537). As an emergent polity with no agreed-upon *finalité*, the European Union generates such contestation. As Leconte notes, this is particularly true for a polity that 'challenges exclusive definitions of national identity, without succeeding in constructing a new European *demos*' (Leconte, 2015: 258). This lacuna facilitated contestation between supporters of European integration and opponents of the process and principle of European integration, legitimised with reference to nationhood as being the site of collective identity and statehood as being the optimal site for democratic participation.

This shift of focus raised another broad research question: what is the source or nature of this embedded persistence? As Sofia Vasilopoulou notes, more research is required on the way that Euroscepticism influences national identity formation (and vice versa) (Vasilopoulou, 2013: 163). Although not the first to make the link between the 'winners and losers' of European integration and globalisation, Robert Ford and Matthew Goodwin's *Revolt on the Right* offered the best-known explanation of support for radical right-wing (and *ipso facto* populist Eurosceptic) parties in the UK. But this important analysis had little to say about the place of nationhood in Eurosceptic mobilisation (Ford and Goodwin, 2014). Employing the concept of the 'left behind' is important but can only be a partial explanation of the appeal of Euroscepticism in England; not all leave voters in 2016 were poorer, less well educated, white men in their fifties (Evans and Mellon, 2016; Hennig and Dorling, 2016). Crucially, Ford and Goodwin sought only to explain support for the radical right rather than Euroscepticism, although the two phenomena overlapped considerably. This was an important element in support for Brexit but cannot do all the explanatory lifting that was given to it in the immediate wake of the surprise result in 2016. To understand Brexit we need to examine the ways that the 'polity contestation' of the European Union was not only provided with an opportunity through the referendum (Oppermann, 2018: 249), but was also framed in terms that took support for UK withdrawal from the EU beyond the committed support of Euro-rejectionists and managed to persuade the uncommitted to vote to leave the EU.

Virginie van Ingelgom similarly focused her research on the 'undecideds', 'don't knows' and 'don't cares', which the results of the 2009 and 2014 elections to the European Parliament revealed were now a solid feature of the political landscape in Europe. Far from becoming politicised after Maastricht, van Ingelgom argued that European citizens largely withdrew their interest and activity from EU politics, creating a new category: 'Euro-indifferents' (van Ingelgom: 2014: 183). What changed was not citizen politicisation, but rather elite polarisation. Thus, although it is plausible that a constraining dissensus emerged at an elite level in the past two decades, van Ingelgom argued it is an overstatement to transpose this model onto public opinion. In this reading, elite contestation becomes an important feature of Euroscepticism. Projecting this elite contestation onto and through the device of a referendum, necessitated elites seeking to influence an electorate that rarely put the issue of Britain's place in Europe high on the list of priorities, meaning that elites needed to find alternative registers through which to pitch their arguments to the peoples of the United Kingdom.

The above conclusions were the product of comparative research. In the United Kingdom's case it is not difficult to construct Euroscepticism as a 'persistent and embedded' phenomenon. The contours of such a narrative are well known. Official scepticism towards the emerging project of meaningful regional integration can be found in Britain since the 1950s when European integration began in earnest. Principled opposition amongst a widening set of interest groups in civil society formed during the first negotiations (Dewey, 2009). In the 1960s and 1970s, Eurosceptics were known as 'Anti-Marketeers' and were principally drawn from the left of British politics with an emphasis on protecting sovereignty in order to defend British socialism from the ideas and policies of the European centre-right. Euroscepticism became characteristic of the right from the mid-1980s, building in support and intensity until the Brexit referendum in 2016.

The emphasis on the continuity of opposition to European integration within and from the United Kingdom led to some fruitful explanations that move us beyond issues of party management. Party management is a necessary but not sufficient explanation for the persistent nature of Euroscepticism in the United Kingdom. The expression 'awkward partner', coined by Stephen George in his book of the same name, appeared first in 1990, with a second edition published in 1998 (George, 1998). The durability of George's phrase rested upon the concept of 'awkward': a concept that not only suggested an uncomfortable relationship with European integration but also suggested a social characteristic observable amongst denizens of the British Isles. Despite this resonance, the link between nationhood and Euroscepticism was not explored in George's seminal work. This was left to later scholars such as Menno Spiering who traced a causal link between national identity and Euroscepticism (Spiering, 2004).

Chris Gifford explains the persistence of Euroscepticism in the United Kingdom in relation to its post-imperial political economy (Gifford, 2014: 15). Gifford cautions against making too close a causal link between Euroscepticism and English nationalism: 'Populism is populism, it's not nationalism' (Gifford, 2015: 363). Nevertheless his focus opens up valuable avenues of enquiry, suggesting a path dependency *out* of the EU (and to somewhere else). With its emphasis on the post-imperial structure of the British state and a missing European 'rescue', Gifford's argument is one that links Euroscepticism with both a populist nationalism and – although he does not use this term – the Anglosphere. This does not happen in a way that is simply nostalgic, regressive or delusional but results from a structural susceptibility to populist Eurosceptic politics embedded in the post-war British political system (Gifford, 2014: 6).

The term 'Euroscepticism' was itself put under strain by Brexit. David Cameron's negotiations in Brussels in February 2016 saw him switch from someone who appeared to be contemplating exit to a man committed to campaign 'heart and soul' to remain in a reformed EU (or rather a reformed UK–EU relationship). The debate in England in the lead up to the Brexit referendum tended – in the conceptualisations outlined above – to be a contest between soft and hard forms of Euroscepticism with little Euro-enthusiasm on offer. In the analysis in this book, the term 'Brexiteer' will denote EU-rejectionists advocating a position of 'polity contestation', whereas 'Eurosceptic' will cover those whose claims are characterised by 'policy contestation'.

The Anglosphere: England's transnational Euroscepticism

Another important insight provided by the recent scholarship on Euroscepticism relates to its pan-European and transnational nature and organisation (Fitzgibbon, Leruth and Startin, 2017). It should also be noted, however, that the transnational dimension of emergent Euroscepticism is not solely a pan-European phenomenon, but extends beyond the borders of Europe. Indeed this extra-European dimension to Euroscepticism became – in the case of Brexit – constitutive of Euroscepticism by suggesting an alternative to the political trajectory of continued European integration and the EU political project as a whole.

Perhaps best seen as a transnational political tradition given life through policy networks rather than as an actually existing entity, the Anglosphere is a relatively novel expression of an older idea in the politics of Anglophone countries. The boundaries of this entity are far from fixed, but the 'core' states are taken to be the United States, the United Kingdom, Canada, Australia and New Zealand. Other countries with an Anglophone heritage or a link to the former British Empire are sometimes included, notably Singapore, India, countries of the Caribbean and – more problematically given its means of exiting the British Empire and non-membership of the Commonwealth – the Republic of Ireland. At an ideational level, three interlinked narratives concerning the development of representative democracy, the positive effects of empire and free trade and the defeat of totalitarianism in the twentieth century bind the Anglosphere.

By 2007, when it entered the *Shorter Oxford English Dictionary*, the term 'Anglosphere' came to represent a mutually beneficial political association of English-speaking countries that built on older political traditions linking the Anglophone world (Vucetic, 2011: 165). It was also imagined as a balancing corrective to the type of polity represented by the European Union. As Daniel Mandel explained in the *IPA Review* on the 200th anniversary of the Battle of Trafalgar in 2005:

> In a world of politically centralising bureaucracies, a vigorously sovereign, free market, democratic Anglosphere might yet prove a corrective. If so, it will be owed in large measure to the British maritime supremacy established at Trafalgar, which permitted the expansion of British influence and institutions via trade and empire. And if not, the fact will remain that British naval power has been on the whole a powerful benign force that helped shape the better contours of our world. (Mandel, 2005: 32)

This was certainly true of the United Kingdom, as Duncan Bell has shown with the idea of 'Greater Britain' (Bell, 2017) and Michael Kenny and Nick Pearce have shown with regard to both that idea and that of the 'English-speaking peoples' (Kenny and Pearce, 2018). But what is often referred to as 'the Anglosphere' in the singular is in fact a multilayered identity that means different things in different places. For Eurosceptics in the United Kingdom, the Anglosphere's main practical attraction was as an alternative to the European Union. As Stefano Gulmanelli has shown, the 'Anglospherist reshaping of Australia' during John Howard's time as prime minister was advanced in the areas of a challenge to existing understandings of multicultur-alism and a realignment of international relations towards those states with 'shared values' that implicitly aligned Australia's foreign relations in a 'transnational cultural space' (Gulmanelli, 2014: 593). These specific areas of activity were bolstered by wider discourses on the right about 'Judeo-Christian', Enlightenment, 'Western' and 'British' civilisation(s) during the years 1996–2007 (Berryman, 2015: 591). It was these networks and ideas that linked debates in one part of the Anglosphere with those taking place in others.

These mutually constitutive transnational links were important for Eurosceptics and Brexiteers in the United Kingdom in helping to them to imagine the UK outside of the EU. Accordingly the idea was attractive to prominent British Eurosceptics and high-profile Conservatives who eventually became Brexiteers. Margaret Thatcher, David Willetts, John Redwood, Daniel Hannan, David Davis, Norman Lamont, Liam Fox, Bill Cash, Michael Howard and Jacob Rees-Mogg wrote or spoke in support of increased cooperation across the Anglosphere, although explicit mentions of the concept diminished the closer to government these figures got. This list of supporters also suggest that the Anglosphere is an idea with friends in high places, but that is also a love that dare not speak its name, except when in opposition or safely on the backbenches.

When exactly 'the Anglosphere' emerged in its contemporary manifestation is hard to say. It is probably safer to suggest that the idea never really went away on the right of politics. If a date were to be chosen, however, two Hudson Institute Conferences in 1999 and 2000 announced the arrival of the Anglosphere as a new concept in right-wing transatlantic discourse in the United States, the United Kingdom and Canada. These two conferences, the first in Washington, DC and the second in Berkshire, brought together an impressive array of conservative grandees. Delegates included Margaret Thatcher, David Davis, Conrad Black, Francis Fukuyama, James C. Bennett, John O'Sullivan, Robert Conquest and Kenneth Minogue. It was here, argued John Lloyd, who attended as an observer for the *New Statesman*, that the vague notion of a return to closer cooperation between kindred English-speaking nations, 'congealed into a movement' (Lloyd, 2000).

The Anglosphere idea represented a push for a realignment of global and domestic politics (and occasionally an international organisation), to be grounded in the history, culture and institutions that many Eurosceptics and especially

Brexiteers believe make Britain different from the Continent (Nedergaard and Friis Henriksen, 2018). As John Laughland explained, the Anglosphere is 'united by an attachment to individualism, the rule of law ... and the elevation of freedom', with the implication that these values were not shared by the 'corporatist, socialist, corrupt and even authoritarian political cultures prevalent on the European continent, and of which the EU is itself an expression' (Laughland, 2008). Since the late 1990s, exponents of the 'Anglosphere' argued that the English-speaking nations were distinguished by a set of institutions and values that other nations of Europe and Asia lacked: 'a common law tradition, respect for private property, continuous representative government, and a culture that nurtures civil society and entrepreneurial enterprise' (Bennett, 2004: 54). With the United Kingdom, the United States, Canada, Australia, New Zealand, India, the English-speaking Caribbean islands and Singapore all being dedicated to free trade and greater military and security cooperation, the Anglosphere would, it was argued, constitute 'a centre of hope in the world ... round which peace, cooperation, and democracy can develop' (Conquest, 2005: 225).

In certain respects, the Anglosphere did not have to be conjured up: it already existed. This was particularly true at the level of intelligence cooperation through the existence of the so-called 'Five Eyes' network of intelligence sharing, which was established between 1946 and 1956 (Vitor Tossini, 2017). Such long-standing cooperation between Anglosphere countries led to what Jason Dittmer described as the practice of 'everyday diplomacy' that looks like a 'civilisational' alliance, but is based on bottom-up and quotidian cooperation (Dittmer, 2015: 605). Tim Legrand's research has shown how these networks and the identities they create extend beyond intelligence sharing and into the realm of policy transfer (Legrand, 2016). The revelations about Cambridge Analytica's involvement in the Brexit campaign, via Aggregate IQ and BeLeave, show that trans-Anglosphere networks were active during the referendum (Cadwalladr, Graham-Harrison and Townsend, 2018).

Whatever their past relationships, five independent nation-states will have their differences. Sometimes these can appear to be shades of grey: literally in the case of the Royal Australian Navy's (RAN) adoption of its own shade of 'Haze Grey' for RAN vessels (more appropriate to Pacific conditions) to replace the British 'Storm Grey' designed for the Atlantic (*Daily Telegraph*, 2016: 11). There are, however, separate if inter-related spheres within the Anglosphere. The Commonwealth is the largest of these and the Anglo-US alliance is the most important for international relations. This 'special' relationship hints at the importance of bilateral relations within the Anglosphere, but also the unique place of the United States, with the presidency of Donald Trump complicating rather than facilitating the idea of the Anglosphere as an emergent unit in world politics. CANZUK (Canada–Australia–New Zealand and the United Kingdom) also emerged as another source of cooperation within the Anglosphere. Such interaction did not always produce a sense of commonality. The Anglosphere contains hierarchies as well as commonalities.

Intra-Anglosphere relations are as important for creating and sustaining national distinctions, as are oppositional and macro-level 'civilisational' identities in creating a sense of commonality, as Steven Loveridge has shown (Loveridge, 2015). Indeed, Brexit led to stronger statements of what we might call 'Anglo-scepticism' amongst some politicians of the English-speaking world as much as it created support for the Brexiteers' grand strategy.

For all its conceptual vagueness, the Anglosphere in British politics represented a response to a dilemma that used historical consciousness and political tradition not only as its point of departure, but as its place of destination too. Its value for Brexiteers was as much ideational as material. As Peg Murray-Evans noted 'the Commonwealth was part of the ideological driving force of Brexit' and an integral part of the government's vision for 'Global Britain' (Murray-Evans, 2018: 197). This was true of the Anglosphere too. The past was used as a political resource: 'Like so much else about the current moment – from the planned restoration of grammar schools to cries for relaunching the Royal Yacht Britannia – the past serves as inspiration and guide', noted Duncan Bell. 'We are invited to march back to the future' (Bell, 2017). Marching back to the future gave Brexit its nostalgic air, but it was a necessary ideological move to imagine the UK outside of the EU. As Andrew Mycock noted, it rested not so much on imperial amnesia, but instead on a form of myopia in which the best of all possible Empires was used to inspire voters to have the national self-confidence to vote 'leave' (Mycock and Wellings, 2017).

The Anglosphere is a growing area of academic attention. Yet, little is known about what Tim Legrand has called these 'elite, elusive and exclusive' networks amongst policy-makers within the Anglosphere (Legrand, 2016: 440). Those who explicitly refer to it as such are found on the right of politics, but such policy networks exist on the centre-left too. Srdjan Vucetic has gone furthest to theorise the Anglosphere and its likely consequences in international relations and politics. According to Vucetic, actions should follow identity despite rational reasons to behave otherwise (Vucetic, 2011: 25). The well-known motto that nations have interests not friends is challenged by this analysis. Yet Vucetic is right to accord identity an important place in explaining politics and one that can be fruitfully applied to the inter-relationship between English nationalism, Brexit and the Anglosphere.

The outline of the book

To make the argument that Euroscepticism provides the most formed-up ideological content for contemporary English nationalism and that the memory of England's historical development inclines the English worldview away from the EU and out towards the 'English speaking peoples', this book is structured into three parts. Part I, 'Discovering England', sets out the dilemmas that have helped create contemporary English nationalism and the ways of understanding this phenomenon that actors and analysts bring to bear on this topic. Part II, 'Three Pillars of

the English Anglosphere', outlines the ideas that animate and link English nationalism, Euroscepticism and the Anglosphere. Part III, 'England's Brexit and the
Anglosphere', examines the way in which English nationalism and the idea of the
Anglosphere informed the politics of Brexit before, during and after the 2016
referendum.

Chapter 2, 'England's Dilemmas', examines the emergence of contemporary English nationalism and adopts a 'traditions and dilemmas' approach to
understanding policy towards England, the European Union and the Anglosphere.
Mark Bevir and Rod Rhodes have argued that when confronted with a dilemma, political actors will be guided in their policy choices by pre-existing political traditions.
One important tradition they overlooked in their analyses was the national one and
it is this that will be applied to the analysis of policy choices and the discursive construction of political Englishness in this book. In other words, nationalism should
not be overlooked as an explanatory factor when seeking to understand the changing
constitutional nature of the United Kingdom, the United Kingdom's changing relationship with the European Union and the United Kingdom's changing relationship
with the rest of the world. The inter-relationships between these major dilemmas
and English nationalism were admittedly complex since the United Kingdom was
both object and agent of change, first in relation to Scottish independence and
secondly in relation to withdrawal from the European Union. Thus an important
sub-claim is that it is impossible to analyse the 'awkwardness' of Britain's relationship with the EU without analysing the 'awkwardness' of Britain itself. Since the
1990s, Euroscepticism and English nationalism have become constitutive of each
other. Again, the historical continuities within English nationalism incline English
nationalists away from Europe and towards the English-speaking world.

Chapter 3, 'Locating England', examines the way in which English nationalism
has been theorised and researched. It argues that the analysis of English nationalism has been trapped between two ideal types of nationalist development and
politics: France and Scotland. The Scottish intellectual and nationalist Tom Nairn
had a major influence on this framing. Situating his analysis of English nationalism
within a Marxist-derived understanding of historical development and ideological
hegemony, Nairn initially described English nationalism as 'absent' in the 'normal'
sense; that is to say in comparison with the historical development of France and its
integrative republican traditions. More recent analyses of English nationalism also
found it to be 'absent' but for different reasons, principally because it did not look
like Scottish secessionism, which is an account associated with Krishan Kumar. In
this way, when theoretically as well as geographically located between France and
Scotland, England appeared to be missing in action. But this was only because the
ideal types used to define English nationalism inhibited a nuanced understanding of
the phenomenon. The 'absence' was only ever a *perception* of absence and it was this
perception that required explanation. Thus another important sub-argument in this
book concerns the merging of Englishness and Britishness that came about through

the tendency in English nationalism to legitimise and defend British sovereignty. Building on the definition of nationalism advanced above we can see not only how English nationalists speak the language of Britishness, but in defending British sovereignty, the English are drawn away from the European Union and propelled towards the English-speaking world.

A crucial element of this English worldview rests on an understanding of the past. Broadly, the English Eurosceptic version of the past rests on three intertwined pillars: the development of representative democracy and the English 'genius' for government; the acquisition and operation of the British Empire; and memory of twentieth-century conflict. Within this political memory, there are 'hard' and 'soft' Eurosceptic interpretations of the past. The 'soft' version of English Euroscepticism suggests that England was the home of representative democracy, which helped create the conditions necessary for an Empire of free trade that, in turn, helped rid Europe of militarism and totalitarianism. In this version, England – usually conflated with the United Kingdom – is distinct but not entirely incompatible with the European Union as long as it is given special recognition for its difference. In this way, it is very much the 'Scotland of Europe'. The 'hard' English Eurosceptic version of the past presents the development of representative democracy in England as incompatible with what is perceived as the anti-democratic development of the EU since 1992 and especially after the Eurozone crisis, which means that the UK should withdraw from the EU and embrace the opportunities presented by globalisation (assuming that European integration and globalisation are incompatible). This reorientation included re-emphasising ties with its former Empire and Commonwealth that helped Britain win the war, but was then betrayed in 1973 by what was presented as a spineless political class that had lost faith in the nation. Both versions crowded out a Europhilic English version of the past and both were deployed by their political supporters to legitimise their projects of reform or exit.

Chapter 4, 'Gift to the World', develops this idea of the importance of English constitutional history as a form of resistance to European integration and for Anglosphere thought. England's constitutional development is the fulcrum that links English nationalism, Euroscepticism and the Anglosphere and serves as the foundation for all three ideologies. Thus Chapter 4 begins by looking at the debate surrounding the re-publication of Henrietta Marshall's *Our Island Story* in 2005 and the subsequent political support for that celebratory Edwardian English constitutional narrative in 2010–14 as a means of cohering Britain and Britishness and suggesting an alternative (global) future to Europe through a 'shared exceptionalism'. In this context, this chapter argues that support for Henrietta Marshall's book was not just a debate about history teaching but suggested the constitutional and global preferences of the Conservative elements of the Coalition Government (even the ultimately pro-Remain ones), thereby reinforcing an Anglosphere narrative in English public life.

Chapter 5, 'Greater Britain', develops this theme and examines England's 'wider categories of belonging', an important element in generating support for the Anglosphere and hence imagining the UK outside of the EU. It argues that, given the importance of sovereignty in England, the boundaries of Englishness were blurred during the historical formation of nationalism that conditions an Anglo-British worldview to this day. Importantly, this historical blurring occurs alongside a conceptual one, whereby sovereignty is equated with 'greatness' that is in turn equated with Empire (or a particular memory of it). The sub-argument is that this imperial dimension to English national consciousness has been reworked and rehabilitated for a global era. Once again, debates about Empire – whether it was a 'Good Thing' or a 'Bad Thing' – were not merely academic (or comedic) but were part of a political project that sought to legitimise a reorientation away from Europe and towards a global policy underpinned by the importance of free trade.

Chapter 6, 'Great Wars', examines the place of war memory in situating England between Europe, the Anglosphere and the wider world, whilst at the same time cohering the United Kingdom around the most commonly shared narrative amongst the nations of the UK. Interpretations of the past as a guide for current and future action are a crucial element of nationalist ontology. The so-called 'second memory boom' beginning in the late twentieth century was not simply a nationalist phenomenon but there were strong affinities between remembrance, commemoration and national narratives. This was especially true for English memory of the wars of the twentieth century. Whereas a Franco-German narrative emerged soon after the end of the Second World War that saw European integration as a logical outcome of the conflicts between 1914 and 1945, a contrary conclusion took root in England. In England, the wars suggested that Continental Europe was a source of threat to England with '1940' standing as a metaphor for the defence of British sovereignty par excellence. British accession to the European Communities in 1973 represented a historical rupture via the United Kingdom's seemingly ever-closer relationship with former enemies at the expense of traditional allies. Thus the accelerating pace of war commemoration at the start of the twenty-first century helped reinforce an English worldview that again favoured the Anglosphere at the expense of Europe.

Chapter 7, 'Leap into the Known', examines the part played by arguments for the Anglosphere in the referendum campaign that began in earnest after the Conservative election victory in 2015. Heavily bound up in ideas about globalisation and at times subsumed amongst alternative 'models' for the UK's relationship with the EU, the Anglosphere exercised a strong ideational pull away from the European Union for pro-Leave elites. In contrast to 1975, when the regime of global governance and free trade was less extensive and the Commonwealth was not a political community that could offer any alternative to Europe, Eurosceptics in 2016 turned to the Anglosphere as a more appropriate cultural and economic 'fit' than the EU and one whose 'muscular liberalism' was a more effective counter to the threats of the twenty-first century than an EU that one Eurosceptic critic described as 'regulated, apologetic, sclerotic and feeble (Hannan, 2013: 356)'. Such a critique and reorientation sat comfortably with English nationalism committed to a defence of British sovereignty and attuned to the (somewhat illusory and certainly not straight forward) sense of commonality with the English-speaking peoples of the world.

Chapter 8, 'Taking Back Control', examines the fate of England during the process of Brexit that began after the referendum vote of 2016. The Brexit referendum was a 'moment' in the history of English nationalism and the vote to leave was built on particularly English issues and worldviews. Yet in the aftermath of the vote, England receded in political importance – at least that accorded to it by senior political actors as the UK Government sought to 'take back control' not only from the European Union, but also from the alternative and potentially competing sources of sovereignty called into salience through the referendum.

Each of these chapters is preceded by a vignette of a commemorative moment from the recent past. These vignettes are designed to highlight the way in which State-sponsored history informs public life in England, which will help to make the link between the past and present, via memory, in this account of contemporary English nationalism.

The book concludes with Chapter 9, 'Interregnum and Restoration: Brexit as English nationalism', arguing that the political memory of England's constitutional development, of its imperial past and of twentieth-century warfare are the cords that unite English nationalism, Euroscepticism and the Anglosphere. If '1688' established the English genius for government, which was exported by Empire and saved in '1940', the lasting result of the endurance of English sovereignty was a blurring of the boundaries of political Englishness. This blurring shaped the national imagination in England in enduring ways. Contemporary resistance to European integration revived and energised this powerful national tradition in England, historically founded on the defence of British sovereignty. Like the words of 'Land of Hope and Glory', which express a particular idea of England without ever mentioning it, England's nationalism should be understood as being constituted in a wide frame. It is both merged with and occluded by these wider categories of belonging. The wide boundaries of this historical imagination inclined English nationalists away from European integration and towards the Anglosphere as an affective political community. This national imaginary framed responses to major political dilemmas, which it also helped cause. English nationalism coalesced around resistance to the European Union and put the United Kingdom on a trajectory that seemingly set England's boundaries 'wider still and wider' at the beginning of the twenty-first century.

2

England's dilemmas: national questions in a global era

The Treaty of Rome, 2017

Some birthdays are a cause for celebration. At others you find yourself in a corner of a room crying into your beer and wondering where it all went wrong. The sixtieth anniversary of the signing of the Treaty of Rome in 2017 was more the latter than the former. In that year, the European Union was in the midst of the most significant and sustained series of crises in its existence since Euratom and the European Economic Community were signed into existence back in 1957.

The United Kingdom was not present at the Treaty of Rome commemorations – or rather it was conspicuous by its absence. For sure, there were the official celebrations, including a Declaration, a white paper on the future of the EU and some sombre speeches from heads of state and government. But the ghost at the banquet was Brexit. If there had been a growing sense of distance between citizens and the European project in its forties, and the Eurozone and migration crises had not been bad enough in its fifties, Brexit really was *la cerise sur le gâteau* as the EU turned sixty.

Although barely mentioned at the anniversary, the secession of the United Kingdom from the European Union denied the EU of one of its three most important member states. This importance was predicated on the UK's economy – the fifth largest in the world in 2016 – and its diplomatic and security capabilities. With a population of 63 million recorded at the census of 2011, the UK also represented 17 per cent of the EU's total population of 503 million. The UK had been one of three states whose accession to the Treaty of Rome in 1973 represented the first enlargement of the European Communities. Notwithstanding Greenland's decision to leave the EEC in 1982, by voting to leave the UK was the first member state to cause the European Union to significantly contract.

With the UK set to leave, the European Union started to look like the united Europe envisioned by Count Richard Coudenhove-Kalergi in his inter-war designs for European unity, published in 1923 as *Pan-Europa*. In this vision, Europe was constituted as a means to recreate prosperity after the First World War and as a bulwark against Bolshevik Russia. Much like Winston Churchill's call for 'some sort of United States of Europe' in 1946, the United Kingdom was not part of this vision. Its interests and inclinations were bound up with its global Empire. Charles de Gaulle shared this view, and it was only the protestations of the Conservative leadership in the 1960s and 1970s – and a much more ambivalent Labour leadership dragging its recalcitrant party along with it in the 1970s – that convinced a majority of the UK electorate in 1975 otherwise.

However, the idea of Britain with a global past (and therefore a potentially global future) never really went away. The low point of this vision was from the 1970s to the 1990s, when the end of Empire and the development of regional forms of integration – the EU, NAFTA, Australian and New Zealand engagement with an emerging Asia – appeared to suggest that Britain's global pretensions had faded like the seafront of an English coastal resort: a site of fond memories perhaps, yet unable to compete with the glamour of a European future.

But Brexit changed that. Indeed Brexit made the return of 'global Britain' an economic and diplomatic necessity. By the time of the sixtieth anniversary of the Treaty of Rome, the United Kingdom's involvement in the historic process of European integration began to look more like an interregnum than the post-war restoration that Harold Macmillan told the British public it represented when his government began to shift British policy away from the Commonwealth and towards Europe in the early 1960s. Whilst European leaders contemplated what the EU might look like after what the European Commission President, Jean-Claude Juncker, called the 'tragedy' of Brexit, the government in Westminster contemplated the political task ahead of it: uniting the (unspecified) country around a withdrawal from the EU whilst simultaneously seeking new allies and keeping the United Kingdom from coming apart at its national seams in the process.

England is a problem. Or rather, Britain's political classes have a problem situating England within the United Kingdom's changing constitutional framework and the UK's shifting position in the global order. England's problematic place in the United Kingdom, and hence in the European Union and beyond, was a phenomenon that commentators found easier to address than politicians. Writing just before the Brexit referendum of June 2016, Fintan O'Toole wrote in the *Guardian* that 'When you strip away the rhetoric, Brexit is an English nationalist movement... The passion that animates it is English self-assertion... Over time, the main political entity most likely to emerge from Brexit is not a Britain with its greatness restored or a sweetly reunited kingdom. It is a standalone England' (O'Toole, 2016). Reflecting on the position of England a year and a half after the referendum as the negotiations to leave the EU reached a critical stage David Marquand concluded that 'Britain's problem is not with Europe, but with England' (Marquand, 2017). This focus on England was belatedly welcome; yet if England was a distinct political entity as in Marquand's formulation, it opened a series of questions and political dilemmas about England's relationship to the United Kingdom, the European Union and the world.

England was also a problem for political science. Political scientists were slow to provide any answers to these conundrums. This quiescence was itself a product of the pluri-national composition of the British state and England's unstated dominance within it. As Ailsa Henderson, Charlie Jeffery, Daniel Wincott and Richard Wyn Jones argued:

> the complexities of a state with four component units become simplified into the study of 'British politics', [and thereby create] a process which has the effect of veiling the characteristics and impact of England, the biggest part of the United Kingdom, at the same time as marginalising engagement with other parts of the UK. (Henderson et al., 2017: 632)

The authors concluded that the result of this was a 'triple effacement' that marginalised Northern Ireland, pushed Scotland and Wales to the edges of research and occluded England, meaning that 'we end up analysing the United Kingdom as a fictive country: Anglo-Britain' (Henderson et al., 2017: 632). This chapter (and this book) seeks to eschew any such misplaced analyses by making English nationalism the independent variable and focus of enquiry. There is, however, no avoiding the continuing elision between England, Britain and the United Kingdom that exists (in political rhetoric) despite twenty years of devolution. Indeed, this is the most salient characteristic of English nationalism, as it is historically constituted. Accordingly, this book and chapter will show how English nationalism is simultaneously expressed by and subsumed within a defence of British sovereignty that leads to a particular framing of major political – and especially constitutional – dilemmas in British politics. This defence of British sovereignty led to a nationalist logic of leaving the EU and reconnecting the UK with a global-era version of the 'English-speaking peoples'.

Nationalism and Britain: evading the 'English question'

One of the most notable things about the aftermath of the referendum on Scottish independence in 2014 was how quickly it became a debate about England. This was because the UK Independence Party (UKIP) was making inroads into Conservative electoral support that threatened to take away votes at the upcoming general election (Jeffery et al., 2016: 346). David Cameron, who had made key interventions about the importance of being British before and during the 2014 referendum campaign, quickly shifted the terms of debate when speaking to the press outside 10 Downing Street in the early morning of 19 September 2014 just after Scotland had voted to remain in the UK. 'It is absolutely right', Cameron said, 'that a new and fair settlement for Scotland should be accompanied by a new and fair settlement that applies to all parts of our United Kingdom ... I have long believed', he continued,

> that a crucial part missing from this national discussion is England. We have heard the voice of Scotland – and now the millions of voices of England must also be heard. The question of English votes for English laws – the so-called West Lothian Question – requires a decisive answer. (Cameron, 2014e)

The 'West Lothian Question' was a means of posing the 'English Question' in British politics without explicitly specifying the nation at the centre of the conundrum. This dilemma – whether or not the Westminster parliament was sufficient to represent England in a devolved United Kingdom – was not initially called the 'English Question' because for a long time in politics and political science England was not deemed to exist as a political unit: it was, in Richard Rose's conceptualisation, a state of mind rather than a self-consciously organised political community (Rose, 1965: 5). Famously exemplifying the tradition of evasion at the outset of the devolution resettlement, Derry Irvine suggested in 1997 that the best way to answer the English question was to stop asking it (cited in Aughey, 2007: 201). Cameron's move to put England into the constitutional politics of the United Kingdom was a significant step. Up until then, none of the major political parties had seen advantage or had the inclination to address the issue of a rising sense of politicised Englishness (Mycock and Hayton, 2014: 267).

This type of habitual evasion contributed to the sense that although other nationalities and identities in Britain and around the world could be celebrated and represented politically, the same was not and could not be true for England and the English: hence Cameron's adoption of the idea that the millions of voices of the English needed to be heard. Yet the Conservatives' 'decisive answer' to the West Lothian question was English Votes for English Laws (EVEL). EVEL passed the House of Commons final reading on 15 July 2015 and received Royal Assent on 22 October 2015. This provision meant that a 'double majority' was now required for those laws that applied to England or England and Wales only: a Bill required a majority of Westminster MPs and those representing English (and Welsh constituencies) to pass. Yet even this attempt to isolate England as a political community led to further elision between England and Britain when Labour MP Tristram Hunt described this solution to the English Question as a 'very British muddle' (Hunt, 2016).

Opposition from Labour and the Scottish National Party (SNP) was predictable to a move that appeared to give the Conservatives a large majority amongst English

MPs and divided members on national as well as party lines. Shadow Leader of the Commons, Angela Eagle, described EVEL in its early stages as a 'back of the fag packet' response to the English question, whilst Ed Miliband argued that EVEL was 'an act of constitutional vandalism' (cited in BBC News Politics, 2015a and BBC News Politics, 2015b). Further muddying the national waters was opposition from an English Unionist perspective. Conservative MP and member of Commonwealth and Foreign Affairs Committee, Andrew Rosindell, was concerned that EVEL might 'damage the fabric of our cherished Union and lead to a situation where this House could be deemed to be the representative assembly of England, rather than the House of Commons of the United Kingdom of Great Britain and Northern Ireland' (Hansard, 2015a, 22 October, vol. 600, col. 1119).

The asymmetrical outcome of the devolution resettlement was initially driven by attempts to contain nationalist politics in Scotland, Wales and Northern Ireland and restore civic government to London. But initial responses to this political asymmetry were themselves conceptually asymmetrical, hoping to resolve a 'national' question with regional governance. This tension was not addressed systematically and a default 'muddle through' position emerged within both major English parties (Mycock, 2016: 389).

Such a position was understandable given the defeat of the referendum on devolving powers to the North-East of England in 2004. New Labour governments were uninterested in questions of political Englishness in the early 2000s, whereas Gordon Brown made Britishness his focus in the latter part of the decade. If plans to devolve power to Scotland were driven by nationalist and civil society pressures demanding a response from Unionist parties, then there appeared to be little such demand or political gain to be had from regional devolution in England. When such devolution came in the form of city governments and metro mayors it was a Whitehall-inspired top-down process of centralised decentralisation.

But for all this the English question did not go away. In opposition there was a cautious embrace of the need to shift Labour from its traditional Unionism to one that acknowledged the need to recognise England and the English more explicitly in Labour's articulations of its Unionism. Encouraged by policy advisor and 'Blue Labour' founder Jon Cruddas and the former cabinet minister John Denham, the Labour leader Ed Miliband argued in 2012 that 'we in the Labour Party have been reluctant to talk about England in recent years'. Noting that 'the English people don't yearn for a simplistic constitutional symmetry', Miliband conjured a future-oriented progressive patriotism founded on a historical memory of tolerance and acceptance and an emphasis on regional identities (Miliband, 2012).

This plan to give more centrality to England in Labour's campaigning was given greater urgency by two events in 2014 and 2015. The first was the reaction to Emily Thornbury's tweet showing a white van parked outside of a house draped with three English flags during the 2014 Rochester and Strood by-election that saw Douglas Carswell re-elected as MP for that constituency, for his new party,

UKIP. Thornberry was a shadow cabinet minister and MP for Islington North and Finsbury and so the selection and tweeting of the image along with the single word 'Rochester' was enough to be read as an act of snobbery on behalf of the metropolitan elite towards the non-metropolitan English that forced Thornberry's swift resignation (Mason, 2014). It illustrated Michael Kenny's point about the politically untenable nature of such attitudes in the face of what was becoming a claim for recognition by or on behalf of the 'white working class': 'the option of screening out these claims, or putting them down to misguided prejudice, is likely to become increasingly incompatible if sections of this constituency continue to detach from parties of the left, and provide support for far-right parties or anti-establishment populists' (Kenny, 2012: 32).

The second event had greater medium-term significance: Labour's loss of all but one seat in Scotland in the 2015 General Election. This collapse followed the Pyrrhic victory in the Scottish independence referendum the previous year. This victory exhausted the Scottish Labour Party and paved the way for the SNP to win fifty-six of Scotland's fifty-nine Westminster seats at the General Election. Much like the Conservatives in 1997, Labour was now a de facto English party. In the wake of the failure to win government at Westminster in 2015, a Labour ginger group called Red Shift made a progressive Englishness the second of their ten recommendations to win power back in England, crucial to the formation of government at Westminster. This group of MPs called on the leadership to embrace the politics of English identity as 'a positive statement of national expression and pride in England' and to stop seeing Englishness as something 'negative, divisive and dangerous' (Red Shift, 2015: 4). Labour's Unionism was born of different material and ideational elements, but like the Conservatives in 1997 the Labour Party's Unionist traditions and instincts ran deep and the political outcome was a largely unaltered defence of the Union. Yet attempts to promote Labour's radical traditions under Corbyn after his election as leader sat in an uneasy relationship with an emerging politicised Englishness envisioned by Blue Labour and Red Shift. As Emily Robinson argued, a politics of radical nostalgia was 'unable to speak to either the competitive politics of nationalism or received understandings of English nationhood' (Robinson, 2016: 386).

This did not prevent political parties and governments from trying to speak to traditions of political Englishness, but the rhetorical response to the dilemma was predominantly British in register rather than English, despite the growing survey evidence of a politicised Englishness (Wyn Jones et al., 2012; Wyn Jones et al., 2013). Solutions to problems of representation are crucially important in nation-states but they must exist in a dialogue with other more symbolic forms of representation in order to resonate with a wider citizenry. This symbolic repertoire was engaged ahead of the European football championships and the London Olympics of 2012 because international sporting events push such questions to the fore. The dilemma in 2012 was which anthem English sportsmen and women should sing during these international competitions: 'God Save the Queen' or some other anthem over which there was as yet no agreement? Cameron had already told ConservativeHome that he preferred 'Jerusalem' as the English anthem (ConservativeHome, 2012). An Early Day Motion was tabled on St George's Day 2012 calling for a specifically English anthem (EDM 2992). In justifying this move, Liberal Democrat Greg Mulholland, the principal sponsor of the Motion argued that it was wrong for English teams to use the UK national anthem when competing as England rather than as Great Britain because this confused England with Britain and the UK and was damaging to the unity of the United Kingdom (Mulholland, 2012).

Mulholland's EDM built on a campaign for an English anthem by British Futures and Anthem4England. The latter described itself as a campaign for 'people who are heartily fed up of *God Save the Queen* being used as the English national anthem' (Anthem4England, 2017). British Futures was a London-based think tank dedicated to identity issues and it assembled a symbolically cross-party group of MPs supported by academics and other think tanks to push for an English anthem. The grounds for this call were essentially Unionist: 'The lack of an English national anthem can lead to complaints about a lack of fair play, while treating the British national anthem as if it belongs to England undermines an equal claim to British identity and the allegiance of other nations within the United Kingdom', claimed the group (cited in ConservativeHome, 2012). By filling this political space with a moderate nationalism (usually constituted as patriotism) it was hoped that an English anthem would also act as a bulwark against extremist nationalism.

The issue of an English anthem was back on the political agenda again in 2016, once again ahead of the European Championships and Olympic Games. Labour MP Toby Perkins sponsored an English Anthem Bill. Two persistent elements regarding solutions to England's political dilemmas emerged in the course of this bill. The first was that regional identities made imagining England as a political community difficult. 'I won't say which area it was that thought the most appropriate choice for an English national anthem should be "Heaven Knows I'm Miserable Now" (it will remain a secret between myself and the listeners of BBC Humberside)' he said, but also noted that such a choice was 'perhaps reflective that each local area has its own sense of what Englishness means' (cited in BBC News, 2016a). Secondly, was opposition from a more strident Unionism than that of British Futures' variety. Anticipating the drive to keep the United Kingdom together whilst seceding from the EU, prominent Brexiteer Jacob Rees-Mogg argued that he opposed the Bill for an English anthem for 'deep and serious reasons'. Subsuming England into the wider categories of belonging denoted by the United Kingdom and the Crown by use of the non-specific term 'country', Rees-Mogg asked:

> What greater pleasure can there be for a true-born English man or true-born English woman than to listen to our own national anthem – a national anthem for our whole country, for our whole United Kingdom, of which England is but a part, but an

important part – and to listen to those words that link us to our Sovereign, who is part of that chain that takes us back to our immemorial history? (Hansard, 2016a, 13 January, vol. 604, col. 866)

The Unionist and monarchist Anthem4England saw Rees-Mogg's interpretation of Unionism as part of the problem. 'While it may be politically convenient for the UK Government to encourage Scottishness and Welshness whilst keeping Britishness to the fore in England', it argued, 'it serves neither Britain nor the monarchy to do so' (Anthem4England, 2017). Yet Rees-Mogg's intervention against an expression of English nationhood that was increasingly suggesting a degree of alienation from the British state and its forms of governance was indicative of another political project – indeed another 'national question' playing out internationally – in which Rees-Mogg and his English compatriots played significant part.

Resistance to Europe: posing the 'British question'

Ahead of the elections to the European Parliament in 2014 and the immanent referendum on Scottish independence, David Cameron said that over the next three years the country had three major political dilemmas to resolve: whether to break up the UK, whether to back ongoing austerity and whether to stay in a reformed European Union (BBC News, 2014). The plan for a referendum on Britain's membership of the European Union (at that time mooted for 2017 in the event of a future Conservative majority at Westminster) would guarantee, it was hoped, that another Conservative government would not be 'obsessed by Europe, divided and distracted from the concerns of ordinary people' (BBC News, 2014).

This did not turn out to be the case. The reference to 'economic policies' (otherwise known as 'austerity') hinted at another major dilemma: what to do about a growing tide of opinion that rejected mainstream political parties and politics (Mair, 2013). Speaking after the Queen's Speech in June 2014 leader of the opposition, Ed Miliband, noted that 'there is a depth and scale of disenchantment that we ignore at our peril' (Hansard, 2014a, 4 June, vol. 582, col. 15). The way to restore trust in politics adopted by the Conservative leadership was to increase the mechanisms of direct democracy in British politics, notably a referendum on the UK's membership of the EU. 'I think that one of the ways in which we can turn people back on to politics' argued David Cameron in the same debate, 'is to make clear that, when it comes to the vital issue of whether or not Britain should be a member of reformed European Union, it is the British people who should have their say' (Hansard, 2014b, 4 June, vol. 582, col. 24).

Referendums assume a settled understanding of which 'people' will be represented by the vote. This was not the case for the United Kingdom as the referendums and elections of 2014 to 2016 had shown. Like the EU, the UK also appeared to lack a unified *demos*. The salience of the third of Cameron's major dilemmas in British politics – what attitudes the United Kingdom should have towards European integration and ultimately whether it should stay in the EU or leave it – sustained the elision of England, Britain and the UK in England, devolution and the Scottish 'Indyref' notwithstanding. It also mobilised English nationalism through the device of a referendum: firstly through calls for such an act at the time of the decision to join or remain outside of the Eurozone and ultimately in the lead up to the Brexit referendum of June 2016. It did so by gradually revealing England as a de facto political community, but one that was only rarely articulated as English. This was a result not only of parties' need to appeal broadly across Britain, but as part of the historical conditioning of English nationalism in its relationship to British sovereignty.

As we have seen in Chapter 1, part of the problem in even conceiving of an 'English question' was the long-standing elision between the concepts of England, Britain and the United Kingdom – and even the 'English-speaking peoples'. This historically informed elision came about due to the defence of British sovereignty that was and is such a notable feature of English nationalism. Placing sovereignty at the centre of an account of English nationalism allows us to understand popular and elite articulations of English nationhood, and its elision with 'wider categories of belonging' such as Britain and the Anglosphere. It also has the advantage of allowing us to understand English nationalism in its integrationist and autonomist-secessionist forms. Although the English defence of British sovereignty within the United Kingdom was important, the second major way that the defence of British sovereignty remained a central element in English nationalism was via resistance to European integration through which contemporary English nationalism developed a secessionist element unheard of in its previous history. Unlike its Scottish counterpart, however, this secessionist element was not directed at the United Kingdom, but at the European Union instead.

There were many drivers of resistance to European integration in Britain dating from the 1960s: the Labour left's fears of economic competition and its critique of the European Communities as a (Catholic) capitalist club; a neo-liberal critique of 'big government'; a Thatcherite critique of economic and monetary union; memory of twentieth-century conflict; and not least popular and elite resentment of the free movement of labour after the 'big bang' enlargement of 2004–07. But what is both 'embedded and persistent' in this Eurosceptic politics is a defence of British sovereignty in order to protect whatever political project or interest is being played out in the UK itself. It is this that gives the appearance of a persistent 'British' quality to resistance to European integration across parties and over time. Without a defence of the UK's sovereignty, none of the diverse political projects noted above could have been safeguarded in the face of the political and economic drivers of European integration. Thus although sovereignty is sometimes portrayed as an abstract concept, it is an often taken-for-granted foundational element of political life. It is a crucial element in understanding nationalism. English nationalism is no exception and within conservative narratives of English nationalism sovereignty takes on a particular quasi-cultural significance as the 'British way of doing things'.

Nevertheless, the Brexit referendum vote illustrated English distinctiveness. England's overall 54–46 per cent vote to leave – London included – contrasted with Scotland's and Northern Ireland's votes to remain: 62–38 and 54–46 per cent respectively. England's vote was more in line with Wales's 52–48 per cent vote to leave, which mirrored the aggregated UK vote. Yet these figures require interpretation and explanation. Using political traditions – and significant changes to them – to interpret the Brexit vote, helps us understand the old and new political cleavages animating the political contestation surrounding ideas of nationhood and sovereignty.

The SNP and Plaid Cymru policies of 'Independence in Europe' adopted in the 1990s, and Sinn Fein's cautious endorsement of the EU in Northern Ireland after 2007, highlighted a different way of viewing European integration in the nationalist politics of Scotland, Wales and Northern Ireland to those articulated in England and amongst Ulster Unionists. In the Scottish case, this policy shift contrasted with what Graeme Morton has called 'unionist-nationalism' which divorced nationalism from secessionist implications and instead highlighted its integrationist qualities (Morton, 1996: 258). That is to say, an ongoing union with England best served Scotland's 'national interest', thus laying the basis for what was for centuries the dominant version of (integrationist) Scottish nationalism. This long-standing assumption in Scottish politics was challenged more recently by a secessionist-nationalist argument that Scotland's national interest (however defined) was best served by independence from the United Kingdom, but not the European Union. Thus outside of England it was possible to find political parties advocating membership of the European Union as something that would *enhance* national independence and sovereignty, rather than – as was the case in England once the decision not to join the Eurozone had been taken – constrain independence and sovereignty. Similarly the part played by the EU in the Northern Ireland Peace Process during the 1990s and afterwards, and the role of European integration in easing movement across the border between the UK and the Republic of Ireland, meant that the EU enjoyed levels of public support in Northern Ireland not seen elsewhere in the UK.

This divergence on the issue of European integration was significant for nationalist politics in England. Resistance to European integration laid the foundations for contemporary English nationalism in two important ways. First of all, the traditional defence of imperial British sovereignty meant that imperial and national discourses were interwoven in expressions of English nationhood (Kumar, 2003; Wellings, 2002). This had the effect of drawing the worldview imparted by the dominant version of English nationalism away from Europe and towards the English-speaking peoples and the Commonwealth. Secondly, the end of empire in the post-war era meant that English nationalism became more concerned with the defence of

British – as opposed to a wider imperial – sovereignty. Membership of the European Communities was supposed to restore the 'greatness' lost with decolonisation, but this only served to institutionalise the English memory of decline in the form of the European Union (Wellings, 2010).

By the early 1990s, British sovereignty was again perceived to be under threat: this time not from Imperial or Nazi Germany but from the process of European integration and – as the decade wore on – from secessionist nationalism, particularly in Scotland. What emerged out of this twin threat – with resistance to Europe being initially far more important to the articulation of English nationalism than resistance to Scotland – was the embedding of Euroscepticism as both a distinctive feature of English political life and the most formed-up and coherent expression of English nationalism; even if it was a nationalism that used the symbolism and rhetoric of Britishness to make its claims for distinctiveness (Wellings, 2012).

This dual defence of British sovereignty from challenges stemming from the process of European integration and the politics of secessionist nationalism illuminated traditional integrationist and novel secessionist tendencies in contemporary English nationalism. The integrationist tendency in English nationalism rested on an often unstated assumption that the Unions with Wales, Scotland and Northern Ireland were in England's best interests and without which the United Kingdom's status as a great power would be diminished. Thus the principles underpinning Graeme Morton's 'unionist-nationalism' could equally be applied to England as much as Scotland. Since the Treaty of Union with Scotland – or more accurately since Jacobite and Wilkite challenges to the Union had been overcome by the late eighteenth century, English nationalism was not defined by secessionism or unification, but rather by the desire to defend a loosely integrated union state from external threats throughout the nineteenth and twentieth centuries until the end of the Cold War. Combined with resistance to the European Union, the challenge of Scottish secessionism from 2007 exposed and reinvigorated these long-standing yet dormant arguments in English nationalism, leading to English nationalism being defined and enacted around a defence against European integration and support for British integration.

William Hague noted the interlinked questions for European and British integration. Hague pitched his argument for remaining in the EU from the perspective of the regional and international orders. 'There is no doubt that without the United Kingdom', he wrote, 'that the EU would be weaker. It would lose the fifth largest economy of the world, the continent's greatest centre of finance, and one of its only two respected military powers'. But the greatest risk of Brexit did not come from its possible impact on the EU he warned, but on the UK:

> We will have to ask, disliking so many aspects of it as we do, whether we really want to weaken it, and at the same time increase the chances, if the UK left the EU, of Scotland leaving the UK. To end up destroying the United Kingdom and gravely weakening the European Union would not be a very clever day's work. (Hague, 2015)

John Major echoed this fear. Framing the dilemma posed by the referendum as a choice between 'Great Britain or Little Britain' Major argued that the slogan 'Give us our country back' was undoubtedly an emotional appeal 'that warms the heart of all those who love our country, as I do', but he cautioned that as a 'meaningless soundbite' it was a 'prelude to disappointment':

> And what country, exactly, will we 'get back'? Will Scotland remain part of the UK? As a Unionist, I hope so – but no one should ignore the threat that if the UK-wide vote is to leave, Scotland may demand another referendum on independence. The UK out of the EU and Scotland out of the UK would be a truly awful outcome. (Major, 2016)

Scottish nationalism was not the only concern, however. What was novel was the development of a *secessionist* element to English nationalism from the 1990s. Importantly, these ideas and arguments were not aimed at the United Kingdom, even if there was disquiet about the financial arrangements of the United Kingdom in the wake of the devolution settlement (Wyn Jones et al., 2013: 20). The secessionist expression of English nationalism was aimed however, not at the United Kingdom, but at the European Union. It was at first evidenced by the creation of UKIP in 1993 and the Referendum Party in 1997. These parties existed at the margins of political life until success at elections for the European Parliament in 2004, 2009 and especially 2014 moved secession from the European Union up the political agenda in the United Kingdom. UKIP's challenge in particular threatened and emboldened backbenchers on the right of the Conservative party and contributed to the concession of what was still called in 2013 an 'in–out referendum' (Lynch and Whitaker, 2013: 306; Tournier-Sol, 2015: 140).

Support for this Euroscepticism was notably English, even if the nation at the heart of the dilemma was rarely named as such. The unstated Englishness inherent in Major's evocation of 'Little Britain' was masked by the rhetoric of Britishness deployed by Brexiteers and the Unionism of the Remain campaign. In the case of UKIP, Richard Hayton has argued that 'although an explicitly politicised Englishness sometimes breaks through into UKIP's rhetoric, the Anglo-British view precludes the wholehearted embrace of the more radical positions favoured by some English nationalists', meaning that a 'full-blooded, politicised English nationalism' has not emerged (Hayton, 2016: 408).

Hayton's conclusion accords with Michael Kenny's view that 'properly nationalist sentiments are held only by a minority of English citizens' (Kenny, 2014: 232). Such preclusions, however, depend on the definition of 'full-blooded' and 'proper' nationalism and assume that England and Britain are conceptually distinct when in fact the two concepts frequently merge. An example of this elision of England and Britain came during the Brexit referendum campaign. Former England cricketer Sir Ian Botham appeared at a pro-Brexit event in Durham, where he observed that 'the people coming into our country, they don't seem to have come over with a job, any qualifications, they just turn up', arguing that as a result the country would 'get cluttered'. 'Personally, I think that England is an island,' he concluded, 'and I think that England should be England; and I think that we should keep that' (cited in Liew, 2016). Botham's logic illustrated the way that dissatisfaction with the European Union – in particular the free movement of labour, one of its fundamental 'four freedoms' – framed England as an 'island', rhetorically extending English sovereignty over the rest of Great Britain, merging the part with the whole.

There was, of course, nothing new in this elision of England and Britain (Smith, 2006: 433). What was truly novel about the articulation of English nationalism – at least as an elite project – in the decade preceding the Brexit vote was a return to an older, nineteenth and early twentieth century, conception of English nationhood that rested heavily on its imperial legacy and historic ties with the 'English-speaking peoples' of the world. Despite being characterised as 'parochial', English nationalism sustains one of the most globalised senses of nationhood in the world, connected in its formative years to other peoples and places across the globe. This element of English nationalism re-emerged through debates about the United Kingdom's place in the European Union, specifically through attempts to address the dilemma of what alternative might exist to the UK's membership of the EU.

The Anglosphere: answering the 'European question'

Responses to the dilemma about the UK's membership of the EU were played out in terms that were resonant with dominant themes of English nationalism whilst at the same time continuing to conflate English nationalism not just with a defence of British sovereignty but also a post-EU extension of it. This was not an extension of British sovereignty in the way that Empire had been, but instead was portrayed as a reassertion of sovereignty outside the EU that would be supported and sustained by what William Hague referred to as 'traditional allies' during his time as Foreign Secretary from 2010 to 2013, as well as the opportunities afforded a trading nation like the UK amongst the 'emerging economies' of Asia (Bevir, Daddow and Schnapper, 2015: 10). This policy reorientation required an ideational shift that simultaneously delegitimised the European Union as an inadequate vehicle for the dilemmas of a global era and also imagined the United Kingdom as an autonomous actor outside of the EU. 'What is so frightening about standing on our own two feet in a developing world, trading with whom we like?' Bernard Ingham asked readers of the *Yorkshire Post*. He continued to delegitimise the European Union in an idiom that only British people could truly comprehend: 'Victor Meldrew could only ever say to all this "I don't believe it" – and tell the EU Emperor he has no clothes' (Ingham, 2016).

This altered global dispensation, was allied with an assumption about the likely support of governments in countries predominantly populated by what were known in the 1960s as 'kith and kin', provided the answer to the most persistent dilemma associated with Euroscepticism: what other option was there but to be in the EU? Speaking in the debate on the Maastricht Treaty in 1992, Tristan Garel-Jones, the Conservative Minister for Europe, posed this very question: 'Can the anti-federalists, the Euro-sceptics and little Englanders offer a positive alternative?' (cited in Congdon, 1992: 14). For a long time this question went an answered. The 1990s were the high point of optimistic views of regional integration. Despite the revivification of the Anglo-US 'Special Relationship' during the 1980s, English-speaking countries each appeared to have their own regional vocations: the United States and Canada in NAFTA; Australia and New Zealand with their Closer Economic Relations and each individually with an economically growing Asia-Pacific region to their north. In this world of regional blocs, the United Kingdom had Europe.

Yet from this unpromising situation an answer to the dilemma of an alternative to the European Union emerged: the Anglosphere. The Anglosphere meant different things in different places, but for Eurosceptics in the United Kingdom it was constructed in opposition to the European Union (Baxendale and Wellings, in press). Although support for this idea came from conservative grandees from each of the Anglosphere's five 'core states' – the United States, the United Kingdom, Canada, Australia and New Zealand – the most sustained articulation of the idea came from Daniel Hannan, a Conservative Member of the European Parliament (EP) who entered it in 2009. Hannan, described by the *Guardian* as the 'man who brought you Brexit' (Knight, 2016), depicted the Anglosphere as 'a devolved network of allied nations' uniquely placed for historic reasons to spread and sustain liberty throughout the world, although this benign ability was under threat from within and without prior to Brexit (Hannan, 2013: 18). Above all, the Anglosphere was promoted as a vastly preferable way of organising geo-political space than the European Union. For this reason, Hannan argued that although the European Union was seemingly underpinned by a common 'Western tradition', the reality was fundamentally different. 'The three precepts that define Western civilization – the rule of law, democratic government, and individual liberty – are not equally valued across Europe' he claimed. 'When they act collectively, the member-states of the EU are quite ready to subordinate all three to political imperatives' (Hannan, 2013: 4–5).

This political subordination of liberty extended to the economy; a key site of the enactment of liberty in the neo-liberal view. Former Chancellor Nigel Lawson, who suggested that the Anglophone neo-liberal belief in the free market had clouded perceptions of the true purpose of the EU, presented this Anglosphere worldview during the Brexit campaign. 'On the European mainland it has always been well understood that the whole purpose of European integration was political, and that economic integration was simply a means to a political end', he wrote. 'In Britain, and perhaps also in the US, that has been much less well understood, particularly within the business community, who sometimes find it hard to grasp that politics can trump economics' (Lawson, 2016). For both Hannan and Lawson, the Anglosphere was a far better 'fit' for Britain – for reasons that were ultimately historical – than the European Union.

Such an argument about the English-speaking world was not – and could not – have been made in 1975 during the first referendum in the UK on membership of the European Communities. The fact that Anglosphere supporters could suggest in 2016 that the Anglosphere (and even the Commonwealth – an example of more blurring of identities in the English-speaking world) could be an alternative to membership of the EU was itself the product of the type of globalisation that Anglophone neo-liberalism helped to spread globally in the wake of the Cold War. According to Sir Peter Marshall, who was heavily involved with the Commonwealth from 1983 to 2003, the Anglosphere concept developed out of 'highly encouraging phenomena' that characterised the post-Cold War world. For Marshall the increasingly free movement of goods, services, capital and people across borders, accompanied by universal, instantaneous communications, 'readily serves to turn a world economy into a global village'. Furthermore, this global community was one in which the English, British and Commonwealth legacies were highly relevant once again: 'The English language is its *lingua franca*. British values, British democracy and the British [*sic*] legal tradition and practice are much admired. London is a prime cultural hub, much favoured by foreigners for business or as a place of residence' (Marshall, 2013: 23). In such ways, arguments about the Anglosphere offered an analysis that appeared both daringly new and reassuring traditional.

This sense of reassurance was designed to soften the sense of rupture that would inevitably attend any thought of leaving the European Union, a polity that had formed the bedrock of British foreign policy since the 1970s. Actions designed to offset this likely sense of dislocation were enacted at the bilateral level as well as more abstract arguments about the existence of the Anglosphere and the values that underpinned it. Boris Johnson's attention to Australia when he was London Mayor was a prelude to his support for Brexit. 'When Britain joined the Common Market', he wrote from Melbourne in 2013:

> it was at a time when the establishment was defeatist, declinist and obsessed with the idea that we were being left out of the most powerful economic club in the world. In those days – when olive oil and garlic had barely appeared on the dining tables of Britain – it was assumed that in order to be 'internationalist' it was enough to be European. Well, it is perfectly obvious, in 2013, that that is no longer enough – and that we need to seek a wider destiny for our country. (Johnson, 2013)

Yet this shift away from Europe required historical atonement and healing as a prelude to increased bilateral cooperation: 'It is time to undo the damage of 1973', Johnson declared. 'It is time for Britain and Australia to set up a bilateral Free Labour Mobility Zone [which] would be an assertion that we are no longer thinking of ourselves as little Europeans, run by Brussels, but as a country with a truly global perspective' (Johnson, 2013). In such formulations of Britain's place in the world the past showed the way to the future.

Not that a 'truly global perspective' was incompatible with membership of the EU for many people in the United Kingdom for whom swapping the EU for Australia may have seen like an odd way to attain such a status. Indeed for those who supported the UK remaining in the EU, membership was a vital pre-condition of the UK's economic strength. In 2014, John Major stressed the free-trade credentials of UK and Germany and the way that the EU amplified the trading strengths of both economies to an audience in Berlin. Major's speech was coordinated with David Cameron's speech to the Australian Parliament ahead of the G20 summit in which Cameron stressed the cultural, political and economic compatibility of the UK and Australia. This coordination of speeches by senior figures was evident the year before when William Hague's 2013 John Howard Lecture on renewed UK–Australia relations was scheduled to coincide with the original timing of what became Cameron's 'Bloomberg Speech', originally intended for delivery in the Netherlands. Even for pro-remain Conservatives, revivified relationships with 'traditional allies' such as Australia formed an import plank of the strategy to reform the UK's relationship with the EU whilst ultimately retaining membership. This two-level game meant that when it came to the Brexit referendum, the British public was offered a choice between soft or hard Euroscepticism and the confusing spectacle of senior figures switching from qualified opposition to the EU to a position of support (Hayton, 2018: 159).

England was never far from the thoughts of those seeking to reposition the UK in relation to the EU and the rest of the world. Major was responding to success of UKIP, not just at the elections to the EP in 2014, but in defections from the Eurosceptic right of the Conservatives and at two subsequent by-elections in the autumn of that year. Following his by-election victory on 10 October, former Conservative-turned-UKIP MP Douglas Carswell, who gained a 44 per cent swing from the Conservatives in the electorate of Clacton, departed from the Burkean understanding of representative democracy and stated that 'I resigned from parliament to face this election because I answer first, foremost and last to you. You are my boss. I will not let you down'. He too illustrated the central yet occluded place of England in his acceptance speech when he told his electors that

> We must be a party for all Britain and all Britons: first and second generation as much as every other. Our strength must lie in our breadth. If we stay true to that there is nothing that we cannot achieve. Nothing we cannot achieve in Essex and East Anglia, in England and the whole country beyond. (BBC News Politics, 2014)

Carswell's invocation of county, region, nation and an unspecified 'country beyond' was a neat summation of the geographic location of UKIP's support. But Carswell was not concerned with Essex alone. His horizons included the Anglosphere. Carswell was credited with coining the term 'Singapore on steroids' to describe his vision of the United Kingdom outside of the EU, although he disliked Singapore's hereditary and one-party 'democracy' (cited in Leonard, 2015). Despite this positive comparison, supporters of the UK's continuing membership of the EU had other islands in mind: Emannuel Macron feared the Brexit would lead to the 'Guernseyfication' of the UK, turning it into 'a little country on the world scale [that] would isolate itself and become a trading post and arbitration place at Europe's border' (cited in BBC News, 2016b). But the invocation of Singapore meant that, even accounting for Carwell's ambiguous relationship with the party, UKIP's policy orientation could hardly be described as parochial. The Anglosphere was an important element in the worldview of its policy-makers. 'Britain is not merely a European country', UKIP declared in its manifesto for the 2015 UK General Election:

> but part of a global community, the 'Anglosphere'. Beyond the EU and even the Commonwealth are a network of nations that share not merely our language but our common law, democratic traditions and global trading interests. From India to the United States, New Zealand to the Caribbean, UKIP would want to foster closer ties with the Anglosphere. (UKIP, 2015)

This view was not the preserve of UKIP alone. It formed a crucial part of both Leave campaigns' 'positive message', although the Anglosphere was rarely mentioned by name. Brexiteers had to counter the notion that leaving the EU would be an abandonment of the 'best of both worlds' (UK Government, 2016) and therefore, in the words of Nick Herbert, MP for Arundel and South Downs, a 'jump into the void' (Herbert, 2016). Iain Duncan Smith argued that 'I am positive about leaving the EU because I believe rather than saying it is a leap in the dark, I think it is a stride into the light. It is about hope versus pessimism and people will vote for that' (cited in BBC News, 2016c).

These echoes of Churchill's 'broad sunlit uplands' connected Brexit with the English-speaking tradition in British politics. Duncan Smith's argument was part of a rhetorical strategy to encourage and normalise an imagined future for the UK outside of the EU in what we might call a 'pre-post-Westphalian' conception of the state system. Nigel Lawson rhetorically posed the Remain campaign's killer question 'what is your alternative to membership of the EU?' to his readers in the *Telegraph* and concluded that it would be hard to envisage 'a more absurd question'. 'The alternative to being in the EU', Lawson pointed out, 'is not being in the EU. And it may come as a shock to the little Europeans that most of the world is not in the EU – and that most of these countries are doing better economically than most of the EU' (Lawson, 2016). Admittedly the argument about peace in Europe after 1945 had to be countered, but Lawson did this in a Realist vein, arguing that European institutions were really created 'to eliminate the threat to Europe and the wider world from a recrudescence of German militarism, by placing the German tiger in a European cage' (Lawson, 2016). Lawson pushed this line further, and in doing so brought the Anglosphere into the campaign. He argued that the real guarantor of peace in Europe was and remained the North Atlantic Treaty Organization (NATO)

> of which the UK is a leading member and the only major EU country with a commitment to spend 2 per cent of GDP on defence, plus our special intelligence relationship with the US, and the wider 'Five Eyes' intelligence agreement, which also includes Canada, Australia and New Zealand, which is crucial for our ability to defend our people against terrorists. None of these countries were members of the EU when I last checked. (Lawson, 2016)

Although the drivers of a politicised Englishness may have been 'devo-anxiety', immigration and resistance to Europe, a politicised collective identity is a necessary but not sufficient element of nationalism. Only the latter – resistance to and rejection of European integration – generated anything like a formed-up and coherent statement of English national*ism* as a political ideology, by uniting an elite project to remove the UK from the EU with popular grievances. This phenomenon was strongest in England, where Brexit mobilised a popular English identity, albeit a mobilisation that was characterised by the rhetoric of Britishness. At the elite level, however, the argument was made that Britain had not benefited *enough* from globalisation and should be exposed to more of it. 'Devo-anxiety' and a nativist reaction to immigration and the free movement of labour within the EU were important, but only in that they violated nationalist principles of self-determination and cultural homogeneity and hence compelled some sections of the English community to examine the political arrangements that governed them, aligning their grievances with (part of) an elite project to take the United Kingdom out of the European Union and realign it with Anglosphere countries. Thus the problem at the heart of Brexit was not the United Kingdom's 'awkward' relationship with the European Union, but England's increasingly awkward relationship with the UK and the dynamic this created in Britain's relationship with the EU and its renewed relationships with the rest of the world.

Conclusion

England is perceived as a political problem. There is no consensus on any potential solutions to this problem because there is no stable consensus on the unit of analysis itself. Academic analysis need not be bound by such constraints, although in practice it has tended to be so. But if we make England the main problem, in other words making it the independent variable, this opens up new perspectives on the three main political dilemmas faced in England – its relationship with and to the United Kingdom, the European Union and the wider world – that animate ideas of English nationhood and nationalism. These dilemmas are a product of English nationalism's historical conditioning: English nationalism is simultaneously expressed by and subsumed within a defence of British sovereignty. These traditions therefore help to frame potential political solutions to those dilemmas. This reflexive defence of British sovereignty led to an ultimately successful nationalist logic in England of leaving the EU and re-connecting with 'traditional allies' within and amongst the 'English-speaking peoples'. This amounted to an expression of English nationalism by allying an elite project to withdraw the UK from the EU with popular grievances felt particularly strongly in England, framed by a view of England's previous and future relations with the wider world and the English-speaking peoples in particular. Identifying contemporary dilemmas from the perspective of English nationalism understood as simultaneously hidden and manifested by ideas of Britishness leads to questions of appropriate research design to explain and illuminate this phenomenon. These questions will be addressed in Chapter 3.

3

Locating England: national traditions and political dilemmas

Bannockburn and Bastille Day, 2014

Two commemorative events in the middle of 2014 highlighted England's peculiar relationship to nationalism. The 700th anniversary commemoration of the Battle of Bannockburn that took place on 27 June 2014 with live re-enactments was given extra frisson by the impending referendum on Scottish independence later that year. Three weeks later, the annual Bastille Day Parade on 14 July not only commemorated the capture of the (almost empty) prison that came to symbolise the start of the French Revolution, but also commenced the First World War centenary commemorations by featuring detachments of troops from the seventy-six countries participating in the internationally coordinated Centenary activities.

England was present at these Scottish and French commemorative events in different ways: as the chief malefactor at Bannockburn and amongst the British detachment on the Champs Élysées. But England itself did not have such commensurate national days to commemorate for two reasons. First of all, expansionist policies since the Norman invasion – within the British Isles and across the Atlantic and worldwide – put the English in the place of colonisers rather than the colonised seeking independence or 'freedom' à la Mel Gibson. Secondly, the veneration of the evolutionary rather than revolutionary nature of England's political development meant that there was no symbolic 'revolutionary moment' to commemorate the creation of a new form of political community notionally based on popular sovereignty as in the French model; a model emulated by national states the world over and which subsequently became the norm.

Of course, the picture of historical development is not as simple as these two commemorative events suggest. Bastille Day was originally celebrated on 14 July 1790 as *la fête de la fédération*, when the Revolution was in a decidedly optimistic and constitutional phase. The Third Republic subsequently adopted it in the 1870s as a compromise solution to create a national day that would not offend the still powerful political grouping of monarchists in the new republic.

Bannockburn may have helped preserve the independence of the kingdom of Scotland from the claims of Edward II (subsequently endorsed by Pope John XXII in 1328), yet the Treaty of Union subsumed Scottish independence in 1707 and thereafter. Until the growth in support for secessionism in the 2000s, Scottish nationalism was characterised by an active participation within the structures and activities of the British state and Empire, leavened with a high degree of autonomy concerning the governance of Scotland itself.

Despite such complications, these two models of nationalism – independence and a transformative revolutionary moment – created important models for national days. England's historical development did not provide such raw materials. For a long while this could be lauded as a constitutive element of English exceptionalism and that 'merely' national commemorations were not necessary for such an expansive and trail-blazing polity as England-in-Britain. Royal jubilees filled the role of national days from the early nineteenth century, but as England entered the 2000s, calls for St George's Day to be made a public holiday grew. The date for this, 23 April, happily brought together England's Patron Saint's Day with William Shakespeare's birthday. But at this time, a push for 'England Day' had to contend with a commensurate push for 'Britain Day', initiated by Gordon Brown, a Prime Minister from Scotland. The day subsequently chosen after a period of consultation with the public was 15 June, the anniversary of the signing of Magna Carta in 1215 – an event very important to the development of English politics but which was not seen as foundational in other parts of the United Kingdom. The overall effect of the push for 'Britain Day' underlined the way that the United Kingdom served as a vehicle for imparting an English worldview to the rest of the UK but at the same time had the continued effect of obscuring England as a political community within British structures. England may have been easy to discern by Scottish nationalists on the field of Bannockburn in 2014, but it was obscured by Britain in the Bastille Day parade and hidden in plain view by the attempt to create a 'British' day.

The Englishness of the vote to leave the European Union in 2016 requires an examination of an elusive subject: English nationalism. There is little academic or political consensus on this topic and whether or not a politicised English identity can be labelled nationalism as such or into what kind of model of nationalism England best fits. Such divergent views depend on definitions of nationalism itself. This chapter argues that one of the most important frames for linking popular grievances and the elite project of leaving the EU was a national one in which a majority of the English electorate sought to defend British sovereignty from the EU. This conclusion can be reached by examining the traditions in English politics and history that frame the dilemma of the UK's membership of the European Union. This historic imperative in English nationalism created a sense of nationhood that was broader than England alone and was constituted through engagement with other peoples across the world, notably the English-speaking peoples. This was a major component of the wider categories of belonging that informed understandings of an English nationhood that was still inflected towards former 'white' dominions and the United States. This merged the content of English nationalism with wider polities and projects, notably Britain and Empire, but not the European Union, for which the Anglosphere operated as an alternative in the nationalist imagination.

Between Scotland and France: abnormal nationalism and England's absence

The point of departure for this chapter is an engagement with comparative analyses of English nationalism that, theoretically speaking, locate England somewhere between Scotland and France. This conclusion was made in slightly differing ways by two important theorists of English nationalism and national identity: Tom Nairn and Krishan Kumar. Both theorists sought to explain the 'peculiarity' of England's political development and the effects of this on expressions of nationalism and national identity in England. Implicit and explicit in both accounts are the concepts of abnormality and absence that powerfully shape how we understand nationalism in contemporary England.

Tom Nairn began theorising English nationalism long before mainstream social sciences in the UK turned their attention to this topic. Political science in particular was largely uninterested in the English dimension to 'territorial politics'. Where it was concerned with nationalism at all, secessionist movements on the periphery – especially violent ones – were taken as the problem under scrutiny rather than the stable core. Richard Rose's description of England (noted above) as 'a state of mind', rather than a nation, unconsciously echoed Metternich's judgement that 'Italy' was just a geographic expression. This gave expression to an assumption in political science (not shared within the discipline of History) that the English nation did not – or had ceased to – exist; an idea not seriously addressed by mainstream political science until the twenty-first century.

Nairn's approach to English nationalism in the same period was notable because it took English nationalism much more seriously as a distinct political ideology. Stemming from a different intellectual tradition to Rose's, it too exhibited an Italian connection though of a different sort: the analytical framework of Antonio Gramsci. Building on New Left debates about the British state (the so-called 'Nairn-Anderson thesis' about the precocious and subsequently arrested democratic development of the United Kingdom) Nairn added the notion of a partial or failed bourgeois revolution to existing work on nationalism outside of the Marxist tradition by Hans Kohn and Ernest Gellner. Kohn formulated an early version of the argument – later advanced by Nairn and Liah Greenfeld (1992) – that England was the first of all modern nations and hence its political development was something to be emulated, aspired to and resented by all subsequent nationalists (Kohn, 2008 [1944]). Gellner's intellectual legacy to Nairn was to link nationalism not to atavistic and nostalgic urges in the human psyche, but to impersonal sources of global change. Gellner argued that the 'great but valid paradox is this: nations can only be defined in terms of the age of nationalism, rather than, as you might expect, the other way round'. He continued as follows:

> It is not the case that 'the age of nationalism' is a mere summation of the awakening and political self-assertion of this, that or the other nation. Rather, when general social conditions make for standardised, homogenous, centrally sustained high cultures, pervading entire populations and not just elite minorities, a situation arises in which well defined, educationally sanctioned and unified cultures constitute very nearly the only kind of unit with which men [sic] willingly and often ardently identify. These cultures now seem to be the natural repositories of political legitimacy. (Gellner, 1983: 55)

For Nairn, already dissatisfied with most Marxist theories of nationalism, Gellner's theorisation was 'the "Eureka!" cry which founded the social-scientific theory of nationalism' (Nairn, 1998: 1). In what Paul James called a 'partial break with orthodoxy' (James, 1996: 107), Nairn fused the neo-Gramscianism of the New Left with Gellner's modernisation theory to open up a new analytical and normative position that displayed far more sympathy for nationalist movements than was customary amongst Marxist thinkers, and was closer to the Austro-Marxist position of the 1900s than Rosa Luxembourg's. This was because, as Jonathan Hearn notes, Nairn saw nations 'not as side effects of modernization, but momentous new forms of historical agency that once formed make history' (Hearn, 2006: 99).

In *The Break-up of Britain*, first published in 1977 and republished in 1981 and 2003, Nairn created an extended conceptualisation of nationalism and its relationship to the transition to modernity as the 'modern Janus' (Nairn, 2003 [1977]: 317). This Roman analogy allowed Nairn to highlight the dual nature of nationalism that complicated any simplistic normative stance on the subject. Reflecting the concerns of the left of the time Nairn argued that 'there are two kinds of nationalism. The main, essentially healthy sort we applaud in Indo-China and Mozambique; and the derivative, degenerate sort we oppose in, for example, the American working class, Gaullism, the Chilean *Junta* and so on' (Nairn, 2003 [1977]: 335). But he added a cautionary note:

> The distinctions do not imply two brands of nationalism, one healthy and one morbid. The point is that, as the most elementary comparative analysis will show, all nationalism is both healthy and morbid. Both progress and regress are inscribed in its genetic code from the start. (Nairn, 2003 [1977]: 335)

During this transition to modernity, pre-national societies tried to propel themselves forward by what he called 'a certain sort of regression', drawing on past victories and defeats as a means of surviving the millrace of development (Nairn,
2003 [1977]: 336). As an ideology it was particularly attractive to peripheral
elites who could see the potential benefits to them of a reordering of domestic and
international politics in their material and psychological favour. However it required
a contingent alignment with 'the masses' to effect such a change: hence 'the nation'
came into to being to bring about change. This need to generate and consolidate a
political community bound by common myths and memories led to the 'necessary
resort to populism' resulting in a cross-class alliance between proletariat, peasantry
and the peripheral bourgeoisie that came to be known in its social and political form
as 'the nation', which also acted as a brake on change once contained within a state
(Nairn, 2003 [1977]: 327).

This materialist interpretation was the source of Nairn's initial – though later
modified – conceptualisation of English nationalism as 'abnormal' when compared
with historically informed ideal types. 'Normal' in this formulation was 'something
like France' (Nairn, 1998: 133), where a bourgeois revolution in the republican tradition had (eventually) overthrown the monarchy and created a unified and medium-
sized state with control over human and natural resources sufficient to guarantee its
viability in international society. England – as part of the expanding British state
and Empire – experienced this transition to modernity during the long seventeenth
century and sustained this position (despite the loss of its American colonies) well
into the twentieth. This precocious and fortuitous development meant that Nairn
was able to argue that the question of nationality in England was never addressed
because it was never seriously raised as a vehicle for modernisation (Nairn, 1993
[1988]: 137).

What was offered in its place was what Benedict Anderson characterised in general as 'official nationalism' (Anderson, 1991: 83). Nairn, returning to Gramsci,
characterised this phenomenon as 'folklore from above' (Nairn, 1993 [1988]: 174).
For Nairn, Britishness – principally expressed via monarchy and Crown-in-
Parliament sovereignty – was a form hegemony that produced an 'occluded multi-
nationalism' (Nairn, 1998: 212) throughout the United Kingdom inhibiting the
development of what was seen as normal nationality politics linked to the emergence of a form of democracy underpinned by the republican tradition (Nairn,
1993 [1988]: 174).

This 'abnormality' eventually fed into perceptions of the 'absence' of English
nationalism, an absence that Nairn ultimately decried. Offering case studies of
nationalism within the United Kingdom, including England, Nairn did not char-
acterise English nationalism as in any way absent in the 1970s; in fact it was in full
voice thanks to Enoch Powell. But in subsequent analyses, he developed the idea
that the British state (including the monarchy and a renewal of Britishness as a
capacious 'civic' identity) 'occluded' the development of republican nationalisms

that would be the agent of democratic renewal in the United Kingdom (Nairn, 2002: 167). Importantly, his initially negative assessment of English nationalism shifted – now the absence of English nationalism (at least in the republican register) was to be lamented and urgently addressed lest the political right should claim it as its own (Nairn, 2001: 15). This shift occurred because of the shift in Scottish nationalism from centre-right to centre-left in the 1980s that allowed Nairn to transpose his support for peripheral nationalist movements of small nations onto the English as a potential – indeed essential – vector of political change in the United Kingdom (Nairn, 2001: 11). At the beginning of the twenty-first century, 'something like Scotland', rather than 'something like France', was the ideal against which English nationalism was measured.

Krishan Kumar likewise located England between Scotland and France, but in a slightly different way to Nairn. Published in 2003, Krishan Kumar's *The Making of English National Identity* sought, like Nairn, to explain the apparent 'abnormality' and 'absence' of English nationalism as a political movement, which by this time had become an important trope for framing analyses of England's 'missing' nationalism. Comparative over time and space and engaging with literatures on the historical origins of nationalism, it located English nationalism not during the end of the medieval period as proposed by Adrian Hastings (1997), the eighteenth century as argued by Gerald Newman (1987), or the nineteenth century as Gellner's theory might anticipate but, counter-intuitively, only at the end of the nineteenth century during a crisis of imperial confidence (Kumar, 2006).

This very specific 'moment' of English nationalism can be contested. It is not clear, for example, why this moment of imperial crisis around the time of the South African War should have produced a politicised Englishness and yet the actual end of Empire from the 1940s to the 1960s resulted in an enhanced Britishness. Like Nairn, Kumar's also concluded that England was 'something like France', but in this explanatory framework it was also something like Russia, Austria and Turkey in that it was a nation at the core of a post-imperial state. Kumar labelled this phenomenon 'missionary nationalism' (Kumar, 2003: 34). Kumar argued that political expressions of English national identity had been suppressed by the structural location of England's place at the demographic and political heart of the British Empire. This inhibited groups and individuals whom the theory of nationalism might otherwise anticipate being 'English nationalists' from upsetting the political equilibrium and weakening the polity that was the source of their 'national pride'. For Kumar, as noted above:

> Empires, though in principle opposed to claims of nationality, may be carriers of a certain kind of national identity which give to the dominant groups a special sense of themselves and their destiny ... The key feature of imperial or missionary nationalism is the attachment of a dominant or core national group to a state entity that conceives itself as dedicated to some larger cause or purpose, religious, cultural or political. (Kumar: 2003: 34)

In other words, the British Empire was England's 'imagined political community'. Combining Kumar's 'certain kind of national identity' with Nairn's 'certain sort of regression' starts to suggest why memory of Britain's imperial past looms large in the contemporary English imagination.

The most important move in Kumar's conceptualisation of English national identity was to take Anthony Smith's concept of a pre-modern *ethnie* and link this to the Empire as well as the English, and later British, state to provide an explanation of an 'abnormally' quiescent English nationalism. The misconception however was to over-emphasise the way that the Empire *subsumed* Englishness (like Nairn's Britain 'occluding' the nations of the United Kingdom), rather than an examination of the ways that empire *informed* Englishness in the creation of its formative national traditions (Wellings, 2002). Yet the greatest value of Kumar's work was his challenge to examine England and Englishness from 'the outside in, from the vantage point of the whole globe, into which the English had spread and which had played a formative part in the making of their identity' (Kumar, 2015: 205). Nationalism in Kumar's reading is not just the political-cultural expression of a particular nation, but serves other political functions that are shaped by contexts outside of the control of the people constituting the nation or even their rulers. Consequently, Kumar was right to insist that we need to place research into English, and other 'missionary nationalisms', into wider historical contexts to fully comprehend this phenomenon. Approaches that do not start by recognising the merged and occluded nature of English nationalism therefore take for granted the very thing that needs investigation: 'the wider world within which "England" and "Englishness" find their meaning. English national identity cannot be found from within the consciousness of the English themselves. We have to work from the outside in' (Kumar, 2003: 16–17). Such an exogenous conceptualisation raised epistemological questions. It called on researchers to lift their gaze from the immediate post-devolution context and seek evidence of the construction and maintenance of English identity through the inter-relationship between the English and their significant others, particularly in European and imperial contexts as well as that of the UK. By so doing, Kumar's call can help to avoid what Arthur Aughey has referred to as 'Singapore syndrome' in explanatory accounts of contemporary English nationalism: that all our intellectual firepower is facing in the wrong direction and is over-concentrated on the UK-context alone when it should be alive to a wider set of possibilities; a point reinforced by Michael Kenny (Aughey, 2013: 115; Kenny, 2014: 132).

National traditions and the legitimisation of British sovereignty

If the ideas of absence and abnormality are only partially helpful in explaining English nationalism (and indeed fell away in the years preceding Brexit), this section argues that examining the political traditions that animate English nationalism is a fruitful avenue of enquiry. It begins with an understanding of nationalism broadly informed by a constructivist view. It does not suggest that opposition to Europe has always defined the English but rather that these ideas are mutually constitutive through their contestation (Colley, 2014: 134–135). It then adapts the 'traditions and dilemmas' approach of Mark Bevir and Rod Rhodes to capture what we will need to understand as the *dominant* national tradition in England that is used to address major political dilemmas. This dominant national tradition will be outlined through an engagement with the important works of Arthur Aughey, Andrew Gamble and Michael Kenny. The section concludes that the dominant form of English nationalism has been and remains today a defence of British sovereignty.

Another source of the assumption of the 'absence' of English nationalism concerned empirical rather than theoretical research. Responding to political cues, survey researchers began interrogating the idea of English nationalism after devolution at the end of the 1990s. By linking questions about English identity to demands for an English parliament or some mechanism of 'home rule', research appeared to confirm an absence where a presence was anticipated (Condor, 2010: 525). Searching for evidence of a politicised English identity, Sir John Curtice noted a rise in English self-identification after devolution, but noted a plateau thereafter and hence questioned the notion of a 'resurgence' of English identity (Curtice, 2018). In the realm of politics itself, the rejection of an assembly for the North-East suggested that there was little appetite for devolution in England (although the establishment of 'metro mayors' were subject to endorsement by referendum in 2012). Yet these 'missing backlash' analyses tended to take 'something like Scotland' as an implicit model for nationalism in England. English nationalists, it was assumed, must want the same thing as Scottish nationalists: home rule or independence. From this position it was not a giant leap to point to the marginal nature of the Campaign for an English Parliament and low levels of support for an English Parliament (19 per cent in 2014) (Park, Bryson and Curtice, 2014: vi) and the low vote share for the English Democrats (whose vote share dropped from 1.8 to 0.8 per cent between the 2009 and 2014 EP elections) to suggest that English nationalism did not exist.

At this point is will be useful to clarify what exactly it is under scrutiny because there are small yet important distinctions in the concepts deployed, notably in implicit assumptions between nationalism and secessionism. Different researchers have analysed related but distinct concepts pertaining to nationalism in England. As we have seen, for Nairn this was definitely an instance of English national*ism*. This stemmed from his analysis of nationalisms in Scotland, Wales and republican-nationalist Ireland that had much more evidently secessionist dimensions, along with his analyses of nationalism in England and amongst Ulster loyalists for whom continued 'union' as a loose form of integration was the main political aim. Nairn's neo-Gramscian concern with ideology facilitated his claim that the historical alliance of Crown and Parliament constituted nationalism 'from above', even if it was therefore *erstatz*. Krishan Kumar's concern was with what he called 'national identity'. This is where Kumar's grounding in comparative historical sociology inclined him towards 'identity' as the unit of analysis. Although the title of his major work reflected EP Thompson's *The Making of the English Working Class*, this was not as grounded in Marxist theory as Thompson's or Nairn's. It was however notably 'Scottish' in the influence of Edinburgh University's research on nationalism and national identity in the United Kingdom, and reflected David McCrone's idea that national identity is the 'hinge' that relates citizen or subject to the state (Ichijo et al., 2017; McCrone, 1998).

The most explicit working through of the nature of a politicised English identity is Michael Kenny's notion of nation*hood* (Kenny, 2014). This concept allows the rich and plural nature of collective expressions of English nationality to emerge and avoids this diversity being subsumed under any one particular interpretation, positive or negative (Kenny, 2014: 241). Initially national*ism* was assumed to be 'proper' only under certain conditions, a point later modified and refined (Kenny et al., 2016). Similarly withholding judgement on whether we can call it nationalism yet, Arthur Aughey, writing in 2007, was concerned with English*ness* (Aughey, 2007). Like identity 'Englishness' implied a passive mode of political being, although not absence per se. As late as 2010, Aughey described English nationalism as a 'mood, not a movement', in this case remarkable for its absence from deliberations about the UK's constitutional future (Aughey, 2010a: 506).

It was from the beginning of the second decade of the twenty-first century, however, that empirical survey research began to pick up a change in politicised expressions of English identity, English nationhood and Englishness that suggested it might be more of a movement than a mood. This required a shift in assumptions about the importance of England as an explanatory factor in contemporary British politics. The Future of England Survey (FoES) – coordinated between the Institute for Public Policy Research (IPPR) in London and the universities of Edinburgh and Cardiff – began from an assumption that politicised Englishness existed rather than was absent and sought out the drivers of this phenomenon. This shift of assumptions opened up new possibilities and over the space of the five years before Brexit illuminated the contours and content of a politicised English identity as the bearer of a distinct political project, driven by disillusion with the political status quo – both in the UK and the EU – and dissatisfaction with immigration to England (Wyn Jones et al., 2012; Wyn Jones et al., 2013). Even the FoES couldn't resist an analogy from a Scottish author – 'the dog that finally barked' – to suggest the significance of the apparent 'absence' of English nationalism that was really the key to the unravelling responses to the major dilemmas of British politics (Wyn Jones et al., 2012).

Taking England seriously as a political community within the UK implied being attuned to both the integrationist and secessionist political projects attendant to nationalism, both of which were in evidence in the United Kingdom up to and during the Brexit referendum. Although secessionist nationalism has the possibility to disturb regional and global political orders and hence captures the attention of policy-makers and public, integrationist nationalism is much the more common of the variants of nationalism although far less noticed. This is because, as Michael Billig showed, nationalism had become routinised in the developed West and was seen as the 'normal' state of affairs (Billig, 1995). This quotidian nationalism permeates and informs notions of citizenship and belonging, creating what is labelled 'everyday nationhood' (see Edensor and Sumartojo, 2018; Skey and Antonsich, 2017). Jonathan Hearn similarly noted the routinised nature of contemporary nationalisms in liberal democracies. Hearn argued that liberal democracies 'do not so much transcend nationalism, as domesticate it, routinizing its dynamic, by channelling it through core political institutions' (Hearn, 2006: 166). For Hearn, contemporary nationalism in the developed west is characterised by contestation over ideas, consisting of

> contending visions of how a population within a given territory should be governed, and such visions are normally underwritten by a certain conception of the population's common *identity*, embodied in shared beliefs and values ... The state must continually reach down into this process of contentious national identity-building in order to renew its legitimacy. (Hearn, 2006: 167).

Although contestation over *contending* rather than shared beliefs and values is more significant in generating nationalist politics in established polities, such conceptualisations had the advantage of pushing nationalism into the realm of ideology; or as Umut Özkırımlı defined it 'a particular way of seeing and interpreting the world, a frame of reference that helps us make sense of and structure the reality that surrounds us' (Özkırımlı, 2005: 30).

In this way, Hearn's definition of nationalism as 'the making of combined claims, on behalf of a population, to *identity*, to *jurisdiction* and to *territory* (Hearn, 2006: 11) called on researchers to be attentive to such discursive claims (which may in fact constitute 'identity' at the moment that they invoke it) that legitimise political projects. Importantly the claims themselves may be to territory and jurisdiction beyond that of the existing state itself, especially for large nations like England within pluri-national states. This poses questions about evidence relating to claims about identity and how sub-state nationalism can – if at all – be separated from claims about the states in which they reside. Charlie Jeffery and Daniel Wincott critiqued the notion of 'methodological nationalism' in relation to research on sub-state nationalism itself. They noted a paradox in the concept, namely that

> the critique of methodological nationalism might reflect, embody or promote methodological nationalism. This paradox is captured in the term itself ... in which 'nationalism' denotes the state, a set of political institutions, rather than the collective goals of a community. (Jeffery and Wincott, 2010: 175)

Linking this to Billig's work, Jeffery and Wincott suggested provocatively that 'Methodological nationalism might even be styled as the form taken by banal nationalism within the academy' (Jeffery and Wincott, 2010: 172).

Jeffery and Wincott's research – along with that of their associated colleagues at the Future of England Survey – opened up important new avenues for understanding the increasing politicisation of English identity. Such research can be fruitfully complimented with 'interpretive' research that attempts to explain what people 'mean' by 'being English' and the origins of what usually turn out to be diverse meanings imputed to single categories (Kenny, 2014: 79). This implies that if we want to understand and explain the effect of English nationalism in framing political dilemmas and thereby foreclosing certain political alternatives, we need to examine the political traditions that inform and legitimise those choices made in response to dilemmas. Drawing on the 'traditions and dilemmas' approach developed by Mark Bevir and Rod Rhodes (Bevir and Rhodes, 2003; Bevir and Rhodes 2006), this analysis of the development of contemporary English nationalism can help explain what Startin and Simon Usherwood called the 'embedded persistence' of Euroscepticism (2013: 13), in this case in England, as well as British Government policy choices towards Europe before and after the Brexit referendum.

Building on a range of research techniques, Bevir and Rhodes argued that when faced with a political dilemma an actor must make a choice that appears legitimate to his or her colleagues and/or a wider constituency in a situation of what Bevir, Daddow and Schnapper later called 'situated agency' (Bevir, Daddow and Schnapper, 2013: 6). This is where the traditions – understood as political ideologies or past practices – of the political actors become important, not in determining the agency of any given actor, but as suggesting a legitimate point of departure for a particular course of action. The 'output' legitimacy of a given policy choice may retrospectively justify any novel departure and silence dissent, but it is continuity that bestows 'input' legitimacy at the moment of decision, hence the importance of traditions in framing political and policy choices. This is not meant to be deterministic: a tradition 'is unavoidable only as a starting point, not as something that determines later performances' (Bevir, Daddow and Hall, 2013: 167).

Bevir and Rhodes 'traditions and dilemmas' approach is very helpful in translating the existence of political ideologies into the actions and choices of individuals and governments, but misses out on an important 'meta-tradition'; that of the nation. In seeking to understand contemporary English nationalism it is important to understand the historical traditions that inform it. That means analysing the historical memories that sustain English nationalism – and what we will subsequently call its 'dominant' form – and the political dilemmas that drive it towards particular outcomes and (re)constitute it thereby. Such concerns lead us to a basic question animating this research: how have traditions contained in thinking about the English nation shaped responses to European integration and Britain's relations with the wider, English-speaking world? Given that these processes are constitutive, the account that follows will be sensitive to the ways that resistance to European integration and commonalities with English-speaking countries outside of the European Union have shaped articulations and understandings of English nationalism 'from the outside in'. By approaching the grand political dilemma of the UK's membership of the European Union in this way, Brexit becomes explicable as part of a longer tradition of constituting English nationalism around a defence of British sovereignty.

Consequently, the 'national tradition', in addition to others identified by Bevir and Rhodes, is important in understanding policy choices as responses to political dilemmas. Although often discounted as ephemeral and although in reality highly contested, the 'national tradition' is crucial for understanding major dilemmas of high politics because it adds an apparent unity of purpose and offers a motive seemingly above party and politics, potentially bestowing further legitimacy on a contentious policy choice. However, this means that the range of possible policy choices is constrained by those that have preceded them, especially if those choices are claimed to align with 'national' values or culture, burdening deviations from such traditions with the taint of illegitimacy.

In this way, explaining and interpreting these political traditions – especially the 'national' one(s) – becomes a crucial element in understanding a major political event like Brexit. Whilst it is true, as Matthew Ryan noted, that all case studies are implicitly comparative (Ryan, 2017: 195), research by interpretive political scientists, as opposed to historical sociologists attuned to politics like Kumar, placed less explicit emphasis on the comparative dimension of analysis and was stronger on traditions of political thought from and within which current thinking about contemporary English nationalism emerged. Making a differentiation between 'politics' and 'the political', this research work on contemporary English nationalism allowed for fine-grained and in-depth interpretations of what Alan Finlayson called 'the contingent outcome of ongoing historical activities' (Finlayson, 2017: 215) and Daigneault and Béland call the 'within-case mechanisms' that lead to an explanation of existing or novel phenomena (Daigneault and Béland, 2015: 386). Although sensitive to the material drivers of change, such approaches help explain the contested ideational expressions of English nationalism in the twenty-first century.

Along with Kumar's 'outside in' suggestion, Arthur Aughey offered a sympathetic external account of Englishness. Aughey displayed a flair for explaining the politics of Englishness in two-word phrases (notably 'anxiety and injustice', as well as the relatively verbose 'mood not a movement') to describe the politics of Englishness (Aughey, 2010a: 506). Like Nairn, Aughey noted the importance of Westminster, underpinned by English consent, to a continuing idea and operation of 'Britishness', but unlike Nairn – with whom he had nothing in common ideologically – Aughey saw a reconceptualised Westminster as crucial to the idea of a renewed political compact that would secure the continuance of the United Kingdom. Updating Richard Rose's idea of Parliament as 'the fifth nation' of the United Kingdom, Aughey argued that whereas post-devolution Britishness was usually spoken of as 'the *collective* values and interests which it is the job of Westminster to express (the fifth nation)', it was now perhaps 'better to speak of it in terms of the *collected* values and interests of a multi-national association which it is the job of Westminster to secure (a fifth nation)' (Aughey, 2010b: 282). This change of emphasis was mirrored in a semantic shift in Prime Ministerial rhetoric that stopped referring to Britain as a nation, but used 'family of nations' instead (Cameron, 2014a), a term previously reserved for the Commonwealth.

Yet as the twenty-first century wore on, Aughey noted that what he called an 'ironic inversion' in assumptions about English governance had taken place. Whereas up to the 1990s the absence of specifically 'English governance' might have been lauded as a political virtue because of the potentially disruptive idea of English nationality expressed and contained in British institutions, by the 2010s the absence of English governance was becoming one of the drivers of the expression of politicised Englishness (Aughey, 2016: 356). This inversion came about because the tradition of equating and defining Englishness through (British) political institutions had been called into question by the changing nature of the British state and the affective alignment of its diverse national citizenries. This inversion also found semantic expression whereby before it was common to use the term 'England' to mean 'Britain', English politicians increasingly used the term 'Britain' to refer to what had in fact become 'England' thanks to devolution and Scottish secessionism. This ideational 'double vision' had sustained the Union in England since the debates about Home Rule in the 1880s and the secession of Ireland after 1921. Yet Aughey was pessimistic about the length of time that this political 'double vision' could hold in the face of a politicised, rather than quiescent, Englishness (Aughey, 2018).

Andrew Gamble gave one explanation for the weakening of this 'double vision' in English political thought. Gamble argued that the twin challenges of the Powellite–Thatcherite traditions amongst conservatives and a reassertion of an English Tory tradition as Conservatism and Unionism fragmented and weakened outside southern England meant that the Union of Great Britain and Northern Ireland lost the sacrosanct position it once held (Gamble, 2016: 364). This conclusion should be read alongside the longer-term search for Britain's place in the world, in which 'Britain' conceived of as a 'world island' (Gamble, 2003) was the rhetorical vehicle for this political project that preceded and overlapped with a renewed English Tory-ism. Not only was this a renewed tradition that made it possible to imagine the United Kingdom outside of the European Union as some sort of 'Singapore on steroids' (an expression attributed to Conservative-turned-UKIP MP Douglas Carswell), it also continued the blurring of English and British identities as what was ostensibly 'foreign policy' became politicised within the new domestic national contexts of the United Kingdom over the issue of EU membership and its potential alternatives.

Michael Kenny also noted that a politicised Englishness was undoing the 'double vision' that had sustained the English understanding of the United Kingdom until the 1990s. When analysing survey research, Kenny noted a quantitative and qualitative change in the political views of those professing an English identity at the end of the

2000s, but he did not link the emergence of politicised expression of what he called nation*hood* to devolution. In a sensitive account of the politics of English nationhood, Kenny stressed the pluralistic nature of nationhood in England and argued that

> the language and sentiments associated with resurgent ideas of Englishness have a more complex set of causes than devolution itself, and have afforded considerable opportunities for those seeking to promote a variety of political agendas and arguments. (Kenny, 2014: 2)

Despite this plurality, the most common manifestation of this politicisation was 'an increasingly dyspeptic, pessimistic, and populist attitude towards current political arrangements' (Kenny, 2014: 91). Although opposed to (early) Nairn's emphasis on a singular – and regressive – English nationalism, Kenny also linked the emergence of a politicisation of English nationhood with structural economic change, although of a more recent provenance than Nairn's 'transition to modernity'. For Kenny, the contemporary politicisation of English nationhood was linked to the changes associated with globalisation and the relative decline in living standards sharpened by – but preceding – the Global Financial Crisis of 2008:

> The combination of gathering economic uncertainty, the decline in living standards experienced by middle and lower income groups from 2004 onwards, and the growing disillusion with a Labour government that was widely perceived as unsympathetic to the people's culture, laid down a pattern of populist-cum-nationalist sentiment within which an appeal to English culture and interests was central. (Kenny, 2014: 93)

This conclusion was supported by Robin Mann and Steve Fenton's research that stressed the intra- and inter-class resentments that resulted from this chronic economic, and attendant social, insecurity (Mann and Fenton, 2017: 7).

Kenny's account was not linked directly to literature on nationalism in the way that Kumar's account was. Yet one of its strengths was its sensitivity to the place of 'culture' in expressions of nationhood. As with patterns of nationalist mobilisation in which culture is politicised before party political mobilisation takes place (Hutchinson, 2005: 65), Kenny noted that 'culture' in England (in this instance sport, music and debates about the countryside and the past) assumed a salience before political parties belatedly responded; and it was this bleated response that made this historic expression of English nationhood different to that identified by Kumar at the turn or the twentieth century (Kenny, 2014: 130–132). Importantly, this politicisation at the party rather than individual identity level was not restricted to the radical right as in Ford and Goodwin's account (Ford and Goodwin, 2014), but was found in the gradual yet potentially radical implementation of English Votes for English Laws (EVEL) by the Conservative Government, following the Scottish independence referendum in 2014 (Gover and Kenny, 2016).

Kenny's English are a more political people than Kumar's quiescent nation and are more politically diverse that Nairn's (early) English nationalists imagined in the Powellite register. With an emphasis on immigration, Europe and free trade, it is easy to draw an ideological line between Powellism and much of the ideas animating UKIP leadership (and possibly other Leave voters). Yet Kenny finds a much richer set of plural political traditions animating the broad church of English nationhood, including 'an emerging discourse of anti-system populism, as well as an embryonic attempt to recast England in a self-consciously multicultural vein' (Kenny, 2014: 2). This may be true, but Kenny's conceptualisation of politics is that of a benign arena of subtle contestation underpinned by the possibility of compromise; a view of politics that Brexit challenged. Kenny's account underplayed the operation of power in expressions of English nationhood; in other words, some expressions of nationhood have greater organisational and institutional support than their competitors and are therefore are more equal than others. Nationhood may be plural but nationalism is a hegemonic project. Thus whilst Kenny is right to recognise the plural traditions animating English nationhood and the political potential they hold, it is worth reflecting on why some versions of nationhood are more dominant than others. England has a very strong radical tradition, yet this tradition does not readily translate into a left-wing political Englishness, because it is too British in its structures, support and ideology (Robinson, 2016: 379). And as Andrew Mycock notes, the strength of regionalism cuts across Englishness as a coherent national ideology (Mycock, 2016: 389).

Neither of these phenomena – regionalism or left-wing scepticism towards the nation as a political project – is unique to England. Nevertheless, together they handed a significant political advantage to those on the right of politics who wished to link their own political agendas to national narratives and traditions of nationhood and express these projects in the language of nation and nationalism. In England's case, this meant that exponents of the Tory and Powellite-Thatcherite traditions (including UKIP) found the terrain of the party politics of nationhood largely uncontested from within England itself, even if the Conservative leadership was reluctant to court politicised Englishness before 2014 (Hayton, 2016; Tournier-Sol, 2015). This matters because in the 'battle of ideas' over nationalism in England, it implies paying particular attention to the interplay between the political projects of elites on the right of English politics and the shifting popular support and political identities that sustain and legitimise such projects. Craig Parsons is right to underscore the importance of ideational contestation to the creations of actors' interests – and that 'the assertion of certain ideas by an elite minority' is not a neutral expression of preferences but a contest that rules out other ideas as active options in the future (Parsons, 2003: 1). Despite the constitutional innovation of EVEL and notwithstanding the development of a politicised English identity, what looks like political Englishness when viewed from 'the outside in' is still largely articulated by elites in the language of what Andrew Gamble calls 'Anglo-Britishness' (Gamble,

2016: 359). It is articulated in defence of what is taken to be 'British' sovereignty in opposition to Scottish secessionism and European integration (including control of UK borders as relates to immigration). This merging of England and Britain, along-side claims made pertaining to England in the language of Britishness, should alert us to the wider categories of belonging that inform the content of the dominant expression of English nationalism.

English nationalism and England's wider categories of belonging

At the elite level, these expressions of English nationalism still relate to defending Britain's (i.e. Westminster's) sovereignty within the United Kingdom and to extending the UK's sovereignty (understood as freedom of action) in the inter-national order. Bringing in this external dimension to our understandings of the construction of English nationalism allows us to place analyses of English nation-alism in wider historical frames.

Robert Tombs has provided an excellent example of this. But he has also provided an example of the analytical perils of being too UK-focused and assuming that nationalism in England is primarily driven by demands for 'home rule' rather than a defence of British sovereignty. In considering (and dismissing) the relationship between Euroscepticism and English nationalism, Tombs (him-self an advocate of UK secession from the EU on the basis of England's historic differences from Continental Europe) began with what appeared to be a curious paradox: 'Euroscepticism is mostly expressed in political terms concerning sover-eignty and law; yet it is strongest in England, which is not of course a sovereign nation.' He continues that there is 'little correlation between Euroscepticism (a fairly broad phenomenon) and English nationalism (a tiny splinter). In other words, Euroscepticism is a form of British nationalism, mostly confined to the most 'British' island nation, the English' (Tombs, 2014: 878).

Such framing does not help us to interpret why a form of 'British' nationalism is strongest in England. Indeed survey research around national identities and attitudes towards European integration showed that the more 'British' a person identified as, the more pro-EU they were likely to be (Lord Ashcroft Polls, 2016). This requires a differentiation between public opinion and elite projects. The latter are articulated in the language of Britishness, yet fully 79 per cent of those who iden-tified as 'English not British' in Lord Ashcroft's exit poll voted to leave the EU (Lord Ashcroft Polls, 2016). The explanation for this English support for a seemingly 'British' political project like (hard) Euroscepticism lies in the paradox that Tombs identifies: sovereignty and law are indeed central to English nationalism, but it is British sovereignty that is the object of political concern, generating the content of English nationalism in its integrationist (Anglo-Britishness) and secessionist (hard Eurosceptic) manifestations.

Definitions are clearly important to help get us out of this analytical complexity. Nationalism has been treated above in Chapter 1, but it is worth recapping at this stage. Nationalism is not just about secession, anti-immigrant sentiment or resentment at the political status quo, although these are all important elements of this phenomenon. Nationalism is also part of the ideological framework of how individuals make sense of the world and constitute their actions accordingly. This framework has a long historical formation, produced by 'global' forms of change in the political economy and attempts to respond to and capture that change to one's advantage (or just cope with it). Managing change to one's advantage implies being in control of the policy-making process. This can mean capturing and creating an entirely new state, but in existing liberal democracies it usually means contestation over policy between or within political parties or, increasingly, votes for insurgent parties or 'protest votes' at referendums.

Nationalism in contemporary Europe is less linked to war and armed conflict than it was in the past. In liberal – or even 'illiberal' – democracies at the beginning of the twenty-first century it tends to be about contestation of the ideas and values that frame ways of being in the world and that at the political level that shape policy-making, which in turn impact people's lives. This ultimately political understanding of nationalism makes sovereignty an important concept underpinning any definition of nationalism. Sovereignty itself is contested too: where it stems from (the state, the People, transnational organisations) and to where it extends (the boundaries of the political community of the nation, competing claims to territory and jurisdiction) are part of this contestation. Sovereignty is the concept that links all three elements of John Breuilly's historical typology of nationalism into secessionist, unification and reform varieties (he does not treat irredentist as a separate category to reform) (Breuilly, 2001: 39–42). When combined with Nairn's insight that nationalism is radical and conservative, as well as progressive and regressive, and requires 'a certain sort of regression' (Nairn, 2003 [1977]: 336) to mobilise and permit the contingent alliance between elites and masses, then we can see how the past becomes important, not just as the source of political traditions that bestow legitimacy on a course of action, as per Bevir and Rhodes, but also a source of reassuring continuity in times of dislocation or disconcerting political dilemma.

A political understanding of nationalism suggests that it is best seen as a legitimisation of sovereignty. The contestation of that sovereignty – where it comes from and where its boundaries lie – becomes part of the ideational constitution of nationhood. What takes it from national identity or nationhood to national*ism* is the hegemonic attempt to impose one version of nationhood over others as a means to frame or capture the policy-making process.

The Brexit referendum of 2016 had this effect. The device of the referendum in 2016 elevated one version of English nationhood, that of the 'Anglo-British' tradition, to a dominant position – although one increasingly contested after the fact. As an ideology about managing change that takes three main forms: secessionism, unification and reform (*pace* Breuilly), we can see that what we can now call contemporary English nationalism displays all three of these traits: it sought secession from the EU; it sought reform of political structures (both in the UK and within the EU, even to the point of leaving it) and – at least as an elite project – it sought a reassertion of the unitary nature of the United Kingdom given the opportunity created by the politics and process of Brexit, alongside a revival of relationships with traditional allies.

This historically informed understanding of nationalism in England with contestation over sovereignty at its heart was usually disaggregated in academic or political analysis. Expressions of nationalism in contemporary England, although driven by novel political developments, were part of a longer historical trajectory that was often overlooked. Analysis of – and anxieties about – Brexit in England tended to emphasise two elements of nationalism: 'nativism' and nostalgia. Secessionism was less often mentioned in England because of the voluntaristic nature of the European Union (even though the United Kingdom itself is understood as a voluntaristic union rather than a unitary nation-state in political traditions outside of England). Reform was contained within the Conservatives' implementation of EVEL and the regional agenda of New Labour and Coalition governments. Unification seemed to fly in the face of the trend towards devolution after 1997. Yet the dominant expression of English nationalism that emerged in the two decades before Brexit and was propelled by a legitimatisation of a defence of *British* sovereignty, as disengagement from the European Union – the politics of which began during the Coalition Government of 2010–15 – required the United Kingdom to seek a revised place in the Atlantic and global orders and forced its leaders to deploy the rhetoric of Britishness at a moment when the affective ties that bound Britain together had never been politically weaker.

This understanding of English nationalism – sensitive to the external as well as internal drivers of its renewed expression – encourages us to examine the effect of the political communities and legitimising narratives that helped define and constitute Britain's place in the post-war world. These communities and narratives became part of the 'wider categories of belonging' that informed English nationalism, especially during and from the period when nationalism became a major legitimising order of political space, internationally and domestically, from the end of the eighteenth century.

This approach is congruent with Kumar's emphasis on the British Empire as a constitutive element in the historical formation of English nationalism, but reaches a different conclusion to his: namely that British imperialism *merged with and informed the content of English nationalism*, rather than inhibited it. Therefore one of England's 'wider categories of belonging' that we should be attentive to was established with the expansion of English sovereignty during the first and second 'British' Empires (noting that the 'first British Empire' was English until the Scots joined after their own colonial ventures in the Panama isthmus failed and union with England took place in 1707). Initially articulated during the second half of the nineteenth century as 'Greater Britain' by the influential politician Charles Dilke (Dilke, 1869), the idea was then conflated with England by the historians J. R. Seeley and J. A. Froude and J. R. Seeley (Seeley, 1882). The former, having visited what he called 'Oceana', came to the conclusion that 'the life of a nation, like the life of a tree, is in its extremities' (Froude, 1886: 387).

As Duncan Bell has shown, this version of Britishness formed an important political tradition in English politics at the turn of the twentieth century (Bell, 2007). Yet non-English nationalists eventually confined this political tradition to an English core in the century after the First World War and most rapidly after the Second. Beginning in Ireland and passing via Egypt, India, Africa and eventually Ulster and Scotland, the idea of Empire as a unifying narrative legitimising the extension and operation of English sovereignty across the globe became politically unfeasible. Empire was replaced by the related but distinct concepts of the Commonwealth and the 'English-speaking Peoples' (Churchill, 1956). During the Cold War, the North Atlantic Treaty Organization (NATO) provided the core of the transatlantic relationship, although even this had periods of relative weakness (the 1970s and post-Iraq) and periods of strength (during the 1980s and the Iraq wars). As Stuart Ward noted, European integration weakened the Commonwealth link in the 1960s–1970s (Ward, 2001), until by the 1990s the Commonwealth was seen as moribund and the futures of its member states were seen in regional terms. From the point of view of imagining England and informing versions of English nationhood, the enlargement and contraction of English sovereignty via the British state and its Empire varied the terrain on which ideas of an English political community could be imagined. Ideas of England could be transposed onto the high seas, the Canadian north, the Australian outback, the Sussex countryside or Wolverhampton South-West, all in interaction with peoples and places which had or were forming their own distinct nationalities and identities, but all of which helped create Englishness – and its blurred boundaries – too.

Approaching English nationalism as a historically inflected defence of British sovereignty, allows us to see how resistance to European integration was a crucial constituent of this latest expression of politicised Englishness, and one that also blurred the boundaries of this particular expression of nationhood. Resistance to European integration was the field on which an English defence of British sovereignty played out *before* devolution made the Englishness of this politics explicit (Wellings, 2012). What we now call 'Euroscepticism' was far from a marginal or fringe element in British politics from the origins of the United Kingdom's engagement with the process and politics of European integration since the 1950s. Instead a sceptical and instrumental attitude towards 'Europe' was both embedded and persistent in political and popular attitudes. Although these attitudes fluctuated over time and place and were associated with Labour and the Conservatives in different periods, the way of seeing European integration as a threat to British sovereignty never went away and re-emerged strongly – and decisively – in the twenty-first century.

Examining resistance to European integration in England through national traditions opens up new avenues of research. One of the major advances on the topic of Euroscepticism by John Fitzgibbon, Benjamin Leruth and Nick Startin was to show that Euroscepticism was not only national but also 'pan-European' and 'transnational'. Indeed Eurosceptic parties and movements often adopted transnational rhetoric so as not to appear nationalist (Fitzgibbon, Leruth and Startin, 2017: 10). This emphasis on the transnational dimensions to Euroscepticism encourages us once again to examine this phenomenon from the 'outside in', and place contemporary Euroscepticism in England in longer historical frames of analysis.

This leads us to examine of what we might call 'the Anglosphere tradition' in British politics and – despite the novelty of the term – note its long historical lineage (Kenny and Pearce, 2018: 3). The 'Anglosphere' is a relatively new word, but it is the most recent expression of the 'Greater Britain' and 'English-speaking peoples' traditions noted above, consisting of five 'core' states and an indeterminate contested number of other states and nations (including Ireland, India and Singapore) plus at times the Commonwealth; and 'CANZUK' (Mycock and Wellings, 2017: 42). For its proponents it is an example of what Srdjan Vucetic calls historically conditioned identity 'fit' in international relations that gives the lie to the old dictum that states have allies, not friends (Vucetic, 2011: 138).

Its definitional incoherence suggests its relative novelty in this most recent manifestation. But this incoherence does not mean it should be dismissed and since its inception in 1999–2000 it had many friends in high places. There is also what we might call an 'actually existing Anglosphere', not just in the form of the so-called 'Five Eyes' intelligence sharing network between the United States, the United Kingdom, Canada, Australia and New Zealand (extant since 1946), but also in the dense array of policy networks between these five countries as Tim Legrand has shown (Legrand, 2016). These living and operative traditions help explain the transnational nature of English Euroscepticism and the ideational terrain of English nationalism by linking English Eurosceptics to elites beyond Europe and reinforcing the image of England (*qua* the United Kingdom) as a global rather than 'merely' regional power.

Furthermore, the development of the Anglosphere helped resolve a political dilemma for Eurosceptics: what alternative did they propose? (Wellings and Baxendale, 2015). But it also operated as the 'certain sort of regression' that Nairn noted was an essential part of nationalist mobilisation and gave Eurosceptics and Brexiteers the 'nostalgic' quality to their political imaginings commented on by their opponents. This should not be dismissed as just post-imperial 'fantasy' (even accepting that fantasy is an important part of politics) but is actually grounded in revived relations: including the possibility of post-Brexit free-trade agreements (FTAs) with Australia, New Zealand, Canada and (maybe) the United States. The element of fantasy comes in hoping that these revived relationships will replace the EU in economic (and diplomatic) terms after Brexit (Ravenhill and Huebner,

2019). But fantasies are important in politics. As we shall see below, the three pillars of the (English) Anglosphere – the origins and spread of representative democracy, the British Empire as a force for progress and the defence of liberty during the twentieth century – played a mutually constitutive role in shaping the content of contemporary English nationalism and making something like Brexit appear not only desirable but possible to its supporters.

Conclusion

By understanding English nationalism as a defence of British sovereignty we can begin to see how the imperatives of English nationalism lead to a blurring of English and other national and (ex-)imperial identities. In this way, seemingly contradictory developments – notably a politicised English identity driven by discontent with the governance of the United Kingdom – can be reconciled with elite projects – notably Brexit – that reassert British sovereignty in the face of the European Union and seek to realign the United Kingdom with 'traditional allies' within a changing world order.

Empirical research shows that those whom we would expect theoretically to be 'English nationalists' articulate England in the language of Britishness. This means we need to seek evidence not just of a self-conscious Englishness, although there are increasing signs of this, but also of an integrative Britishness that is designed to defend British sovereignty, keep the UK intact and retain its place amongst the major world powers. This is an elite English project. Researching England 'from the outside in' allows us to appreciate the Englishness of Brexit and place it within an explanation that prioritises the political tradition from which conceptions of the UK outside of the EU sprang: that of the English-speaking peoples, or the 'Anglosphere' in contemporary parlance. English nationalism is therefore neither 'abnormal' nor 'absent', but can be located in the English political traditions that inform and legitimise political actions.

Part II

Three pillars of the English Anglosphere

4

Gift to the world: England's shared exceptionalism

Magna Carta, 2015

In 2015, Magna Carta celebrated its 800th anniversary. This, according to Magna Carta Trust, was 'a global event to which the whole world is invited' (Magna Carta Trust, 2015). As part of these global commemorations, text from Magna Carta was projected onto the façade of Parliament House in Canberra, where a copy of Magna Carta from 1297 is on public display. This copy was found in the attic of the King's School, Somerset sometime in the 1930s and sold to Australia in 1952 ahead of the Coronation and the first of Queen Elizabeth II's Royal Tours. The effect of such narratives was to link England's constitutional development with nations outside of the EU, simultaneously stressing commonality with non-EU nations and differentiation from EU nations.

The global dimensions of the commemorations of the events at Runnymede should alert us to an important fact: England was a very 'global' nation and not all Brexiteers were 'Little Englanders', however much their opponents tried to land this opprobrium on them. An important part of their vision for the United Kingdom outside of the European Union was based on their view of the past and the long development of England's representative democracy and sovereignty of Parliament.

This development and the imperial trusteeship that helped spread it was described after the First World War as England's 'gift to the world' (Morris and Wood, 1924: vii), a refrain adopted by senior Brexiteers in 2016. Despite this seeming universalism, the parliamentary version of representative democracy paradoxically formed the basis of English exceptionalism whilst simultaneously being exported across the globe. This represented an unusual form of exceptionalism whereby the original was emulated in places where the 'national character' allowed for such institutions to take root, but never to the point of depriving it of its originality.

Constitutional development and national character were closely related in the Whig and Tory traditions. Writing an Introduction to a new edition of Bagehot's *The English Constitution*, Earl Balfour (1936 [1867]) argued that 'It matters little what other gifts a people may possess if they are wanting in those which, from this point of view, are of most importance. If, for example, they have no capacity for grading their loyalties as well as for being moved by them; if they have no natural inclination to liberty and no natural respect for law; if they lack good humour and tolerate foul play; if they know not how to compromise and when; if they have not that distrust of extreme conclusions which is sometimes mis-described as want of logic; if corruption does not repel them; and if their divisions tend to be too numerous or profound' (cited in Bagehot, 1936: xxii).

This was not how representative democracy and national character were presented in 2016. The incompatibility between the English-derived Westminster systems and the European Union's representative mechanisms were framed in the language of the EU's 'democratic deficit', arguments developed initially by pro-Europeans to bolster the powers of the European Parliament. But the defence of the United Kingdom's parliamentary sovereignty via the device of a referendum created paradoxes of its own. Using popular sovereignty to bolster parliamentary sovereignty, an outcome interpreted and enacted by executive government, raised the question of who was in charge after the Brexit vote. Magna Carta may have been England's 'gift to the world', but as it turned 801 the Kingdom was once against discontented as the body politic searched for new rules of engaging with itself and the wider world.

Chapter 4 develops the idea of the importance of English constitutional history as a link between English nationalism, Euroscepticism and the Anglosphere. It argues that England's constitutional development of serves as a point of commonality for all three ideologies. The process of disengaging from the European Union – evident during the Coalition Government of 2010–15 even before the Brexit referendum itself – was bound up with debates about England's constitutional development, its consequent ties to the Anglosphere and England's uncertain constitutional position within a changing United Kingdom; debates re-energised by the Eurosceptic wing of the Conservatives in the decade pre-dating Brexit. To illustrate this argument this chapter looks at the debate surrounding the re-publication of Henrietta Marshall's *Our Island Story* in 2005 and the subsequent political support in 2010–15 for that constitutional narrative as a means of cohering Britain and Britishness. By simultaneously suggesting an alternative (global) future for the United Kingdom, Anglospherists in England articulated arguments about Britain's place in Europe in English national frames that in turn linked Britain with the Anglosphere.

England's history wars: imagining a better yesterday

Such an argument rests on the importance of what Krishan Kumar calls the 'mobilizing and integrating function' of political myths (Kumar, 2015: 203). For Kumar 'national myths are not simply normative or descriptive. They are also mobilizing and energizing devices'. According to him, 'In their telling and re-telling, in the memories and emotions they evoke in their invocation at particular critical moments in a nation's life they summon up energies and commitments that make difficult tasks easier, and apparently impossible ones feasible' (Kumar, 2015: 201). It is in this light that debates about England's political development, its place within the United Kingdom and it relationship to the rest of the world through its outward-facing form (the United Kingdom) take on greater importance in the project of integrating and mobilising nationhood towards a historic political goal (leaving the EU). Support for the republished *Our Island Story* was not solely a way of getting parents to read 'history' to their children, but was part of a three-level game concerned with keeping the UK united whilst disengaging it from the EU and reconnecting with 'traditional allies' in a world beyond Europe. England's constitutional development was not only important in cohering a particular understanding of British politics but it was also the fulcrum that bound English nationalism to Euroscepticism and the Anglosphere.

There were unintended consequences, however, to this political strategy. The salience of referendums in British politics since 1997, but especially since 2010 on the issue of Europe, is in part explained by the need to re-invigorate the links between citizens and representative government. This set up a tension between parliamentary and popular sovereignty at a historic moment in which the existence of a British or UK-wide *demos* could no longer be assumed. The promotion of 'constitutional Englishness' was one of the dominant forms of this national consciousness to emerge after 2010, but it also sustained a particular reading of Englishness that linked – and merged – England with wider categories of belonging, especially those English-speaking countries claimed as legatees to the development of English constitutional history.

This articulation of English nationhood along constitutional lines sheds new light on the Brexiteers' main campaigning message. The slogan 'Take Back Control' was effective on two levels. The first was that of control over borders and was designed to resonate amongst those concerned about levels of immigration (from the EU and elsewhere) into the United Kingdom. The second was a slightly more esoteric argument about the right form of democracy and representation that ought to pertain to Britain. Between them, these two issues accounted for 82 per cent of Leave voters' stated reasons to vote leave: 33 and 49 per cent respectively (Lord Ashcroft Polls, 2016). The language of democratic self-government was important in the Brexiteer arguments in favour of leaving the EU: 'When you pick up your ballot paper this Thursday', wrote Boris Johnson four days before the 2016 referendum, you have it in your hands to transform Britain's current democratic arrangements for the better. You can change the whole course of European history – and if you vote Leave, I believe that change will be overwhelmingly positive ... When in the history of this country have we gone wrong by believing in self-government? (Johnson, 2016b)

Yet for all such arguments about self-determination, the referendum introduced uncertainty and tension into British politics. The tension between the popular sovereignty implied in a referendum and the place of parliamentary sovereignty in the 'British Political Tradition' had been manifest in 1975. This tension returned to the centre of British politics once the Coalition Government introduced the EU Bill in 2010 and David Cameron pledged a referendum on membership of the EU in 2013 (Wellings and Vines, 2016). The novelty of a UK-wide referendum on EEC membership in 1975 had set an important precedent: that it was only 'the People' who could decide on a matter of such national and constitutional importance as this; and that they had to do so through a referendum. This precedent resurfaced when pressure mounted for a referendum on the UK's membership of the European Union after 2010. In moving a motion in favour of an in–out referendum in the House of Commons on 24 October 2011, Conservative MP for Bury North, David Nuttall justified this move with reference not only to popular sovereignty, but popular culture too:

> At a time when people pick up their phones and spend their own money voting week in, week out to keep their favourite contestants on programmes such as 'Strictly Come Dancing' and 'The X Factor', many will be baffled as to why the Government and all those who oppose this motion seem keen to prevent them from having their chance to vote on Britain's future relationship with the European Union. (Hansard, 2011, 24 October, vol. 534, part 1, col. 48)

Yet the innovation of the EU Act and the calling of a referendum effectively undermined that which it sought to protect: parliamentary sovereignty was significantly challenged by the popular sovereignty implicit in the referendum device.

This was another instance of Arthur Aughey's 'ironies of inversion' in the way in which the English constitution was imagined and understood in the lead-up to Brexit (Aughey, 2016: 356). The long-term process of disengagement from the European Union was bound up with debates about England's constitutional development. These debates had the effect of linking England with other parts of the Anglosphere and thereby helping to imagine the UK outside of the EU. The link between politics and the past is an important one in the generation of coherent and consistent national narratives underpinning the integrative function of nationalism (Smith, 2014: 21). This is as true for England as for any nation, but England's historical peculiarity lay in its entanglement with other nations. England's constitutional history was the dominant frame for understanding England's past when the study of history was first incorporated into the academic life of England's universities during the nineteenth century and also a significant source of this entanglement. But as history was 'modernised' after the Second World War, English constitutional development became the epitome of dull, 'boring' history; the type of subject forced upon disengaged schoolchildren and avoided by university students and lecturers interested in the new frames of class, race and gender (Bentley, 2005: 19). In politics, however, a different direction emerged in the latter years of the twentieth century. The changes associated with European integration and devolution in the United Kingdom gave new life to constitutional questions in Westminster and beyond.

The past weighed heavily on future directions of British politics in the second decade of the twenty-first century. In characterising both Theresa May and Jeremy Corbyn as leaders ideally suited to 'create a better yesterday' (Ascherson, 2016), Neal Ascherson's critique expressed how competing of visions of the past that had seized the ideational commanding heights of the Conservative and Labour parties. Before Brexit brought these two leaders to power, Nick Cohen noted the link between a desire to leave the EU and a particular vision of the past and future amongst (predominantly right-wing) Eurosceptics:

> Voters who do not give Europe a thought from one month to the next do not realise how large [the EU] looms in the right wing imagination. To Conservative minds, the EU is an aggressive, imperial power. Fighting it compares with the fights against Hitler and Stalin. The EU is all that stands between us and the chance of becoming a sovereign, unregulated country: a new Victorian Britain. (Cohen, 2015: 21)

This vision of the past and future had a long political lineage. Since the United Kingdom embarked on accession to the European Communities, the past was an important marker of differentiation between Britain and Europe for Anti-Marketeers, Eurosceptics and Brexiteers alike. Hugh Gaitskell, Enoch Powell, Margaret Thatcher, John Major and David Cameron all used the past to frame criticisms of the European project. For all of them, the past was a key source of differentiation between the United Kingdom and the European Communities. Brexiteers carried this tradition to its logical extreme in 2016. The memory of twentieth-century conflict will be dealt with fully in Chapter 6. For now, it is important to note the persistently differing trajectories between English and European narratives. In this telling of the European twentieth century, European integration made war in Europe – or rather between European states – 'not only unthinkable, but materially impossible' as Robert Schuman put it in 1950 (European Union, 2018). For Brexiteers, the twentieth century represented an apogee followed by decline.

This idea was given a forceful endorsement by the awarding of the Nobel Prize for Peace to the European Union in 2012. This 'EU-ropean' version of the past found only limited traction within English versions of history and the politics surrounding those interpretations that surfaced in the decade before Brexit. Even ostensibly pro-Europeans, such as Tony Blair, did not endorse or use this narrative in salient ways after 2003 (Daddow, 2018). Post-material politics have been characterised by 'identity politics' and clashes over values at the domestic and international levels and the intersection of both (Huynh, 2016: 76). This meant that the politics of identity became an increasingly important marker of political positions, filling the void of what used to be determined far more by class and socio-economic status. Yet New Labour governments were reticent to fill this identity politics space in England, choosing to re-emphasise Britishness in its place, especially during the Brown administration of 2007 to 2010. Giving journalistic expression to this vacuum in the wake of the EVEL debates, Raphael Behr pointed out that once institutional structures underpinning national identity have eroded – in England's case Church and Empire – then what was left was only harping on 'harmless idiosyncrasy: moaning about the weather, queuing, ambivalence towards Marmite' (Behr, 2015: 31). The decline of institutions as the pillars of national identity left space for political entrepreneurs: national values were reasserted to fill this ideational vacuum. This is one of the reasons that the teaching of history became politicised in the decade before Brexit. This version of England's past pointed England away from the EU and (back) towards other English-speaking countries.

As in other Anglophone countries, the past was an important site of ideational conflict played out between politicians and historians. Such 'battles of ideas' were fundamentally about using the past to cohere a national community around a vision of a better yesterday and therefore a more comfortable present and future (McKenna, 2018: 75). Each debate was refracted through the politics of each Anglosphere nation. There was a debate about slavery in the United Kingdom (as we shall see in the following chapter) and an official apology in 2009 to the 'Forgotten Generation' of post-war child migrants from the UK to Australia who suffered institutional abuse after their arrival. However, the delegitimising debates about the effects of settler society on indigenous peoples in Australia, Canada, New Zealand and the United States did not directly affect the United Kingdom. What it did have in common with other Anglosphere nations ahead of a particularly intense period of public commemoration that included the 800th anniversary of Magna Carta was the attack on 'experts' and the marginalisation of 'expert opinion'. This critique of 'experts' was a feature of the Brexit referendum campaign. Writing in his blog, UKIP MP Douglas Carswell sought to delegitimise expertise as politically compromised: 'Many of Remain's "experts" were wrong about the euro. Some directly benefit from the EU's lobbyist-friendly regulatory regime. Several owe their positions to George Osborne. Infallibility and integrity can't just be taken on trust' (Carswell, 2016). Devaluing 'old' expertise and filling this void with a link to a national narrative was an important part of the Brexit project. Writing about the sense of collapse and absence of political leadership that attended the immediate aftermath of the Brexit vote David Frost argued that 'In reality, the only collapse is among commentators whose world view has disintegrated and experts whose expertise is suddenly a lot less valuable … A new chapter is opening in our national story. We are a great country – all of us: all of our political parties, all of our nations' (Frost, 2016).

This tendency to prosecute the battle of ideas by devaluing expertise had been observable across the Anglosphere for some years prior to the Brexit vote. It was a common feature of alt-right activity from anti-vaccination campaigns to campaigns against climate change. In England the debate about re-establishing an older narrative of Britain's past and its constitutional link to Anglosphere countries occurred in England in the decade leading up to the Brexit vote. This debate was part of a broader conservative critique of New Labour's civics education curriculum established in 2002 and a broader critique of pedagogy, particularly the 'themed teaching' of subjects at primary school: 'Critics of the approach', wrote Laura Clark in the *Daily Mail*, 'warn it smacks of 1970s-style teaching methods' (Clark, 2009). The reference to the 1970s was important. For hard Eurosceptics, the 1970s represented the moment when Britain lost its sovereignty to the European Communities. It was the moment when, as pro-Brexit MP Richard Shepherd put it in the debates about an in–out referendum during 2013, 'the national, constitutional history [of] the most remarkable and ancient of all the democratic communities in Western Europe' became critically threatened with extinction, a situation brought about by 'the cravenness of a generation of British politicians who did not think they could govern their own land or believe in their own country' (Hansard, 2013a, 5 July, vol. 565, col. 1202). Rescuing the past from left-leaning elites and inculcating constitutional history amongst pupils in England was the educational corollary of this political drive (Christinidis, 2015: 211).

This long-standing argument about replacing empathy with narrative was restated in the years leading up to the Brexit referendum. This politics, as we shall see below, was focused in particular on the re-publication of Henrietta Marshall's *Our Island Story* in 2005 by the centre-right think tank Civitas. There was also support from other organisations. Part of this push to bring the teaching of narrative (constitutional) history back into the classroom was led by the Prince of Wales through the Prince's Teaching Institute, described in the *Telegraph* as 'a charity established by Prince Charles to protect traditional subjects from the rise of "trendy" teaching which puts more focus on "skills" than knowledge' (Henry, 2011). In 2010, Prince Charles himself expressed concern that 'in the 1960s, anything which might conceivably be described as a timeless principle was abandoned on the basis that all we had known and learned had suddenly become irrelevant, old-fashioned, out-of-date and definitely not modern' (cited in Henry, 2011).

More directly, support for such a change in emphasis in the teaching of history and civics came from the Conservative ranks of the Coalition Government, when this was formed in 2010. When in government, the contest with professional associations – particular those concerned with the teaching of history – was pursued with vigour by the Secretary of State for Education, Michael Gove. Gove's vision, formulated during the period of Conservative opposition, was that he regarded 'education as the means by which individuals can gain access to all the other goods we value – cultural, social and economic – on their terms', allowing individuals 'to become authors of their own life story' (Gove, 2009). But it was Gove's view that 'we fail to give our children a connected sense of the narrative of our islands' (Gove, 2009) that drew most ire from the historical profession when he was Secretary for Education in England and Wales from 2010 to 2013. This anger arose because it came with a simultaneous devaluation of the methods and expertise of the historical profession (Priestland, 2013). In a joint open letter to the *Times*, the Historical Association (HA) argued that

> Mr Gove would have us believe that the HA is an ideologically motivated organisation dedicated to the erosion of academic standards. In fact, its 6000 plus members have widely divergent political views but are united by their love of history and their devotion to bringing high quality scholarship to schools and the wider public. The key skill that the study of history teaches is the ability to evaluate evidence. Regrettably, what Mr Gove has demonstrated in his speech is a remarkable capacity for manipulating and distorting it. (Ward, 2013)

When Richard Evans, the Regius Professor of History at Cambridge University, asked readers of the *New Statesman* in which other academic discipline would a return to the state of knowledge as it was one hundred years ago be advocated (Evans, 2012), it was a good point but one which also missed its target. The debate was not so much about History as it was about International Relations. The battle of ideas in England's history wars was fought on the terrain of narrative history. This was a field that – if successful – would allow people educated in England to understand a particular version of England's constitutional development that linked England to parts of the world largely outside of the European Union. The narrative was intended to establish secure and stable version of the past in which Europe was a peripheral and secondary part of Britain's world. In doing so this vision of the past thereby helped imagine a future in which the UK's membership of the European Union was a mere interregnum. Taking the UK out of the EU was – in this view – a restoration of England's established historical trajectory.

Our Island Story: the Anglosphere and British integration

A reasserted constitutional historical narrative created a potent ideational argument that supported the integrationist and secessionist elements within English nationalism. It supported the secessionist element in English nationalism by downplaying the significance of Europe in the development of democracy in England. This contrasted with the place of European integration in consolidating democracy in post-fascist and post-communist Europe that was a strong element of the EU narrative. It contributed to the integrationist element of English nationalism by suggesting that England's constitutional history had more in common with forms of representative democracy in English-speaking parts of the world, both within the United Kingdom and beyond.

The lightning rod for this political push came with the re-publication of *Our Island Story* in 2005. The deployment of, support for and debate about *Our Island Story* illustrated and reasserted the wider categories of belonging that historically framed understandings of political Englishness. The in-group invoked in the title was that of 'Greater Britons' *à la* Charles Dilke and J. R. Seeley. The latter's 1883 lectures popularised the notion that Greater Britain was 'a real enlargement of the English state' carrying across the seas 'not merely the English race, but the authority of the English Government' (Seeley, 1971 [1883]: 38). Furthermore, the British community described in *Our Island Story* was one bound together by England's con-stitutional development, a product of, in Enoch Powell's phrase 'the slow alchemy of centuries' (cited in Heffer, 1998: 336). It was this governance, part design and part accretion of conventions, which created a form of British commonality across the globe at the historical moment when nationalism was becoming the principal ideology used to legitimise the ordering of geo-political space. As such, 'official nationalism' in England became heavily inflected with British and imperial language and symbolism at this historical moment.

This push in the battle of ideas about Britain, Britishness and the UK's place in the world began at a low point of Conservative fortunes before David Cameron's 'modernising' project began in earnest (Bale, 2010: 284) and before UKIP made its electoral breakthrough in 2009–14. At first the debate surrounding *Our Island Story* was linked to arguments about the best ways of writing and teaching history. Lady Antonia Fraser noted in the Foreword to the republished book that 'Much has been written about the decline in the learning of "chronological history", of the fading out of narrative history, of the rise, at the cost to all, of social history that seeks to pro-mote "empathy" yet robs history of its context' (cited in Marshall, 2005 [1905]: xv). This argument was something of a straw man since, as Marilyn Lake argued, few historians or educators would argue against coherent and engaging narratives per se, but rather against *which* narratives should be privileged (cited in Abjorensen, 2009: 155). But the re-publication of *Our Island Story* had not only the virtue of bringing 'the way that history is taught back into sharper focus', it also evoked (for Fraser at least) 'the warmth of childhood memory' (cited in Marshall, 2005 [1905]: xv). This nostalgic element of its appeal underscored Helen Brocklehurst's argument that a clear narrative was supposed to bring about an enhanced sense of nostalgic 'security' to the receptive reader (Brocklehurst, 2015: 54).

The 'story' in Marshall's book that seemed to offer such a sense of nostalgic security was that of the development of England's and subsequently Britain's consti-tutional liberties. Published originally in 1905, *Our Island Story* was the type of cele-bratory, Whiggish, constitutional narrative history that the modernisers of English history so reviled (Bentley, 2005: 5). It was a tale of England's – and Britain's – constitutional development told through stories about English and British kings and queens (Scotland makes its first appearance via James VI and I in chapter 74 of 110). The story begins with the Romans and ends with the South African War and the death of Queen Victoria at the outset of the twentieth century. It is quite explicitly sub-titled 'A History of Britain for Boys and Girls' and the author adds a further qualification that 'this is not a history lesson, but a story book' (Marshall, 2005 [1905]: xxi). Despite the author's intention, its advocates saw it as a means to shore up a form of British integration that they saw as under threat from multiculturalism and nationalism.

Even if Marshall herself claimed no political intent, others used the idea of Britain possessing an 'island story' that made it distinct from, or even incompatible with, the EU as a lesson in politics. By 2012–14, the book's narrative was deployed as a political device not only as a way to cohere children of diverse backgrounds in English schools but also as a way to cohere the United Kingdom while simultaneously imagining a looser relationship with a reformed European Union. The way to do this was by promoting a narrative that re-emphasised a global past as the affirming outcome of England's distinct constitutional development. For Eurosceptics this global past positioned the United Kingdom on a trajectory towards a global future. For Brexiteers, 'global' and 'Europe' were mutually incompatible concepts.

Picking up on the 'island story' narrative, the *Daily Express* formally launched its campaign to get Britain out of Europe in 2010. Conflating Britain and England, it described England/Britain as 'a precious stone set in the silver sea, as Shakespeare so evocatively put it; a realm with a glorious island story stretching back a thousand years, with links to every continent and a language taken up throughout the world' (*Express*, 2010). The link to English as a global language was important suggesting the broad, sunlit uplands of a global future rather than the deadening confines of a regional past to which England, in this reading of history, only temporarily belonged. History was then combined with the Conservative (and UKIP) critique of the pre-Thatcher British ruling class. Citing the lack of a popular mandate for remaining in the EU since the referendum of 1975 (subsequent general elections notwithstanding), and arguing that in post-Eurozone crisis Europe there was no longer a good economic argument for remaining a member, the newspaper launched its 'crusade' for British withdrawal. Whilst the *Express* conceded the historic reasons for seeking European unity in the wake of two world wars it noted that 'Britain is a land apart' that was never entirely a part of the historical trajectory that propelled the Continental powers towards integration. Tacking the Thatcherite critique of the political class onto a maritime metaphor, the *Express* argued as follows:

> Our political class bought into the European experiment after losing confidence in our nation and accepting the inevitability of decline. They viewed Europe as a life raft and clambered on board. The British people never took that view. Now it is

Europe that is in decline and Britain that is being held back. It is time to break free. (*Express*, 2010)

This push for what was until 2015 known as an 'in–out' referendum had not been mollified by the introduction of the EU Act of 2011. The EU Act was an attempt to counter public disengagement with politics after the parliamentary expenses scandal of 2009. It was at the heart of the official reasoning given in defence of the novel incorporation of referendums into English law. When introducing the European Union Bill to Parliament in 2010, David Lidington, Minister for Europe, argued that 'There has been a profound disconnection between the will of the British people and the decisions taken in their name by the British Government in respect of the European Union'. He added that

> This Government is determined to reconnect with the British people by making itself more accountable for the decisions it takes in relation to how the EU develops. We plan to decentralise power from the Government to the British people, so the people can make the big decisions on the direction of the EU. This Government is committed to allowing the British people to have their say on any future proposals to transfer powers from Britain to Brussels. (Lidington, 2010)

Yet despite the passing of the EU Act demands for an in–out referendum did not disappear. A politics of accelerated disengagement from the EU began as Cameron sought to manage and placate the Eurosceptic backbenches and growing challenge from UKIP (Lynch, 2015: 192). This disengagement was framed by the 'island story' version of Britain's past. In January 2013, Cameron reversed the government's policy of the previous two years and conceded a referendum on EU membership if the Conservatives formed a majority at the 2015 election (an unlikely scenario when the speech was given). In the 'Bloomberg speech' that announced the referendum, Britain's island story again framed reasons for seeking a distinctive approach to European integration, but stopping short of advocating exit (although this possibility was implied if his suggested reforms did not occur). Acknowledging that 'the United Kingdom is sometimes seen as an argumentative and rather strong-minded member of the family of European nations', Cameron claimed that this was owing to the psychology produced by geography: 'We have the character of an island nation – independent, forthright, passionate in defence of our sovereignty. We can no more change this British sensibility than we can drain the English Channel' (BBC News Europe, 2013). At this stage of the Brexit démarche, the island story narrative was used by David Cameron to link Britain to the wider world without yet claiming that a more globally oriented United Kingdom and the EU were incompatible polities as Brexiteers did in 2016. 'The fact is that ours is not just an island story', Cameron argued, 'it is also a continental story. For all our connections to the rest of the world – of which we are

rightly proud – we have always been a European power and we always will be'
(BBC News Europe, 2013). This Janus-faced position was difficult to maintain
during the referendum campaign itself, when the switch from Eurosceptic Prime
Minister to champion for Remain undercut the credibility of pro-EU statements
from the highest profile member of the Remain campaign.

Yet before the secessionist nationalism of the Brexiteers gained momentum after
the Conservative general election victory in 2015, the island story narrative had to
be deployed in defence of the United Kingdom's unity ahead of the Scottish referendum on independence in 2014. Linking the 'feel good factor' of 2012 which
witnessed the Diamond Jubilee as well as 'Team GB' finishing third at the London
Olympics (effectively first place given the habitual US and Chinese dominance in
the medal tally), Cameron began the campaign to keep the UK together in earnest.
'The best thing about the Olympics wasn't the winning', he told an audience at
the Lea Valley Velodrome in February 2014: 'it was the red, the white, the blue. It
was the summer that patriotism came out of the shadows and came into the sun.
Everyone cheering as one for Team GB. And it's Team GB I want to talk about
today: our United Kingdom' (Cameron, 2014a). The debate about *Our Island Story*
that was played out in the realm of history teaching in English schools, now shifted
into the realm of nationalist politics as Cameron sought to defeat Scottish secessionism and manage the hard Eurosceptics in his party worried by the success of
UKIP. The future of British unity was endorsed by reasserting past greatness direct
from the pages of Marshall. 'I have an old copy of *Our Island Story*, my favourite
book as a child', Cameron told the Lea Valley audience, 'and I want to give it to my
three children, and I want to be able to teach my youngest, when she's old enough
to understand, that she is part of this great, world-beating story' (Cameron, 2014a).

Although England's constitutional history was being deployed to keep Britain
together, it had another integrative function to perform. This integrative function
was part of a critique of multiculturalism, which had been declared dead by Cameron
at a security conference in Munich in 2011, but which still required effort to keep it
buried. In explaining his rejection of 'state multiculturalism', Cameron argued that
'we have allowed the weakening of our collective identity':

> Under the doctrine of state multiculturalism, we have encouraged different cultures
> to live separate lives, apart from each other and apart from the mainstream. We've
> failed to provide a vision of society to which they feel they want to belong ... instead
> of encouraging people to live apart, we need a clear sense of shared national identity
> that is open to everyone. (Cameron, 2011)

Amidst concerns about the growth of 'home-grown terrorism' amongst susceptible
(predominantly male) populations in disadvantaged areas of the United Kingdom
(predominantly in England), England's constitutional history became part of the
Conservative push to create a more unitary articulation of Britishness. This time the

link was not just with the imperial-global expansion of this form of governance but also with the value of Magna Carta itself. One of Cameron's responses to the 'Trojan Horse' controversy within Birmingham schools was to bring Magna Carta to bear as a source of unity in contemporary England. Commenting on the 'Trojan Horse' issue on the 799th anniversary of the signing of the first Magna Carta, Cameron used language redolent of the nineteenth century when he argued that 'I believe we need to be far more muscular in promoting British values and the institutions that uphold them' (Cameron, 2014b). This more 'muscular' approach suggested two inter-related courses of action. The first was to ensure that new immigrants speak English 'because it will be more difficult for them to understand these values, and the history of our institutions, if they can't speak our language'. The second action was to bring 'proper narrative history back to the curriculum, so our children really learn our island's story – and where our freedoms and things like our Parliament and constitutional monarchy came from' (Cameron 2014b). This policy linked the English language with British political culture, seeking to create and develop an affinity 'not just of the language itself', as the Australian novelist David Malouf noted at the start of the second Iraq War, but the 'peculiar habit of mind and all that goes with it' (Malouf, 2003: 3).

This peculiar habit of mind – created by Britain's geographic location in Cameron's telling – appeared again during the Brexit referendum campaign. In his so-called 'World War III' speech delivered at the British Museum on 'Europe Day' 9 May 2016 Cameron attempted to make a claim for continued British membership of the EU in terms of security and history, again in the context of Britain's 'island story'. 'If there is one constant in the ebb and flow of our island story', said Cameron, 'it is the character of the British people.' He continued as follows: 'Our geography has shaped us, and shapes us today. We are special, different, unique. We have the character of an island nation which has not been invaded for almost a thousand years, and which has built institutions which have endured for centuries' (Cameron, 2016). Confusingly, the island story narrative – used in 2013 to suggest that Britain should have less to do with the European Union and more to do with its pre-EU allies – was now being used to frame arguments by the Prime Minister to keep the United Kingdom in Europe. The geography implicitly underpinning the narrative was also confusing and revealed the Englishness of this narrative. The use of the singular 'island' story left Northern Ireland in an uncertain relationship to the rest of Great Britain as the contest over EU membership neared the June 2016 vote. Similarly, Magna Carta did not hold the same foundational position in Scottish national narratives as it did in the UK Government's English one.

Given that the United Kingdom was under threat of break-up as well as effecting a secession from the EU of its own, political commonality had to be sought at a higher level of abstraction than the salient moments from a narrative of English constitutional history. In this political context the reassertion of interpretations of the development of what Krishan Kumar calls the 'British [*sic*] constitution' as a 'meta-narrative' of English identity were underpinned by a concomitant reassertion of a Whig history narrative that was in fact a 'self-flattering national myth' about English aggrandisement (Kumar, 2015: 207). Crucially, this particular national narrative performed the mobilising and integrating functions of political myths and linked England with other parts of the world: 'What the narrative announces is that this people, with these virtues and capacities, will mark out for themselves a particular place in the world. They will have a future that the past already presages, in laying down the basic elements of the national character and the forms of national life' (Kumar, 2015: 202). The idea of 'liberty' was crucial in this articulation of commonality across different national traditions within the United Kingdom, but it also had the effect of linking the United Kingdom with the Anglosphere through a story about the development of representative democracy, of which Magna Carta was presented as the wellspring.

Liberty, according to Linda Colley, was 'a multiform master narrative whereby varieties of Britons over the centuries have been able to tell and organise stories about themselves and their state' (Colley, 2014: 37). This master narrative does not apply to (English) 'Britons' alone, however. Magna Carta is the font of the idea of liberty in Anglosphere thought and the fulcrum of English nationalism, Euroscepticism and the political traditions to which the Anglosphere was heir. 'In every generation', wrote Daniel Hannan, 'the English-speaking peoples have tended to treat [Magna Carta] as their Torah, the script that sets them apart' (Hannan, 2013: 110) thereby setting them on the path to the invention of freedom.

Magna Carta is even celebrated in the United States, which is the Anglophone nation most politically distinct from England. In 1965, US Secretary of State Dean Rusk accepted an acre of the field at Runnymede from Queen Elizabeth II as a gift from the British people to the United States (US Senate Joint Resolution 150, 1991). Ten years later, the US Congress sent a delegation to the UK to borrow an original copy of Magna Carta for the Bicentennial of the Declaration of Independence in 1976 (US House of Representatives Resolution 458, 1975). In 1991, Congress declared 15 June Magna Carta Day and called on the President 'to issue a proclamation calling on the people of the United States to observe the day with appropriate ceremonies and activities' (US Senate Joint Resolution, 150: 1991). Although US Senate Resolution 155 of 10 November 1997 stated that 'the Declaration of Arbroath, the Scottish Declaration of Independence [*sic*], was signed on April 6, 1320 and the American Declaration of Independence was modeled on that inspirational document' (US Senate Resolution 155, 1997), this influence was corralled into the particularism of 'Tartan Day' (6 April). There would, however, be no concomitant 'Tweed Day' for the English in America. Magna Carta was more universal in its implications as a Senate Resolution explained:

> Magna Carta was exceptional in its prolonged influence on legal and constitutional thought in England and among the English-speaking nations as a statement of fundamental law, enshrining principles of human freedom and liberty ... [It] subsequently

provided historical precedent for the powerful stream of thought emphasizing the natural rights of the individual that is expressed in the United States Constitution. (US Senate Joint Resolution 150, 1991)

It was this transnational and exemplary understanding of liberty that allowed Brexiteers to present voting to leave not only as a benefit for Britain but for the EU too. In April 2016, Michael Gove argued that

> For Britain, voting to leave will be a galvanising, liberating, empowering moment of patriotic renewal … But for Europe, Britain voting to leave will be the beginning of something potentially even more exciting – the democratic liberation of a whole continent. If we vote to leave, we will have – in the words of a former British Prime Minister – saved our country by our exertions and Europe by our example. (Gove, 2016)

In this view, the democratic liberation of Europe was a happy by-product of Britain's withdrawal from the EU. But the concern with Europe was an afterthought. The shared exceptionalism that underpinned this English worldview was precisely the thing that inclined both Eurosceptics and Brexiteers away from the European Union and towards the English-speaking peoples.

The promotion of *Our Island Story* and its grounding in the English constitution illustrated the overlapping functions that the government hoped that promoting such narrative would provide. It was used in arguments to keep the United Kingdom united and to distance the United Kingdom from the EU, by the 'soft Eurosceptics' in the Remain camp and by Brexiteers. It also tapped into a persistent construction of English identity that linked it with the political development of other English-speaking peoples. This construction of Englishness helps explain what McGowan and Phinnemore describe as the 'profound discomfort with the concept and realities of integration' (McGowan and Phinnemore, 2017: 80). This version of Englishness carried significant implications for the UK's membership of the European Union. *Our Island Story* and the narrative of English history that it carried was used to reinforce British integration, but by reasserting an English version of British commonality, it also ultimately contributed to European disintegration by highlighting the British difference from Europe in an English idiom. It did so by providing a vision of England's constitutional past that linked it with Anglophone nations and thereby enabled citizens to imagine a constitutional future outside of the European Union.

Traditional allies: liberty and the Anglosphere

This constitutional narrative was not formed in isolation as a response to a perceived crisis of teaching in 'Broken Britain' alone. It was allied to a reinvigoration of diplomatic relations with what Foreign Secretary William Hague recast in 2010–13 as 'traditional allies' (Hague, 2013). *Our Island Story* created a discrete narrative loop. It was at once a tale whose field of reference was bigger than England itself and yet connected English and British history with other parts of the world (outside of Europe) whilst at the same time relating world history and global development back into the earliest episodes of England's past. In this telling of English history, the development of forms of governance and representative democracy were emphasised linking the Anglo-Saxon *witan* with the establishment of representative government and liberal democracy in the present day. Like recurrent themes in expressions of English nationhood, it is both expansive and diminutive. Arguments in favour of *Our Island Story* therefore served to emphasise a significant tradition in English thought that situated England as the dominant partner in an historic political-economic and cultural enterprise with a global legacy and, therefore, a global future.

As part of their argument to convince voters to leave the EU, the Brexiteers needed to defend and promote Westminster as a model of democracy even as they prosecuted a referendum that undermined parliament's sovereignty, simultaneously lauding and sidelining the institution they upheld as preferable to the European Union's representative mechanisms. In doing so, Westminster-style representative democracy and the ideals and practices such a system entailed, were remembered as a political system that was both exported and emulated throughout the former British Empire and amongst the English-speaking peoples. 'It is frankly shocking', argued Liam Fox,

> that the other side is proving so dismissive of the success of democratic self-government. This principle was once seen as Britain's gift to the world, yet now the leaders of our country are willing to sacrifice it to the interests of bankers and continental politicians. (Fox, 2016)

In this reading, Westminster, like its European counterpart in Brussels-Strasbourg, had also been a supranational parliament governing a diversity of peoples. The difference was that sovereignty was shared only in the sense that the model was emulated in jurisdictions that were given – or won – increasing degrees of autonomy or outright independence from the United Kingdom.

Despite the effects of such colonial nationalism, England's constitutional development serves as the foundation for Anglosphere interpretations of liberty. It is a shared exceptionalism that links all Anglosphere nations. An understanding of the past – or more specifically an ability to recall episodes of a particular national narrative – is a crucial element in the ideology of nationalism. No less is true of a trans-nationalism like the European Union or the Anglosphere. Each must have its foundational myths. England's constitutional history is absolutely central to the Anglosphere view of the world: without England's history the Anglosphere makes no sense. The political culture that is said to bind the Anglosphere is a product of English history within the 'British world' and the United States, a world in which

Europe – in the Anglosphere reading – is a best peripheral and at times a source of threat rather than security: 'How long before the ECJ starts undermining the Five Eyes intelligence sharing agreements that have been a foundation of British security since 1945 and which are the source of jealousy and suspicion in Brussels?' asked Gove during the referendum campaign (Gove, 2016). Gove's argument contained explicit reference to Anglosphere countries and linked governance to prosperity. 'Under democratic self-government', he argued, 'countries such as Australia, Canada, the USA and New Zealand all enjoy excellent economic growth and global influence', including 'the ability to control their own borders' (Gove, 2016). The explicit and implicit links between England, Britain and other English-speaking peoples around the globe simultaneously re-emphasised England's exceptionalism from Europe and linked it to the Anglosphere.

This historical trajectory made a return to a re-articulated version of Churchill's 'English-speaking peoples' seem like a desirable *and possible* alternative to membership of the EU. It also re-emphasised a construction of Englishness around institutions and symbols that further inflected English nationhood with wider categories of belonging. Monarchy was the vehicle by which Britishness was made personal throughout the Commonwealth after the Statute of Westminster in 1931 and its subsequent ratification in the Dominions. The *Royal Titles Act* (1951) accepted the principle of 'divisibility' and that the Monarch should adopt a title appropriate to each self-governing nation-state in the Commonwealth. These charges, noted Ben Pimlott, 'accelerated a movement away from the notion of the British Monarch as sovereign over "dominions" and towards a personally-based link, in which the monarch enjoyed a separate identity in each' (Pimlott, 1997: 182). As the self-governing Dominions accrued more and more independence in domestic and foreign policy matters in the second quarter of the twentieth century, the Monarchy formed more and more the 'dignified' part of government and state identified in Bagehot's *The English Constitution* (1867), with the modification that it was now the 'dignified' part of the English Constitution that held the Commonwealth together after the Second World War. Hence the political importance of Royal Tours such as that of 1953–54 that both cemented loyalty in the Commonwealth and projected visions of loyal friends and allies back into England.

In this worldview, the Commonwealth was distinct, but not quite foreign: the relevant government department for relations with such countries was, after all, the Foreign and Commonwealth Office (FCO) suggesting that Britain and Britons had more in common with Commonwealth countries, which remained a category distinct from other foreigners. Although often derided as anachronistic, the Commonwealth experienced a political revivification in official British eyes during 2010–15 and especially after 2016 when it became an important vehicle for the UK Government's strategy for economic life after Brexit (Fox, 2018). Yet the signs of this re-engagement with the Commonwealth countries were evident before the Brexit referendum and were part of the Conservative disengagement from the EU in 2010–15. Symbolically, William Hague left the House of Commons for a Commonwealth Heads of Government (CHoGM) meeting in Perth, Australia midway through the in–out referendum debate of October 2011 in order to pursue better relations with 'traditional allies'. An analysis of the revival of bilateral ties with Anglosphere states suggests as many points of tension as of commonality that undercut this idea as a realistic alternative to membership of the EU. Nevertheless, the Anglosphere and Commonwealth – partially overlapping entities – retained a powerful affective pull for those seeking British disengagement with or withdrawal from the European Union (Murray-Evans, 2018).

Ties with English-speaking countries were revivified at a bilateral level during 2010–15 too. Although the Anglo-Australian relationship maintained intelligence links through the 'Five Eyes' network noted by Michael Gove above, it had assumed a 'taken-for-granted' aspect during the 1990s when regional integration was strongly advocated in both countries (Major, 1993: 91). Yet this changed in 2006 when the UK and Australia announced the establishment of annual meetings of foreign and defence minsters ('AUKMIN') after the conclusion of the Commonwealth Games in Melbourne that year. The focus on the relationship intensified under the Coalition Government. Speaking to the Australian Parliament ahead of the G20 summit in Brisbane in November 2014, David Cameron stressed the personal links between Britain and Australia, noting that almost 600,000 Britons visited Australia each year, as well as acknowledging his Australian aunt in the gallery. He was also keen to stress the common values that formed 'the very bedrock of our relationship' and that linked Britain and Australia historically and in the present day:

> We have stood together so often, and do so today, not just because we faced common threats, but because we believe in the same things: In the rule of law; in the fundamental right of individuals to choose and to change their governments; in open societies and economies and free trade as the only route to thriving, stable societies ... My argument today is that it is these values, the values that bring us together and that have made our countries great, these are the values which should guide us through the challenges we face today. (Cameron, 2014c)

Once again, the shared past of the two countries was the guide future joint action.

Cameron's speech also showed how 'values' rather than institutions bound together Anglosphere countries more so than their previous relations as 'English-speaking peoples'. But there were tensions in the concept for those seeking to use Anglosphere countries as a counterweight or alternative to membership of the EU. Arguments for the Anglosphere – even with Magna Carta-inspired liberty at their heart – need to account for the development of nationalism and expressions of independence within their own legitimising narratives, so that – like Anglo-Saxonist arguments of the nineteenth century – all narrative roads lead to liberty through the development of representative government.

The American War of Independence (1775–83), subsequent Anglo-US tensions during the nineteenth century, and the US eclipse of the UK as the world's pre-eminent power in the twentieth, required the greatest explanation. The American Revolution thus forms a moment of tension within Anglosphere thought. However, the meta-narrative of 'liberty' is the device that allows this conflict to be recast as an Anglosphere 'civil war' in a way similar to that espoused by pro-Europeans who recast the conflicts of 1914–45 in such terms (McCormick, 2014: 29).

This reinterpretation of the past was also part of a pattern observable in the re-articulation of 'fraternal conflict' in a manner similar to the memory of the American Civil War outlined by Susan-Mary Grant, whereby former enemies came to be remembered as co-nationals divided (Grant, 2005: 510). Thus the conflict was described as a 'civil war' in *Our Island Story* (2005 [1905]: 436). One hundred years later Niall Ferguson described the revolutionary wars as 'the moment when the British ideal of liberty bit back' (Ferguson, 2003: 84). Closely related to Ferguson's argument was Daniel Hannan's reconceptualisation of the American War of Independence as the 'Second Anglosphere Civil War' (Hannan, 2013: 209), with the first having been the Wars of the Three Kingdoms in the mid-seventeenth century. 'It cannot be stressed too strongly', argued Hannan, 'that the American Revolution was an internal argument followed by a civil war' and that the American Revolution was 'made by Englishmen who, as their ancestors had done during the 1640s, asserted their rights against a monarchy that they viewed as alien and innovatory' (Hannan, 2013: 209–214). It was this reconceptualisation that allowed Hannan to conclude that the 'constitution was not just an American achievement. It was, as its authors were keen to stress, the ultimate expression and vindication of the creed of the English-speaking peoples' (Hannan, 2013: 241).

Similarly, James Delingpole, writing for Breitbart UK ahead of the first Fourth of July holiday after the Brexit referendum told his audience that despite a history of conflict at a founding moment, 'At heart, you Americans and we British are instinctive patriots: heirs to the traditions established by Magna Carta' (Delingpole, 2016). 'For me', he continued:

> Independence Day means the birth of the Anglosphere. As an Englishman, I don't feel at all resentful that you triumphed over George III's Redcoats, nor do I count it as a defeat. It was a victory for all of us: the settlers in the thirteen colonies got to forge their own destiny; the mother country could focus her attentions elsewhere, notably India; we could all enter a new mature relationship as free traders (bringing both parties massively increased prosperity); and, best of all, it resulted in the US Constitution. (Delingpole, 2016)

There are good reasons to avoid imposing an anachronistically nationalist framework onto this conflict. It was indeed a civil war fought in the Thirteen Colonies that caused great political divisions within the United Kingdom. Yet we must also be wary of evincing one anachronism only to replace it with another, in this case, the Anglosphere. What is important for the argument in this book is the linking of elements in the dominant version of English nationalism with wider categories of belonging. The process that Benedict Anderson termed 'the reassurance of fratricide' helped create this ideational linkage. This process was one that Anderson identified as characteristic of the construction of nationalist genealogies that turned past sources of division in to present-day pillars of commonality (Anderson, 1991: 199–201).

Memory of conflict with European powers looms large in collective remembrance in England. Memory of conflict with the United States is less prominent, having been displaced by memories about common endeavours in the twentieth and early twenty-first centuries, as we shall see in Chapter 6. Although never resulting in major international conflict like that between Britain (including Upper and Lower Canada) and the Thirteen Colonies and the United States between 1775 and 1815, the development of nationalism in the other 'core' Anglosphere states was not without tensions that required managing. UK–Australia relationships were not always characterised by an alignment of interests and identities, particularly from the 1890s to the period of British disengagement 'East of Suez' in the 1960s and Australia's turn to America, culminating in the UK's accession to the European Communities in 1973. The domestic manifestation of this 'Anglo-scepticism' in Australia was the growth of the Republican movement in the 1990s leading to the 1999 republic referendum. This meant that Australia was the location where the binding concept of the Crown was most recently and significantly tested.

The republican challenge in Australia during the 1990s forced the monarchy's defenders to articulate anew the value of this institution in national terms. Although always at pains to stress that the monarchist movement was defending *Australia's* monarchy, not Britain's, the links were unavoidable. Writing in 1995 as Executive Director of Australians for Constitutional Monarchy, Tony Abbott – later to be Prime Minister of Australia 2013–15 and a leading advocate of the Anglosphere – admitted that 'the Crown is not now – and probably never has been – at the forefront of Australian consciousness', yet he argued that 'it is still part of our cultural furniture as well as our legal structure. The Crown is no more alien to Australia than cricket and Shakespeare' (Abbott, 1995: 137).

Although Australia voted to retain the monarch as head of state in 1999 by a 55–45 per cent popular majority across all states and territories, one must be careful not to impute this victory to the appeal of monarchism alone (Holmes, 2013). The outcome of the Republic referendum – which required a double majority of states and electorate to pass – was an early example of the same tensions and social divisions that characterised Brexit: an elite project (monarchism) eventually won out through an unanticipated alliance with populist resentment against another elite project (republicanism). The politically literate and economically affluent Australian Capital Territory was the only mainland state or territory to vote in favour of a republic.

This victory for an ambivalent, Australian version of monarchy underscored the fact that the Anglosphere means different things in different places and tends to be characterised in speeches as bound by ephemeral 'values' rather than institutions. Despite the post-AUKMIN emphasis on commonality, David Cameron did not refer to the Crown or the monarchy in his speech to the Australian Parliament in 2014: indeed Cameron's aunt got more mentions than the Queen. The limits to popular monarchism in Australia were further underscored in 2015. The controversy surrounding Tony Abbott's unilateral decision to award a newly reinstated Australian knighthood to Prince Philip, the Duke of Edinburgh on Australia Day 2015, illustrated the uneasy relationship between nationalism and monarchy in Australia and almost cost Abbott his role as Prime Minister through the disquiet this action caused on the Liberal-National backbenches (Sheridan, 2015). Despite this, the result of the 1999 referendum could be read as another popular and democratic endorsement of the English Constitution in England. The nomination of Prince Philip as a knight of Australia in 2015 could be seen as another endorsement of that tradition, but such overt Anglospherism could be misinterpreted in England as much as it was resented and ridiculed in Australia.

Conclusion

At the most fundamental level of commonality, it is a narrative about 'liberty' that binds the Anglosphere. Thus England's constitutional development is the fulcrum of English nationalism, Euroscepticism and the Anglosphere and serves as a point of commonality for all three ideologies. Political support for this narrative before and after Brexit had consequences for the expression of political Englishness and underscored Henrietta Marshall's twenty-first-century publisher's concern with the European Union's effect on British liberties and the British constitution. The content of the narrative, English constitutional history with a British veneer, blurred the boundaries of political Englishness and Britishness. Thus the text should be seen as part of a wider battle of ideas, using England's constitutional past to help imagine the United Kingdom outside of the European Union.

Despite the Anglo-centric bias that was typical of the writing of British history in 1905, Marshall's version of history was too expansive to be called 'English' in any simple way. But in being deployed to this purpose it blurred England's political boundaries with older and wider categories of belonging. It merged England with Britain and linked Britain with the Anglosphere. In sum, *Our Island Story* was not just a vehicle for debates about the past and future of the United Kingdom and a means to cohere political and social unity. Marshall's version of England's political development – written by a Scot in sojourning in Australia, who had also lived in California and London – was used to suggest a future for the United Kingdom outside of the European Union. The global future implicit in stories about a global past provided a historical trajectory that was portrayed as incompatible with the political project of European integration with its own uncertain (and to Eurosceptics, threating) *finalité*. Its Anglosphere narrative implied a British, not European, future in tune with English history, one in harmony with the linguistic and political cultures that were a legacy of Britain's imperial past.

5

Greater Britain: England's wider categories of belonging

Bicentenary of the abolition of slavery, 2007

The year 2007 was an important anniversary. It represented the tercentenary of the Act (or Treaty) of Union between Scotland and England. Three hundred years is a long time in politics and few other states could boast such longevity and political continuity. Given this – and in an age where commemorations were commonplace – it was all the more surprising that there was no official attempt to commemorate this historic anniversary. Instead, the United Kingdom's commemorative time and energy went towards commemorating the bicentenary of the abolition of the slave trade within the British Empire.

The centrepiece of commemorative events was the ceremony at Westminster Abbey in August, which was most notable for the incursion by Toyin Agbetu who made his protest so close to the person of the Queen. There are several explanations for the elision of the tercentenary of the Union between England and Scotland by the bicentenary of the abolition of slavery. The first was that for an external audience the abolition of slavery was a more significant global event than the creation of the United Kingdom of Great Britain. Secondly, the early form of 'humanitarian intervention' represented by the campaign to end the transatlantic slave trade and its subsequent suppression by the Royal Navy sat well with the New Labour Government's priorities, notably its emphasis on overseas development aid, whilst also being something that appealed to the right of British politics.

The cosmopolitanism of the abolition movement appealed to progressive political traditions. It could be presented as a humanitarian, ethical and moral Parliament triumphing over a social evil buttressed by economic interests; an argument, moreover, carried in 1807 by moral rather than physical force (unlike in the United States). It allowed New Labour to acknowledge the negative aspects of Britain's global role and how it came to such pre-eminence whilst at the same time presenting a redemptive narrative about Britain's relations with the transatlantic world and Africa.

But at a deeper level it also represented an important occlusion and illustrated some of the reflexes that conditioned English nationalism at the outset of the twenty-first century. These reflexes were in turn conditioned by understandings of Britain's past that limited what was or was not possible to commemorate in order to legitimise not just government policies but the British polity itself. That polity was entering a significant period of strain based on political de- and realignments amongst the nations of the United Kingdom. In 2007 the Scottish National Party formed a minority government in Holyrood. Having a secessionist party at official commemorations for the tercentenary of the United Kingdom would certainly have been awkward. The result was a commemorative moment that looked outwards rather than inwards in an attempt to define Britishness as a globally engaged and cosmopolitan identity.

This official legitimisation of Britain as a global actor also came at a moment when England was emerging as a de facto political community. Yet as so often England was an absent presence during these commemorations. The English could – and were indeed forced to – draw upon 'wider categories of belonging' than England itself when legitimising the sovereignty of the British state – both internally and externally. This situation developed not only the elision between England and Britain, but also associated 'Great Britain' with greatness and 'Little England' with diminutive parochialism.

Avoiding the tercentenary and emphasising the bicentenary meant not talking about England at a moment when it was coming ever more sharply into political view. In 2007, the UK Government at Westminster was already wary of drawing too much attention to the pluri-national make-up of the Union for fear of highlighting national differences over the value of that Union. Instead it sought to commemorate a version of what we might now call 'global Britain'. As Englishness became politicised, the UK Government offered up a memory of Empire to paper over the emerging cracks in the Union state.

The years leading up to the Brexit referendum were also years of debates about Britain's imperial past. The conclusions made about this topic were fairly one-sided: in 2014 59 per cent of respondents to a YouGov poll said that the British Empire was something to be proud of and 44 per cent thought that the world was better off for its existence (YouGov, 2014). This represented a polarisation of more balanced views of the past presented in 2011 (YouGov, 2011), but was sustained through debates about the idea of pulling down Cecil Rhodes' statue at Oxford University and into January 2016 when once again 44 per cent of respondents said that the Empire was something to be proud of (YouGov, 2016). This chapter establishes why political and strategic ties to the English-speaking peoples resonate in English nationalism and why they can be presented as a reassuring, if perhaps less obviously viable, alternative to European integration. Much of the current attempts to determine the boundaries of 'political Englishness' are concentrated and focused within the political frame of the United Kingdom. On one level this is obvious, but on another it misses something important about the historical development of England's dominant national tradition and therefore the boundaries that this important tradition sets on the opinion, attitudes and actions of actors and voters.

The important element here is that the sovereignty that 'English nationalists' chose to defend was always more geographically encompassing than the nation of England itself. The enduring political legacy of this historic development was that English nationalists could always – and had to – draw upon 'wider categories of belonging' than England itself to explain and justify England's place in the world. This imperative not only deepened the elision between England, Britain and Empire, but also associated 'Britain' with greatness during the nineteenth century and 'England' with parochialism in the twentieth. This diminution of England was compounded when after years of anti-racist struggle so-called BME (Black and Multi-Ethnic) groups in the United Kingdom adopted a 'British identity' over an English identity that was considered too heavily inflected with concepts of race and 'whiteness'. This was compounded by the increasing use of a British identity to signal pro-EU and anti-separatist sentiments. But when nationalist movements within the United Kingdom challenged a common British identity, English identity re-emerged as a political identity by default. It was, furthermore, one that seemed to be inflected with resentment and anger. But in articulating England anew at the beginning of the twenty-first century, political actors drew heavily upon established ways of understanding Englishness that were not based on multiculturalism but that rested upon with notions of England's wider categories of belonging contained in memories of empire and arguments about the Anglosphere in refashioning Britain's place in the world.

Little Englanders: defending British sovereignty after empire

Political myths, as we have seen, have mobilising and integrative functions. They need to both resonate with popular conceptions of being in the world whilst at the same time marginalising or silencing competing explanatory and justificatory narratives. In this way, the constitutional narrative of England's political development articulates well with narratives that explain and justify British imperialism. As Srdjan Vucetic argues, the 'gift to the world' of Anglophone forms of representative democracy provided the ultimate justification for empire: responsible government always corrected irresponsible land use by indigenous peoples and justified dispossession (Vucetic, 2012: 108). Although less contentious than Rhodes' statue in Oxford, a monument such as that of Boudicca located on London's Embankment within view of the Houses of Parliament can create a sense of divided loyalties amongst the English. Although the statue was designed to venerate the queen of the Iceni, the statue raises questions about whether ultimately she was just on the wrong side of 'progress'. Turning to Henrietta Marshall for guidance, we find that Marshall presciently sides with the Iceni: 'The Romans were a very greedy people', she explained. 'They wanted to take away the freedom of Britain and make the island into a Roman province' (Marshall, 2005 [1905]: 17). It was easy to draw a Eurosceptic conclusion from this version of the past.

Yet such a Conradian moment on the banks of the Thames illustrated another historic dilemma for English nationalists: whether to side with Empire or nation; or whether seek a reconciliation between the two concepts that came to be seen as antithetical throughout the nineteenth and twentieth centuries – even amongst the nations at the core of dynastic empires themselves. Krishan Kumar is right to suggest that imperialism offered a 'mission' to groups who we might otherwise expect (under 'normal' conditions) to be English nationalists (Kumar, 2003: 30). Yet in the dominant expressions of English nationalism, nation and empire are not opposed, but merged. Although expressions of England shorn of imperial distractions and free of the burdens that imposing liberty on unsuspecting peoples incurred were articulated throughout the Empire's existence, it was a minority position. Given the need to legitimise Britain's far-flung sovereignty the dominant expressions of English nationalism were infused with imperial language and symbols. Imagining England meant imagining Britain, which meant imagining the Empire and Commonwealth until those political communities disappeared and were replaced – unsatisfactorily for many – with the European Union. Importantly, when England was imagined in contradiction to Britain and Empire, the detractors of this vision could easily paint it as both parochial and lacking the esteem that great power status brought to a people inhabiting the southern part of a small set of islands in the North Atlantic. England was often imagined as a nice, bucolic place (Luton, for example, rarely featured in such constructions); Britain implied something grander, worthy of the respect and resentment due to a formerly great power.

In this way, the expression 'little Englander', originally a label for anti-imperialist, pro-Boer sympathisers during the South African War of 1899–1902 became imbued with a more modern form of contempt. Speaking to the Liberal Democrat conference in the year before the referendum campaign, Nick Clegg noted the strains on the United Kingdom that were emerging after the SNP's impressive showing in the 2015 General Election and asked conference delegates 'Do we want our children and grandchildren to live in a once great country now pulled apart? A Great Britain turned into a Little England, drifting friendlessly somewhere in the mid-Atlantic?' (cited in Liberal Democratic Voice, 2015). In debates about Brexit, 'Little England' was used in attempts to delegitimise political visions of the UK outside the European Union; even though the latter was presented – confusingly – by Remainers as both the vehicle for twenty-first-century greatness and a dead weight on Britain's global ambitions. David Cameron and George Osborne used the term 'Little Englanders' during the Brexit campaign to suggest – erroneously – that those who wanted the UK to leave the EU were isolationist and parochial. Mark Leonard described Farage's political vision as that of a 'little England that restricts migration and withdraws from the common market to regain control of sovereignty', noting that 'he appeals to the socially conservative instincts of people left behind by globalisation' (Leonard, 2015). When he finally made a contribution to the campaign, George Osborne argued that Brexit was 'a battle for the soul of the country', adding that he did not want to live in 'Nigel Farage's vision of Britain. It is mean, divisive and it is not who we are as a country' (cited in BBC News, 2016d). What Farage's vision of the country was, explained David Cameron, was 'Little England'. Cameron urged voters to 'to fight for a Great Britain inside a European Union, and *not* to take the Nigel Farage "little England" option' because it was 'the right thing to do, the British thing to do' (cited in ITV News, 2016).

But such criticisms of the Brexiteers as parochial did not ring quite true. This was because the Vote Leave senior campaigners (possibly in distinction to their supporters) were such committed advocates of globalisation and free trade that it was hard to portray them as parochial. At the elite level, Brexit was not a revolt against globalisation, but an attempt to expose the UK economy to more of it. Indeed the Brexiteers quite effectively – if equally erroneously – turned this accusation of parochialism on the EU and its supporters. But more fundamentally, such claims to parochialism failed to resonate because England's nationhood is historically one of the most 'globalised' in the world. During its formative years, English nationhood was framed and conditioned in relation to the experience of Empire. English people emigrated to, populated and helped colonise – along with their Scottish, Welsh and Irish co-imperialists – large parts of the globe. In a well-worn statistic that operates as its own political myth of past greatness, at its height the British Empire covered one quarter of the world's land area and contained one third of the world population. This global status is usually accompanied by a 'humble brag' that inflates Britain's historical importance at the same time as emphasising its diminutive stature. The blurb on the back cover of Niall Ferguson's *Empire* serves as a good example of the genre: 'Brilliantly telling the story of Britain's imperial past [*Empire*] shows how a gang of buccaneers and gold-diggers from a rainy island in the North Atlantic came to build the most powerful empire in all history, how it ended and how – for better or worse – it made our world what it is today' (Ferguson, 2003: back cover). By containing Britain to a single island the blurb excludes Ireland (including Ulster) from this historical endeavour, an error not replicated in Ferguson's subsequent analysis.

Yet this diminutive greatness illuminates one of the central and determining conundrums about English nationhood – the tension between the local, the national and the global in expressions of English nationalism. If, as we have seen in Chapter 4, representative democracy was presented as England's 'gift to the world' how did the English people come to be in a position to make such an offer in the first place? The answer, of course, was through Britain and its Empire. Along with a defence of British sovereignty, English nationalism – amplified through the British state and Empire – was heavily inflected with notions of greatness. When combined with the meta-narrative of liberty, the idea of greatness complicated membership of the European Union at an affective level. European integration was, as Leo Amery put it in 1931 when presented with an early proposal for European unity, for countries of a 'reduced and diminished status' (HAEU, 1931). Amery (best known for his plea in Parliament on the eve of the Second World War, 'who will speak for England?') summed up in the haughty phrase 'reduced and diminished status' just what was so unsatisfactory about European integration when approached from a political tradition that put such value on Britain's great power status. In this reading of Britain's place in the world after the Second World War, England – contained in the United Kingdom – lay trapped between the receding memory of Empire and the waking reality of deepening European integration. Neither 'Little England' nor European unity offered the prospect of greatness which was so emphasised in English and British national narratives. At the outset of the twenty-first century, the corollary of defending British sovereignty at home and abroad became a quest for something that would not – like the European Union – serve as a daily reminder of Britain's own 'reduced and diminished status', but that could lead to a restoration of global freedom of action (a sort of national liberty) after a European interregnum. It was in this context that the Anglosphere emerged on the right of politics across the Anglophone world and became attractive to Eurosceptics in the United Kingdom.

The Anglosphere may have been attractive to those Eurosceptics seeking to reposition the UK in relation to the EU, but it still left England in an awkward state. One of the tensions in Anglosphere thought is that between the nation and the broader category of 'civilisation' that the Anglosphere itself represents. On the one hand, the predominantly conservative supporters of the Anglosphere have traditionally been strong supporters of the nation-state and nation – in its guise as an international actor and an affective entity binding a citizen to his or her state. On the other hand, the nation is in many ways a lesser category than empire and civilisation, suggesting a diminutive parochialism at odds with imperial grandeur. Examining this tension between nation and a wider category of belonging like 'greater Britain' helps explain why England is not a sufficiently grand nation in Anglosphere thought as an international actor, despite its absolutely crucial place in the Anglosphere narrative as the fount of English-speaking liberty. It is the 'expansion of England' in J. R. Seeley's phrase, which both magnifies and subsumes England's importance. This makes the Union of England and Scotland in 1707 an important way station on the path to greatness and another crucial step in the development of the Anglosphere. Daniel Hannan argued that 'the story of the amalgamation of Scotland and England is worth retelling, for it refutes the idea that the Anglosphere is somehow an amplification of England' (Hannan, 2013: 244).

This convergence between English and Anglosphere narratives is often overlooked. As Mike Kenny has noted, although post-colonial analyses have not found much space within the traditional concerns of British political science, they have contributed a great deal to the notion of a post-imperial English identity in the social sciences more broadly and amongst political commentators on the left (Kenny, 2016: 330). Contributions such as Paul Gilroy's post-imperial 'melancholia' have echoed with the literature on decline stemming from political studies (Gilroy, 2004). Christopher Gifford provided an exception to this standard. Explaining the persistence of Euroscepticism in British politics as a product of imperial and post-imperial strategies, Gifford argued that there was a 'missing European rescue' of the British nation-state at the relationship's troubled core (Gifford, 2014: 15–19). The result of this absence was to distinguish the UK from its European counterparts and to embed a 'structural susceptibility to populist politics' in British politics (Gifford, 2014: 6). Gifford's approach was a rare marriage of a post-imperial and political science analysis. Although not his main concern, his research pointed to a fruitful avenue of enquiry into the nature of politicised Englishness, with the ideas and concerns animating elite political projects and the historical structures shaping scope for legitimate action.

This leads to one of the persistent difficulties with disentangling expressions of English nationhood from their British and imperial contexts. Such a methodo-logical problem was outlined in Chapter 3 and lies in finding *explicit* expressions of Englishness. Although, as we have seen, a politicised Englishness emerged in the late 2000s, little political effort was made to form this into a coherent way of explaining England's place in the world to the English. If the 'Little Englander' trad-ition represented one form of anti-imperial sentiment, another articulation of post-imperial English had a far greater and wider impact on British politics, underscoring the link between England and Euroscepticism.

It is difficult to understate the importance of Powell's political journey from what Paul Foot described as 'grand imperialist to little Englander' for post-imperial Englishness (Foot, 1969: 11). In the absence of effective counter-narratives Powellism 'enjoyed a posthumous success' in Brexit England (*Economist*, 2017). Powell was unusual in that he was a conservative who tried to outline a coherent Englishness based on an uneasy blend of popular and parliamentary sovereignty, early neo-liberalism and racialised meanings of Englishness (Wellings, 2013). Powellism was also important for being 'proto-Thatcherism' in its neo-liberal and Eurosceptic guises. Yet although Powell at times blurred the boundaries of Englishness and Britishness, he was more explicitly pro-English, post-imperial and anti-American than Thatcher and her Eurosceptic successors, despite – or maybe because of – his early years in Australia and India.

The guiding thread of Powell's Englishness was an understanding of the four elements of sovereignty infusing the body politic: parliamentary, popular, commu-nity and individual. His neo-liberalism grounded his view of liberty in the individual as an economic agent, free of the constraints of the post-war British economic com-pact. His sense of community sovereignty underpinned his racism: the 'Rivers of

Blood' speech's narrative tension hinged on the unresolved fate of isolated whites surrounded by thousands of black people. His popular sovereignty was expressed through the idea that governing elites had conned the populace into accepting mass immigration. Yet parliamentary sovereignty was the fulcrum of his Englishness that ultimately trumped his populism. As Emma Vines has shown, it was this defence of parliamentary sovereignty grounded in a post-imperial (but not post-colonial) vision of England, that allowed his political Englishness to become not only anti-Common Market sentiment but to lead logically to a defence of the UK's borders in Ulster (Vines, 2015: 545).

As the controversy over the BBC's decision to dramatise Powell's 'Rivers of Blood' speech on its fiftieth anniversary in 2018 showed, Powell's vision of England always contained a major fault line. His racism and the racialised imaginings of England made him one of the most divisive figures in post-war British politics. The 'execration' that he prophesied his views would attract has echoed down the decades although the racialised bloodbath did not occur. Tom Nairn's description of Powellism as an expression of an essentially 'regressive' English nationalism in the 1970s endured. Furthermore it shaped progressive views about English nationalism from then on, even after Nairn himself had shifted his views on English nationalism as a force for democratic renewal from the late 1990s (Wellings and Kenny, 2018).

Yet Powellism sat uncomfortably within the Conservative Party too. Powell eventually broke with the Conservatives over its pro-EEC stance in 1974–75. His defence of British sovereignty in Ulster was not as a Conservative MP but as an Ulster Unionist member for South Down. If Thatcherism left a difficult legacy for the Conservative Party under Cameron (Heppell, 2014: 178), Powell was even more problematic. When Theresa May told the Conservative conference in 2002 that many in the electorate thought of them as the 'nasty party', it was Powell's legacy of immigration, low taxation and Europe that she was describing (cited in Bale, 2010: 164).

Powellism re-emerged as a political force via the politics of Euroscepticism with the rise of the UK Independence Party. The links between UKIP as it emerged as a political force after the 2009 elections to the European Parliament and Powellism were made in public, but usually by critics rather than supporters of this insurgent party. Speaking after UKIP came first in the 2014 European Parliament elections in the UK with twenty-four of the UK's seventy-three seats and 27 per cent of the UK vote share, Russell Brand described UKIP leader Nigel Farage as 'a pound shop Enoch Powell' (cited in BBC Politics, 2016a), inadvertently revealing some of the snobbery of the 'global elite' that would play a part in the Brexit vote. This accusation did not seem to hurt Farage and – like Bob Geldof's intervention on the Thames in 2016 – could be brushed off as an 'ex-pat' millionaire telling those who did not have the wherewithal to leave England how to think and vote.

UKIP's version of Powellism became especially disruptive when the party leadership linked an anti-immigration rhetoric to the European Union via a critique of the EU's free movement of labour (Ford and Goodwin, 2014). In adopting this tactic, UKIP aligned itself with a broader 'populist *zeitgeist*' in the developed west (Mudde, 2004) that intersected with Euroscepticism over the issue of sovereignty and borders (Leconte, 2015). Yet unlike their Eurosceptic fellow travellers in the European Parliament, UKIP's stated policies were not protectionist like the *Front National*. Instead it was a keen supporter of free trade in keeping with the Powellite tradition (UKIP, 2015).

This re-emergence of updated Powellism in England (it gained little traction in Scotland and nationalist Ireland) continued the conflation of the emergent political community of England with 'wider categories of belonging' of Britain and the Anglosphere. The Englishness of UKIP's support was underscored by their success in the 2009 and 2014 elections to the European Parliament. Even with a proportional representative voting system, all but one of their thirteen seats in 2009 and all but two of their twenty-four seats in 2014 were located in England. Such outcomes led researchers for the Future of England Survey to identify what they called a 'national project' emerging in England, with UKIP supporters forming an important core element of this new politics. This politicised Englishness – supporting the conclusion drawn by Michael Kenny using a different methodology – was driven by 'devo-anxiety', concern over immigration and, in a related sense, resentment at European integration (Jeffery et al., 2016; Wyn Jones et al., 2012; Wyn Jones et al., 2013). Yet the major parties were wary of adopting this groundswell. From the moment they became the de facto English party on 1 May 1997 until 19 September 2014, the Conservative leadership shied away from using English nationalism as part of their electoral politics, despite a growing sense of Englishness amongst grassroots supporters (Hayton, 2012). As we have seen, David Cameron reversed this trend on the morning after the referendum on Scottish independence, although the answer provided to the newly invoked 'English question' was a technical one to do with English Votes for English Laws (EVEL). The Labour Party was also wary of adopting an explicitly English politics, despite advice from the 'Blue Labour group' that was close to Ed Miliband, culminating in his speech on Englishness by the Labour leader in 2012.

Even UKIP were reluctant to adopt this English constituency *explicitly*. In 2014 and 2015, they clung to the notion that their name suggested that they were a UK-wide party and fielded candidates throughout the UK, making gains in Wales. Yet despite its origins in an emerging English critique of European integration and its voter base across the Midlands, South-East and East of England, the UKIP leaderships' instincts were firmly in the English-speaking tradition. In its foreign policy – an expression of its foundational core issue – UKIP rejected UK membership of the EU in favour of existing ties with the Commonwealth and the United States. By 2015 this reorientation was explicitly referred to as 'Anglosphere' in the party's manifesto. At the 2015 General Election, UKIP retained 3.9 million of the 4.3 million voters they had claimed at the 2014 EP elections; an impressive retention of voters from a proportional to a first-past-the-post system, suggesting a high degree of loyalty before the Brexit referendum itself, notwithstanding the collapse in support in 2017. But the novelty of the 'revolt on the right' should not obscure its continuities with long-established political traditions in British foreign policy. As noted in Chapter 1, UKIP explained in their 2015 manifesto that Britain was 'not merely a European country, but part of a wider community, the Anglosphere'. The phrase 'not merely a European country' was significant for the implications about Europe and idea of 'greatness' that Europe inhibits in the Anglosphere imagin-ation. It denoted exactly the idea that Leo Amery put down in writing to Richard Coudenhove-Kalergi in 1931 noted above: European integration was for countries of 'a reduced and diminished status'. Britain's imperial (and later Anglosphere) ties meant that a complete reconciliation with the goals and spirit of European integra-tion was hard if not impossible.

UKIP's explicit embrace of the Anglosphere – an ideology that dared not speak its name in the Conservative manifesto of the same year, despite support for the idea amongst the Free Enterprise Group of MPs who wished to see 'Britannia unchained' from the EU (Kwarteng et al., 2012) – had two important effects in terms of the construction and expression of contemporary English national consciousness. On the one hand this conflation of England and the UK and the ideological alignment of England and Britain with the Anglosphere continued the merging of England as a political and cultural community with 'wider categories of belonging'. Indeed it suggested not nostalgia for the imperial past – although it provided reassuring con-tinuity – but that the *future* lay in a return to renewed relationships with Anglosphere nations. On the other hand, in articulating such ideas and visions of the past and future, it also renewed and revitalised that element of English national conscious-ness that underpinned this dominant form of English nationalism and enabled Brexiteers to imagine the United Kingdom outside of the European Union.

Three English circles: Britain, Europe and the Anglosphere

This English worldview had been muted – rather than entirely lost – in the immediate post-Empire period. English nationalism's greatest ideologue, Enoch Powell, was not really concerned with foreign policy beyond the EEC and Southern Rhodesia, a favourite topic of the Conservative Party's Monday Club. To understand the place of Empire and foreign policy in English nationalism, we need to turn to another renowned statesman, but one who, as David Cannadine has pointed out, almost personified the English-speaking people as both agent and historian: Winston Churchill (Cannadine, 2003: 1).

Churchill, despite being pushed into second place as the greatest ever Briton by William Shakespeare, remained popular in the Brexit era despite – or possibly because of – his imperial rather than post-imperial Britishness. Boris Johnson wrote a best-selling, self-referential (auto)biography of Churchill that claimed to show

how one man could make history (Johnson, 2014). Churchill's championing of the Anglo-US 'Special Relationship' placed him in an important position with regards to England, Europe and the Anglosphere. This is because Churchill set down in writing the idea that when the English-speaking peoples cooperate, the world is a safer and better place:

> For the second time in the present century the British Empire and the United States have stood together facing the perils of war on the largest scale known among men, and since the cannons ceased to fire and the bombs to burst we have become more conscious of our common duty to the human race. Language, law and the processes by which we have come into being, already afforded a unique foundation for drawing together and portraying a common task. (Churchill, 1956: vii)

He was also a great champion of European integration. 'Thinking primarily of the English-speaking peoples', he wrote, 'in no way implies any sense of restriction. It does not mean canalising the development of world affairs, nor does it prevent the erection of structures like United Europe or the similar groupings which may all find their place in the world organisation we have set on foot' (Churchill, 1956: vii). European integration, in his view, was ultimately for proper Europeans rather than Britons. His articulation of a 'three circles' framework for understanding the United Kingdom's post-war place in the world make him – and public memory of his contribution to public life – important point of reference for the external articulations of English nationalism.

Foreign policy – past, present and future – had the advantage of being a realm wherein a common 'British' identity could be articulated in a less problematic way than at the 'domestic' level. Importantly, the return to Atlanticism that was championed by Margaret Thatcher and consolidated against initial expectations by New Labour in Iraq, laid the foundations for a disengagement from the European Union. This disengagement opened up the possibility of a major foreign policy reorientation legitimised with reference to Churchillian formulations of Britain's place in the world. This articulation of Britain's place in the world was Churchill's 'three circles'. This placed the United Kingdom at the centre of three overlapping yet discrete geo-political areas: the Atlantic, Europe and the Commonwealth. Churchill's preference was for the former and latter, but he felt that all three could be managed and maintained successfully. This was not a conclusion that was endorsed, nor its policy implications pursued, by either New Labour or the Coalition governments. For Oliver Daddow, what he calls New Labour's 'policy failures' were explicable in two ways: 'structurally by the conditions within which its discourses were devised and reported; and agency-wise by the recidivist elements within New Labour's supposedly progressive, enlightened European discourses' (Daddow, 2011: 231). Overtly or implicitly, with their grand strategies guided and structured by a particular reading of the national past, both New Labour and Coalition governments pushed the United Kingdom further away from the ongoing project of European integration.

Thus despite Tony Blair's support for Britain's membership of the European Union during and after the Brexit referendum, this disengagement from the EU began under New Labour, suggesting structural reasons for this reorientation. This outcome appeared unlikely when New Labour came to power in 1997. New Labour appeared to have resolved the Atlanticist–Europeanist tension as part of its 'third way' politics. Tony Blair was the most pro-EU leader since Ted Heath and was at pains to point this out in speeches ahead of the Amsterdam Treaty in 1997 and to the *Assemblée Nationale* in 1998. Famously, Blair outlined what he called the 'Doctrine of the International Community' in Chicago on 24 April 1999. Blair told his audience in Chicago that 'for Britain, the biggest decision we face in the next couple of decades is our relationship with Europe'. Positioning the United Kingdom as a 'bridge' between the United States and the EU, he argued as follows:

> For far too long British ambivalence to Europe has made us irrelevant in Europe, and consequently of less importance to the United States. We have finally done away with the false proposition that we must choose between two diverging paths – the Transatlantic relationship or Europe. For the first time in the last three decades we have a government that is both pro-Europe and pro-American. I firmly believe that it is in Britain's interest, but it is also in the interests of the US and of Europe. (Blair, 1999)

Extolling the 'Third Way in Europe as much as in Britain', Blair felt that 'the tide of Euro-sclerosis has begun to turn' (Blair, 1999).

Neo-imperialism complicated this picture. Critiques of neo-imperialism grew in the 'global' era that at first conceptualised 'empire' in terms of reformulations of global governance, rather than gunboats and free traders (Hardt and Negri, 2000). However, the US-led invasion of Iraq in 2003 (one of the Anglosphere's formative moments) led to another reassertion of British 'greatness' and a distancing from 'post-war' and 'post-national' narratives that were so fundamental to what Donald Rumsfeld called derisively 'old' Europe (cited in Levy, Pensky and Torpey, 2003: xxi). This was part of a broader right-wing critique of the EU and its supposedly 'core' European values. Anglosphere thinkers rejected such ideas and produced their own values, which positioned the UK outside of the collective consciousness, and political myth-scape that legitimised European integration that they characterised as a product of defeat in 1939–45. It also led to the popularisation of a set of concepts used to explain the growing strains within the Western alliance, including that of 'soft power', 'core Europe', Americans being from Mars and Europeans from Venus, and the characterisation of the EU – at the height of David Beckham's celebrity – as a 'metro-sexual superpower'.

Domestically, Englishness was the absent presence in New Labour's 'governing populism'. Any consideration of capturing and developing political Englishness was subsumed within an appeasement of the right – encompassing the Conservatives and the pro-Conservative press – through Eurosceptic rhetoric (Daddow, 2011). English nationalism was portrayed as a post-imperial relic tinged with racism and thus discouraged. New Labour's 'governing populism' did not extend to England but two important substitutions were offered in its place from 1997 to 2010: Robin Cook's 'chicken tikka masala' articulation of a collective yet diverse British identity from 1997 to 2002 and Gordon Brown's version of Britishness after 2005. These versions of British identity owed much to the anti-racist campaigns of the 1970s and 1980s. But Englishness was only weakly articulated in these visions. Despite New Labour's 'pro-European Britishness' (which can be easily overstated), even this substitution for political Englishness was driven by an Anglophone rather than a European consciousness. As Chris Gifford argued, by positioning itself between Europe and America, New Labour was set on 'asserting a vision of an Anglo-Europe, rooted in an Anglo-American approach to globalisation, and with it a revival of British influence and leadership in the EU' (Gifford, 2014: 146).

Yet the positioning of the UK as a bridge between the United States and the EU came under severe strain after the terrorist attacks of 2001 and the controversy over the subsequent invasion of Iraq in 2003. It was this event that pushed the Anglosphere out from the think tank milieu and into a wider public realm, although still on the right of politics. The 'Coalition of the Willing', assembled to invade Iraq in 2003, was a continuation of that informal understanding of the Anglo-American worldview (endorsed and adopted in Australia) that maintained continuity from the twentieth century. The Australian Prime Minister John Howard was the first to use the term 'Anglosphere' explicitly in political discourse (Gullmanielli, 2014), but always at sympathetic events rather than when articulating grand strategy to a wider public.

The idea of Britain as an 'Atlantic Bridge' had also been developed in an anti-European direction after 1997 by Liam Fox, who was the chair of a charitable foundation of the same name, which had been set up to promote pro-Atlanticism in Britain and the United States. It was dissolved in 2011 after controversy over its funding. When in power, the Coalition Government sought to maintain this position as an 'Atlantic Bridge', but came under increasing pressure from the backbench Eurosceptics to go further and promise a referendum on EU membership. This concession was finally wrought from the government in 2013. By this stage, William Hague had already, as Foreign Secretary, reset the UK's foreign policy priorities along a new set of three circles: 'traditional allies', 'emerging economies' and the European Union (significantly the latter being neither of the former).

If the UK was a bridge between Europe and America then the span to France was getting politically longer the more the Coalition Government disengaged from the EU. But this did not mean that governments of the Anglosphere were keen to see Britain out of the EU or that their own relationships were not unproblematic. When senior members of the Obama Administration voiced the consistent US policy in favour of Britain's membership of the European Union, their interventions revealed an ambivalent attitude towards the United States on the right of British politics. Brexiteers already displayed a range of attitudes towards the US president Barack Obama from professed support to hostility born of differing ideological positions. Boris Johnson suggested that the long-standing US position towards UK membership of the EU was hypocritical. 'I just find it absolutely bizarre', he told the BBC, 'that we are being lectured by the Americans about giving up our sovereignty and giving up control when Americans won't even sign up to the international convention on the law of the seas, let alone the International Criminal Court' (cited in BBC News, 2016e), with the latter being an important pillar of US idealist internationalism since before the outbreak of the First World War (Mazower, 2014).

Yet it was the furore over the bust of Winston Churchill in the White House that provided the richest episode for illuminating the place of the British Empire in the Brexiteer imagination and the transfer of ideas across the Anglosphere that animated senior members of the Leave campaigns. In the midst of the 2016 referendum campaign, Boris Johnson responded to Barack Obama's intervention in support of Remain by joining the attack on the US President that the right in the United States had maintained since before Obama's election. Johnson wrote in *The Sun* that 'on day one of the Obama administration [Churchill's bust] was returned, without ceremony, to the British embassy in Washington' suggesting that this action was a symbol of the 'part-Kenyan President's ancestral dislike of the British empire of which Churchill had been such a fervent defender' (cited in Cowburn, 2016).

Tony Blair gave the bust in question to George W. Bush as a symbol of transatlantic fraternity. The symbolism was highly appropriate given that what we might call Churchill's 'part-American ancestry' as well as his politics was a near-perfect embodiment of the Anglo-US relationship. Gordon Brown and Barack Obama did not share the personal chemistry of Blair and Bush. The allegation that Obama had the bust of Churchill removed when he assumed office in 2009 connoted that one of the most significant promoters of the English-speaking peoples had been demoted in American eyes. Further insult was felt when Gordon Brown's official gift of a seven-volume biography of Churchill plus a pen holder made from the timbers of the sister ship of the *Resolute* from which the Oval Office desk was made was reciprocated with a boxed set of 25 DVDs (*Telegraph*, 2011).

Moreover the controversy illustrated the transnational nature of the rehabilitation of empire as a force for good in international relations. Criticism about the bust's removal appeared to suggest that Obama hated the British Empire and by extension contemporary Britain, or at least a post-imperial Britain that was not constrained in its room for manoeuvre by membership of the European Union. This idea was associated with an emerging figure on the 'alt-right' in the United States, Dinesh D'Souza. D'Souza, reported to be 'America's premiere conservative troll' (BBC News, 2016f), made the link in 2012 between Obama's Kenyan roots and the removal of the Churchill bust from the Oval Office with a desire to 'downsize'

America for what he described as the 'sins of colonialism' in a documentary called *2016: Obama's America* (Mungai, 2012).

Across the Atlantic, the memory politics of empire in England rested heavily on the notion that the Empire's negative aspects were mitigated or obscured by the fact that imperialism was apparently worse elsewhere. In this memory, troubling episodes such as the Bengal famines of 1877 and 1943 or mass deaths in concentration camps in South Africa in 1900–02 could be relativised against other atrocities associated with European imperialism. In this way, guilt and responsibility were usually displaced onto the Wilhelmine German Empire in South-West Africa and King Leopold of Belgium's personal colony in the Congo basin (Hochschild, 1999: 282).

Yet in the same year that Civitas re-published *Our Island Story*, Caroline Elkin's research unsettled congratulatory views about the benevolence of British imperialism. *Britain's Gulag: the Brutal End of Empire in Kenya* (Elkins, 2005) made a direct comparison between the British Empire and the Soviet apparatus of terror. Her research revived the moral debates about British policy involved in suppressing the Mau Mau rebellion of 1952–59. This was not new. Parliament debated the 'Hola Camp scandal' throughout the night of 27–28 July 1959, during which a young Conservative MP, Enoch Powell, spoke against the existence and operation of the camps. 'The Kenyan concentration camps', wrote Michael Burleigh, 'bear comparison with the worst, excepting Nazi death camps' (Burleigh, 2013: 385). The whole Kenyan episode, concluded Burleigh, was a moral and political disaster that the British had brought upon themselves, after which there had been an attempted cover-up until official files were released in 2012 (Burleigh, 2013: 388).

Two things can be concluded from the Churchill's bust episode. First of all, that it would not be unreasonable for someone with a Kenyan background to take a different and negative view of British imperialism and one of its foremost proponents like Winston Churchill than those who were legatees of the British Empire's benefits. Secondly, the attempt by Johnson and his supporters to place Obama on the 'wrong side of history' was an attempt to delegitimise his pro-Remain intervention in the Brexit campaign as we shall see Chapter 7. By reviving the issue of Churchill's bust, the Brexiteers were able to make a point about who their 'true friends' really were; however, it was neither the EU nor Barack Obama. One of Donald Trump's first actions as president was to return Churchill's bust to the Oval Office (cited in Milward, 2017).

Greater Britons: re-remembering 'Anglobalisation'

Brexit required and was preceded by a re-evaluation of Empire in public life. It was this that gave it a seemly 'nostalgic' air, but was in fact part of an elite project focused on free trade. At an elite level, Brexiteers were far from being 'Little Englanders', as their detractors had claimed. Brexit's supporters were 'global' rather than parochial. In their view, freedom from the EU's teleology towards ever-closer union would allow Britain to pursue ever-freer trade. In this worldview the Anglosphere stood ready to provide renewed markets with a twist of Chamberlain-ite imperial preference. Not preference in the sense of an imperial federation or customs union, but in the sense of a predilection for the former Dominions (minus South Africa which had dropped from its once pre-eminent place in the English Anglosphere imagination) which, for historical reasons, understood the correct relationship between states and markets. This back-to-the-future reorientation had the additional benefit of allowing Eurosceptics and Brexiteers to strengthen claims to Britishness as they sought to distance themselves from or leave the EU: an outward perspective was safer territory on which to attempt to unite Britons rather than seeking 'domestic' sources of commonality in a United Kingdom in which national divisions were increasingly salient. It also formed a heuristic discursive terrain on which critiques of the present could be articulated and citizens exhorted to be 'greater Britons' than they currently were.

Post-War debates about Britain's Empire were conducted in the shadow of Britain's loss of pre-eminent status to the United States. Dean Acheson's well-remembered remark that Britain 'had lost an empire' is constructed too passively: the UK actively surrendered its status during and after the First World War (Tooze, 2014: 401). After the Second World War, the United States was keen to dismantle the British Empire to its own advantage. This was not an inadvertent 'loss' by policy-makers, but a conscious letting-go in the face of a push from anti-colonial movements and US governments alike.

Until the radical-conservative challenge to the post-Cold War order, Britain's memory of greatness rested on a sense of precedence: if you can no longer claim to be the best, you can at least claim to have been the first. The embedding of policies of globalisation in the late 1990s allowed new ways of thinking about Britain's imperial (now recharacterised as a 'global') past. Niall Ferguson's history of Empire was both a reflection on globalisation and – like Tony Blair's speech in Chicago in 1999 – a call to arms for the United States to 'bear the burden' of empire and its global responsibilities (Ferguson, 2003: 377); something the Project for a New American Century-inspired George W. Bush administration seemed to need little encouragement to do once it came to office in the new millennium.

Such managed decline equated to the 'reduced and isolated' position that Leo Amery dismissed as the basis for participating in the process of European integration back in 1931. The end of Empire pointed disconcertingly in the direction of European integration, a policy turn complicated by de Gaulle's blocking of accession during the 1960s. However Britain's place in the modern (global) world was characterised, it was important for both Eurosceptics and Brexiteers that the Empire be rehabilitated as one of history's 'good things' to allow Britons to imagine themselves distanced from, or completely outside of, the EU. Rehabilitating Empire was less contentious when there appeared to be no international alternative to the current status quo. Simon Schama's characterisation of the nineteenth-century British imperium for his landmark BBC series as the 'empire of good intentions' neatly reconciled the conflict between those who saw the Empire as one of history's forces for good and those who saw it as a shameful episode in world history (Schama, 2003: 195). This dichotomy of view was discernible from the time of high imperialism itself. J. R. Seeley identified two broad yet differing attitudes towards the empire in his 'Expansion of England' lectures in 1881–82. These opposing views are discernible down to this day, but with difference that the 'Little Englanders' were the anti-imperialists, rather than those in support of the Empire. These two views he identified as the 'bombastic' and the 'pessimistic'. The first, he said were 'lost in the wonder and ecstasy of [the Empire's] immense dimensions, and the energy and heroism which have presumably gone into the making of it':

> this school therefore advocates the maintenance of it as a point of honour or senti-
> ment. The other is in the opposite extreme, regards it as founded in aggression and
> rapacity, as useless and burdensome, a kind of excrescence upon England, as depriving
> us of the advantages of insularity and exposing us to wars and quarrels in every part of
> the globe; this school therefore advocates a policy which may lead at the earliest pos-
> sible opportunity to the abandonment of it. (Seeley, 1971 [1883]: 231)

The post-Powellite right inclined towards the bombastic memory of Empire. This view was ultimately endorsed by David Cameron when Prime Minister. Speaking at Amritsar in 2013, Cameron put the official line: 'I think there is an enormous amount to be proud of in what the British empire did and was responsible for. But of course there were bad events as well as good events. The bad events we should learn from and the good events we should celebrate' (cited in Watt, 2013). On the more difficult diplomatic issue of the massacre of 1919 the memory of Churchill was used to offset the memory of the massacre. Like John Howard before him in Australia, Cameron refused to apologise for something he and his contemporaries had not done: 'In my view, we are dealing with something here that happened a good 40 years before I was even born, and which Winston Churchill described as "monstrous" at the time and the British government rightly condemned at the time'. This conclusion led to masterly inactivity: 'So I don't think the right thing is to reach back into history and to seek out things you can apologise for' (cited in Watt, 2013).

Memory of Empire, like that of twentieth-century warfare (which is discussed in Chapter 6), is not neutral and is skewed in the service of wider political projects. Domestically, the Empire came to be seen as a peculiar (and regrettable) preserve of the English (Condor and Abell, 2006: 453). Robert Tombs noted that the English were under-represented in the imperial project compared to other nationalities from the United Kingdom (Tombs, 2014: 782). Yet this was not how the British Empire was remembered at the turn of the twenty-first century. Despite the involvement of Catholic and Protestant Irish men and women in the establishment, development and maintenance of the British Empire and their significant contribution to the British war efforts in both world wars, the Nationalist memory of Ireland's relationship to the Empire is dominant (McCauley, 2014: 131). In Scotland, nationalist memory gained the upper hand after the mid-1990s, where the Empire was remembered along Irish lines as something that the English did to the more peripheral nations of the United Kingdom (Edensor, 2002: 150). Much as asymmetrical devolution created England as a political community by default, this nationalisation of imperial memory left the British Empire to the English without much alteration in the language used to describe it. Britishness was once again a peculiarly English quality.

Thus Charles Dilke's characterisation of the British Empire in 1869 as 'Greater Britain' carried a double meaning in the Brexit era of British politics. The original meaning of the term linked geographically dispersed populations whose common-ality was based upon a shared British origin but whose transnational distinctive-ness was articulated as a peculiar and exemplary 'genius' for government. A century and a half later, the idea of transnational commonality across the English-speaking world was re-energised, but was now expressed in terms of 'values' in international relations. Tony Abbott reflected this narrative back at Britain in 2015, arguing that these commonalties (he described them as 'blessings') were not the accidents of history but 'the product of values painstakingly discerned and refined, and of practices carefully cultivated and reinforced over hundreds of years' (Abbott, 2015). Such values were usually deployed in defence of the neo-liberal status quo that emerged triumphant from the Cold War and became dominant – though not uncontested – in the years afterwards. However, Brexiteers used these value narratives to push for a major reorientation of UK foreign policy outside of the European Union.

The second reinstatement and reinterpretation of the idea of 'Greater Britain' was more evident in domestic political rhetoric that sought to alter the post-Cold War status quo by challenging the UK's membership of the European Union. This narrative was effectively a national heuristic calling on contemporary Britons to be 'greater' than they currently were by aspiring to be what they were in the past. Although in a different register even the minority Labour Leave position drew on articulations of national improvement through revived Commonwealth links, part of a long-standing Labour tradition (Schnapper, 2015: 159–162). 'In the event of a Brexit', argued the pro-Leave Labour MP Kate Hoey:

> we can trade and co-operate with other European countries not involved with the EU, and reach out globally, particularly to the bloc of Commonwealth countries in Asia. We face a great opportunity if we leave. We can stop being Little Europeans and become Internationalists again. (Hoey, 2015).

For Brexiteers, leaving the EU was an important precondition for this restoration of national energy. Its ideational corollary was a rehabilitation of Empire that was both a memory of the national past and political goal to be attained in the future. By imagining a global future, Eurosceptic Anglosphere enthusiasts exhorted the elect-orate to be 'greater Britons' than they currently were.

Thus what eventually emerged after Brexit as a reimagined and rebranded 'global Britain' – sometimes characterised as 'Empire 2.0' (Parris, 2017) – led to an English view of the world into which 'Global Britain' once again sought to insert itself as a fully sovereign political actor in global affairs. This view, in turn, rested the myopic perception that other peoples liked Britain and the British because Britain had colonised their countries in the past. This perception did not always match reality (as we shall see in Chapter 8), but it was a significant idea on the right of British politics in the years leading to the Brexit referendum.

Re-energising the relationship with such countries required restitution for past wrongs. This did not take the form of apologies for slavery or the forced removal of mixed-race indigenous peoples from their families as happened in Anglosphere countries. Instead it meant acknowledging the 'betrayal' of the turn to Europe in the 1960s and 1970s. In the Australian and New Zealand cases this meant atoning for the 'betrayal' of 1973, whilst presenting a return to the centrality of these relationships as a return to a wider world. Writing from Melbourne in 2013, Boris Johnson spoke of the 'historic and strategic decision that this country took in 1973' in which 'we betrayed our relationships with Commonwealth countries such as Australia and New Zealand' (Johnson, 2013). If apologies were required for Australian and New Zealand this this was doubly true for India, truly one of the emerging economies of the twenty-first century. Decolonisation and partition in 1947 left millions of dead on either side of the new border between India and Pakistan. But in the new foreign policy environment established by William Hague from 2010 to 2013, India could be portrayed as both a 'traditional ally' *and* an 'emerging economy'. Ahead of Narendra Modi's visit to UK in November 2015 Jeremy Warner underscored the narrative of an inward European turn in the *Telegraph,* arguing that 'Many British companies shamefully neglected their one-time Commonwealth partners after joining the EU'. With specific reference to India he continued that

> politicians were equally careless with this precious legacy of empire. But this neglect was hardly a pre-condition of EU membership. In large measure, it was home-grown. As for India, the hurried and deeply destructive manner of British disengagement from the subcontinent – the cause to this day of deep resentment and even hostility among many Indians – was perhaps the primary cause of subsequent deterioration in relations. (Warner, 2015)

But it was not just the manner of departure that was resented in India, but also the history of colonisation. Warner was astute enough to recognise that that the manner of decolonisation in the subcontinent was the primary cause in a subsequent deterioration in trade and diplomatic relations, but ultimately this was the wrong sort of memory to accompany the imagining of a post-EU global Britain. Historical tensions could be overcome by a belief in globalisation and the adherence to free-trade policies that would be a rational response to the opportunities unleashed by a UK withdrawal from the EU:

> declining freight rates, mass travel and the connectivity of the digital revolution make interaction with far away places much easier than it used to be. With luck, globalisation might eventually shift the entire world towards free trade practice, rendering the original purpose of Europe's single market obsolete. (Warner, 2015)

Such optimism (the reference to 'luck' was significant) was less realistic when viewed from perspectives of parts of the world where imperialism was not remembered so fondly. The failure of the UK Trade Mission to India in November 2016 was not so surprising when taking an Indian memory of Empire as one's framework. Protectionism was designed to help fledgling industries in newly independent states such as India re-establish markets and industries that had been eliminated by the operation of British imperialism. Furthermore, as Eurosceptics rightly point out, the period of the UK's accession negotiations was one of managed decline. Yet the idea that the Commonwealth and its constituent nations could have been a political and trading community for Britain in the 1960s belied the diplomatic reality of that period. This was something the hyper-globalist wing of the Conservative party chose to forget.

Conclusion

The twenty-first-century rehabilitation of Empire followed the victory of neo-liberalism in the 1990s, exposing public life in Britain to repeats of arguments close to the People's Front of Judea's equivocation over the benefits or otherwise of empire. Yet the Englishness of this debate was masked – as usual – by the British idiom in which it was conducted. As Brexiteers sought a redefined role for the United Kingdom, they sought a past that would inspire them – and by extension the British people in whose name they spoke – to deeds commensurate with their historic forebears, those 'Greater Britons' at the stable centre and dynamic frontiers of what was frequently remembered as the greatest empire that the world has ever seen.

Re-remembering the Empire was an important part of the ideological project that oriented the UK away from, and ultimately out of, the EU. Memories of Empire – like memories of twentieth-century conflict – served as a national heuristic and a reminder of a time when Britons were 'greater' than they were currently. The link between Empire and Brexit was not a straightforward nostalgic reworking of 'Empire 2.0'. Instead, it offered an important narrative that promised to resolve the most important political dilemma of the day by linking England's past, present and future and thereby softening the rupture associated with withdrawal from the European Union. That it did so in a revived language of Britishness only occluded England further in the grand strategies and narratives deployed to refashion Britain's place in the world.

6

Great wars: England and the defence of British sovereignty

Battle of the Somme centenary, 2016

At 7 a.m. on the morning of 1 July 2016 railway stations and public places in England began to fill with silent figures dressed in khaki. Making no attempt to speak with or engage the public directly, the actors in the public art ad-vention *We're Here Because We're Here* marched, stood and waited at the moment when – one hundred years before – Kitchener's volunteers went 'over the top' at the Battle of the Somme. Finally the actors broke into the fatalistic song *We're Here Because We're Here*, before dispersing amongst the commuting crowds.

Commemorative activities are designed to collapse time and permit the participant to empathise with the situation of their forebears. The Somme had been chosen as one of three focal points for the UK Government's commemorative activities as the most iconic of the battles in Britain's First World War: the moment when the volunteer army of the 'Pals Battalions' died in great numbers as the 'Big Push' faltered in the face of German resistance. But as the ad-vention played out on 1 July 2016, the British electorate and especially the political class were grappling with their own once-in-a-century moment. On 23 June – one hundred years to the day after the artillery barrage on the Somme began – the UK electorate had voted by 52–48 per cent to leave the European Union. Not since the Suez Crisis of 1956 had a political defeat implied such a major policy reorientation; not since the pre-First World War crises over the House of Lords, trade unionism, votes for women and looming civil war in Ireland had the political unity of the United Kingdom hung so visibly in the balance.

We're Here Because We're Here followed on from the success of Paul Cummins' and Tom Piper's *Blood Swept Lands and Seas of Red* at the Tower of London, which ran from 4 August to 11 November 2014, itself the product of the symbolic accretion of the layers of the past provided by the permanence of the Tower and the transience of the installation. Other battles had been commemorated – notably Jutland in May 2016 – but these commemorations had been far from the major population centres and the sea battle did not loom as large as the fighting on the Somme in popular memory. Despite the efforts of some historians and politicians, the memory of the Somme as senseless slaughter in the mud stuck.

Traceable to some of the writings of the later war poets and, in particular, a cynicism towards the war from the 1960s associated with *Oh What a Lovely War*, this memory of the Great War was the one that most closely aligned with the founding myth of European integration. But in contrast to the 'European' idea that the two world wars represented a catastrophe followed by renaissance, English memory of the conflict of the first half of the twentieth century was dominated by apogee and eclipse: 1940 and the defeat of Nazism was the apogee of British greatness; membership of the European Union came to be seen as an eclipse of great power status and an institutionalisation of British decline. It was also a memory in which 'Europe' figured as much as an 'other' against which to define England and Britain as a post-war political destination. The fact that it was the English-speaking peoples that had done so much to defend British sovereignty from a Continental threat in 1914–45 was also reinforced by the four years of the First World War centenary. It was a centenary that also obscured England in its wider categories of belonging amongst the English-speaking peoples of the Anglosphere.

Early in 2016 during David Cameron's pre-referendum negotiations at the European Council, the *Daily Mail* headlined its 3 February edition with the line 'Who will speak for England?' Noting that one of the EU's achievements (along with NATO) was the creation of a lasting peace in Europe, the *Daily Mail* continued that 'as in 1939, we are at the crossroads in our island history' because voters would soon be asked 'what sort of country we want to live in and bequeath to those who come after us' (*Daily Mail*, 2016). This rhetorical ghost dating from the outbreak of the Second World War linked Brexit with that existential struggle and – although the article went on the say that 'England' of course meant 'Britain' – highlighted the place of an English historical and national imaginary in the campaign to get the United Kingdom out of the European Union. This was not a new development. In 2006 Oliver Daddow noted that 'themes and images from the nationalist history of the nineteenth century continue to feature prominently in early twenty-first-century discussions about Britain's role in Europe' (Daddow, 2006: 321). Advanced by the *Daily Mail* and the *Sun* these war narratives 'select a limited set of historical facts which they organise for their readers into stories with a singularly recognizable plotline, centering on a nation continually "at war" with mainland Europe' (Daddow, 2006: 319).

This chapter examines the place of war memory in situating England between Europe, the Anglosphere and, in this case, local neighbourhood. The memory of twentieth century conflict is the 'third pillar' on which Anglosphere thinking rests and a major point of intersection between Englishness and Euroscepticism, but one that again occludes England. It positions Anglosphere countries on the side of 'right' in the pivotal conflict of the twentieth century against Nazism, totalitarianism and militarism; a conflict remembered as a straightforward contest between good and evil compared to the more complicated memories of conflicts of the Cold War era and afterwards. In the Anglo-British memory, the Second World War also serves as a point of difference between the EU narrative of 'never again' and an English worldview that represents '1940' as the apogee of Britain's greatness. If in the 'European' narrative the Second World War represents a catastrophe followed by a renaissance, then in the dominant English narrative it represents an apogee followed by a decline: a decline, moreover, institutionalised in the form of the European Union.

Like the memory of Empire, war memory operates as a national heuristic, used by politicians to solicit support for political projects aimed at restoring past greatness. Thus twentieth-century conflict looms large in the legitimacy of European integration and, for different reasons, in the continuing legitimacy of the United Kingdom. Overcoming Franco-German enmity (and by extension wider inter-state conflict throughout Europe) is often presented as the original 'core business' of the European Union (Barroso, 2007). In Britain, the two world wars – especially the Second – posed existential threats to the British state. The victories in 1918 and 1945 appeared to confirm the quality of 'endurance' that distinguished the United Kingdom from its European counterparts and constituted Britain as 'freedom's own island' (Bryant, 1944: 1). The memory of twentieth century conflict plays an important part in legitimising both the European Union and the United Kingdom but in crucially different ways. At times, these memory traditions reinforced each other, but they also pulled apart. The memory of twentieth-century conflict was a major point of commonality between English nationalism and Anglosphere ideology; and indeed helped constitute that memory during inconclusive conflicts in Iraq, Afghanistan and the wider 'War on Terror'. Working back from the present into the past, this chapter shows how the accretion of symbolic meaning of memory of these conflicts provided a teleological trajectory out of the EU and provided a vision of the English future grounded in the English-speaking past.

No longer in retreat: post-war decline and European integration

In addition to the Falkland Conflict and Northern Ireland, the United Kingdom's main 'hot' conflicts during the Cold War included the Suez Crisis of 1956, the Mau Mau rebellion during the 1950s and the Malayan 'Emergency' of 1948–60. Yet two main memories of Cold War conflict compete in contemporary English memory. The first is that of a conflict that did not occur: the 'Third World War' commemorated through the peace narrative of European integration. The second is that of the Falkland Campaign of 1982. Memory of this latter conflict laid important groundwork for creating a distance between Britain and its EEC partners that – when combined with overlapping memories of decline and renaissance in relation to other twentieth century conflicts – created a differing historical trajectory for England as opposed to the European Union.

Memory and politics are closely intertwined. Political projects play out at the intersection of acts of collective and individual commemoration in civil society and the invocation of historical memories by political actors (Winter and Sivan, 1999: 17). These political projects happen at different levels of organisational scale: nation-state, international, regional, local and community (Wellings, Graves and Sumartojo, 2018: 16). But they are political projects nonetheless because the memories of the past that are publically enacted have been chosen over potentially competing narratives that have been thereby excluded from the public domain (Gillis, 1994: 5).

Such contestation was observable between the European and British Eurosceptic memories of the Cold War era. Along with the Falkland Conflict, the year 1982 also marked the twenty-fifth anniversary of the signing of the Treaty of Rome. This anniversary was not much commemorated. The need for intensified commemorative activity was not as urgent; nor was the competence and capacity of the EEC in 1982 as great as it would later become. By 2007 in contrast, the leaders of the now European Union felt it necessary to make a far greater commemorative effort for the fiftieth anniversary of what was now understood as the EU's foundational moment (although it shared that commemorative place with the Schuman Declaration of 9 May 1950). Driven by the apparent need to reconnect with EU citizens in the wake of what was seen at the time as the unprecedented crisis caused by the French and Dutch rejections of the Draft Constitutional Treaty in 2005, as president of the European Council, the German Government issued the 'Berlin Declaration'. This Declaration placed a particular interpretation of war memory at the heart of the legitimacy of the European project. Speaking on behalf of the EU and its citizens in March 2007, Angela Merkel declared that

> For centuries Europe has been an idea holding out hope of peace and understanding. That hope has been fulfilled. European unification has made peace and prosperity possible. It has brought about a sense of community and overcome differences. Each Member State has helped to unite Europe and to strengthen democracy and the rule of law. Thanks to the yearning for freedom of the peoples of central and eastern Europe the unnatural division of Europe is now consigned to the past. European integration shows that we have learnt the painful lessons of a history marked by bloody conflict. (European Union, 2007)

There was nothing much new in this narrative, but it was consciously re-emphasised after the political shocks of 2005 and was connected to a particular teleology.

Noting in 2001 that the enlargement of the European Union was now 'irreversible' the European Council declared at its Laeken summit that

> For centuries, peoples and states have taken up arms and waged war to win control of the European continent. The debilitating effects of two bloody wars and the weakening of Europe's position in the world brought a growing realisation that only peace and concerted action could make the dream of a strong, unified Europe come true. (European Council, 2001)

The Laeken Declaration picked up on a major legitimising theme in the narrative of European integration that had been outlined in the Declaration that began them all: Robert Schuman's in 1950. But it also planted the seeds of future British objections to the *finalité* of European integration. With Jean Monnet at his side, Schuman argued that the creation of a unified Coal and Steel Community between France, West Germany and any other west European country that wished to join would result in 'the realisation of the first concrete foundation of a European federation indispensable to the preservation of peace' (European Union, 2016).

The goal of 'peace through Europe' was never a given political outcome and had to be fought for politically during the war years and after. Writing in secret from the prison island of Ventotene off the coast of Naples from 1941 to 1943, Alteiro Spinelli and Ernesto Rossi argued that by the mid-twentieth century the nation was no longer viewed simply as 'the historical product of co-existence between men who, as a result of a lengthy historical process, have acquired greater unity in their customs and aspirations and who see their State as being the most effective means of organizing collective life within the context of all human society'. Instead it had become 'a divine entity, an organism which must only consider its own existence, its own development, without the least regard for the damage that others may suffer from this' (cited in Eilstrup-Sangiovani, 2006: 37). Such analysis put nationalism and state sovereignty in the place of chief adversary for European federalists such as Spinelli. Similarly, Walter Hallstein, the first President of the European Commission, cited the chief adversary as the 'national selfishness which divides peoples and which still has allies in all of our countries'. He continued as follows:

> We are realistic enough to know that our project has not destroyed that adversary. But if, in the future, this accomplishment takes on life in the acts of men who are animated by a really European spirit, we shall have mortally wounded the adversary. What we seek is a unified Europe in which all free peoples will be able to live and work in a peaceful community. It must never again be possible for war to separate us. (HAEU, 1951)

This, then, was the ideational backbone of the EU's initial claim to 'input' legitimacy whereby an institutional identity based upon European integration as a peace project operated in lieu of other elements of input legitimacy, notably the ability to change a government or leader directly through elections (Hix, 2010). Although this argument had a long pre-war history even before the creation of the European Coal and Steel Community in 1951, it was increasingly deployed after the Draft Constitutional Crisis of 2005 and linked with the commemorative moment of 2007. The greatest international endorsement for this narrative of European integration came at the end of 2012 when the Nobel Prize Committee awarded the Prize for Peace to the EU. Noting that the EU was 'undergoing grave economic difficulties and considerable social unrest' the Norwegian Nobel Committee chose to focus on what it saw as the EU's most important legacy: 'the successful struggle for peace and reconciliation and for democracy and human rights' that had helped to 'transform most of Europe from a continent of war to a continent of peace' (Norwegian Nobel Committee, 2012).

This theme was re-emphasised five years later when the European Union was both commemorating the sixtieth anniversary of the Rome treaties and seeking to shore up its legitimacy under the challenge of the shock of Brexit and other populist-inspired critiques. 'European unity started as the dream of a few, it became the hope of the many' declared the European Union. 'Then Europe became one again. Sixty years ago, recovering from the tragedy of two world wars, we decided to bond together and rebuild our continent from its ashes' (European Union, 2017). The institutions of the European Union and twenty-seven member states countersigned this Rome Declaration. It did not include the United Kingdom, whose historical trajectory now lay officially outside the European narrative.

Here then is an outline of what Ian Manners and Philomena Murray have called the 'noble Nobel narrative' of the European Union (Manners and Murray, 2016) and what has also been called the real 'Euro-myth' (Wellings and Power, 2016: 157). An important part of this narrative is that the two world wars – and the Second in particular – represent a historical nadir of a pre-existing community divided by nationalism and war. 'In historical retrospect', argued the German historian Peter Stadler, 'the two world wars have grown into a new unit, a kind of second Thirty Years' War' (Stadler, 1999: 101). Post-War integration re-unified this broken European community. The trajectory of such a narrative may seem uplifting, yet as a guide for future-oriented political action it falls short. This legitimising narrative suggests that no matter how bad one thinks Europe is today, one should remember how truly bad it was before. Historically this is undeniable, but politically it closes down the debate. The political intent of the narrative is what Bo Stråth and Hagen Schulz-Forberg have called an 'utmost truth claim' (Schulz-Forberg and Stråth, 2010: 16). That is to say that it is designed to silence the 'national selfishness' of competing conceptualisations of Europe's past and future and the place of nations and states within the European Union.

This element of the 'Nobel narrative' did not sit well in the English national imaginary where the Second World War represented the 'finest hour' and what came *after* was 'decline'. Memory of the Falkland Islands conflict provided a counterpoint to this politics of decline. On 14 June 1982, the Union Flag was raised once again over Port Stanley in the Falkland Islands. Although there were elements of Wolfe's decisive tactical move at Quebec in the yomp from Goose Green to Stanley, compared to the sweep of British military history – victory in 1945 and 1918; the defeat of Napoleon; the repulsion of Philip II's Armada – this was not an escape from an existential crisis. Yet it was very quickly presented this way. From this per-spective the decisive political moment of the Falkland campaign came not in the military operations from April to June, but in the speech given at the Conservative rally in Cheltenham on 3 July 1982.

Seeking out those in the national community who may have believed 'that our decline was irreversible' and that 'we could never again be what we were', Margaret Thatcher situated the Falkland victory in the shadow of the Second World War and the sense of decline that followed it:

> There were those who would not admit it – even perhaps some here today – people who would have strenuously denied the suggestion but – in their heart of hearts – they too had their secret fears that it was true: that Britain was no longer the nation that had built an Empire and ruled a quarter of the world. Well they were wrong. The lesson of the Falklands is that Britain has not changed and that this nation still has those sterling qualities which shine through our history. This generation can match their fathers and grandfathers in ability, in courage, and in resolution. We have not changed. (Thatcher, 1982)

Most importantly, a conclusion seemingly confirmed by the election landslide of 1983 (although academic and practitioner debate exists about this), Thatcher set the seal on the dominant memory of the Falkland Campaign by stating that Britain had 'ceased to be a nation in retreat' (Thatcher, 1982).

This was a nationalist auto-critique of the present that conjured up an image of a better past in order to inspire believers to work towards a better future. In 1982, this narrative that invoked an image of British decline in order to overcome it was not yet primarily directed at the European Communities in the way that it was in the twenty-first century. Thatcher noted the diplomatic support from the EEC member states in the Cheltenham speech. However this view was also met with some scepticism. 'The half-hearted support we got from [EEC countries] in the Falklands conflict was an insult' noted one respondent to a Mass-Observation survey on attitudes towards EEC membership conducted in 1982, 'especially when compared with our old, true friends in Australia and New Zealand' (M-OA, 1982: EEC Membership, Respondent 110).

The Thatcherite memory of the Falkland Conflict was not just about reversing decline domestically, but also about restoring the 'Special Relationship' with the United States to its (from the Anglosphere perspective) 'ideal' place in the United Kingdom's foreign relations hierarchy. But the Anglosphere came with its own hier-archies. The sixtieth anniversary of the Suez Crisis was not much remarked on in the United Kingdom given its origins, outcome and competition with First World War

Centenary events and the political preoccupation with Brexit. Yet it found echoes in the chair of the European Research Group, Jacob Rees-Mogg's fears that any plans for a 'soft Brexit' would lead to the United Kingdom becoming a 'vassal state' of the EU (cited in BBC News Politics, 2017). During the Suez Crisis, just such concerns about 'vassal' status had been expressed by the Cabinet but in relation to the United States rather than Europe (National Archives, 1956). Whereas in the late 1950s, European integration seemed like a way out of subordination to the United States, in 2016 the situation was reversed in the minds of Brexiteers.

Most importantly, European integration generated a memory of war in England that was different to that developed in Cold War Western (and certainly Eastern) Europe. At the ideational level, pro-Europeanists argued that European integration was a historic way to transcend the history of war between countries that were now member states of the European Communities. Pro-Europeanists in the United Kingdom used this argument too. However, resistance to European integration tended to generate opposite memories of intra-European conflict in the United Kingdom. Although the 1975 referendum returned a 67–33 vote in favour of continued membership, an entangled memory of war and resistance to European integration remained. 'I am of the opinion that the Treaty of Rome was devised to find a market for German engineering and the inadequate agricultural skills of the French', wrote one respondent to the Mass-Observation survey on ten years of EEC membership in 1982. But this specific conclusion analysis rested on historical memory:

> My dislike of the French goes back to the 1914–1918 War when the British soldier was fighting in France to liberate that country from the Germans and the French civilians were out to relieve our soldiers of every *sou* they had, this I have heard from the lips of my Father and thus I am very much biased against that country. (M-OA, 1982: EEC Membership Respondent 116)

Thatcher's Falkland narrative was aimed at regaining the wartime spirit of national unity (itself a memory rather than complete historical truth) in the service of reorienting the political economy from Keysianism to neo-liberalism. Yet in contrast to the populist *zeitgeist* of the Brexit era, the enemy was not the EU or the 'elites'. In the 1970s and 1980s the decline narrative had to be deployed to save Britain from itself. But by the 2010s it was the EU that was portrayed as being in decline and Britain that required independence to realise its full potential; or as Daniel Hannan put it, the EU was 'sinking, dragging us with it like so many chained galley-slaves' (Hannan, 2011).

Finest hour: the Second World War and England's apogee

The Second World War is the conflict with the largest imprint on English memory as well as a crucial moment in Anglosphere cooperation in which the United

States – unlike the First World War – was engaged for most of the conflict and the fragile peace thereafter. Yet, for English national narratives concerned with 'greatness' the Second World War is potentially difficult territory. On the one hand '1940' is remembered as Britain (and England's) 'finest hour'. Yet on the other, the war confirmed Britain's decline from great power status, not least in relation to the United States – a decline, moreover, that led to the United Kingdom's accession to the European Communities. Hence the emphasis in Conservative national mythology is always on '1940' (Dunkirk and the Battle of Britain) rather than the aftermath of the war, which is emphasised in Labour mythology about the welfare state.

The memory of the Second World War developed two main strands in the Cold War era and after. The first was as a defence against totalitarianism led by the English-speaking peoples. The second was the moment of national apogee in need of frequent emulation to restore greatness defined through the exercise of sovereignty: in short, a national heuristic. Yet the Second World War contained ambivalence in terms of Britain's status. 'At the end of the war', noted Michael Burleigh, 'Britain was both triumphant and prostrate' (Burleigh, 2013: 121). In this regard, a triumphal narrative that adhered to the Second World War had its own redemptive purpose: Britain's decline, lamentable in national terms, had been for a higher noble cause.

This noble cause did not put England on the path towards European integration and in fact allowed for a delegitimisation of the cause of European unity. Given this predilection to view the Second World War as a crusade for an English-speaking version of liberty, it was inevitable that memory of Adolf Hitler would play some part in discussions as the debate about Britain's place in the European Union intensified in the spring of 2016. The *Fuhrer's* first appearance came during the elections for the Mayor of London, when Ken Livingston was suspended from the Labour Party suggesting (erroneously) that Hitler was a Zionist (Wright, 2016). An anti-fascist memory was evident after the Brexit referendum in 2016. When convicting Jo Cox's murderer, Thomas Mair, Justice Wilkie claimed that Mair's inspiration was not love of country but admiration for Nazism. Wilkie argued that Mair's actions amounted to a betrayal of the efforts of a previous generation of Britons. 'Our parents' generation made huge sacrifices to defeat those [Nazi] ideas and values in the Second World War. What you did, and your admiration for those views which informed your crime, betrays the sacrifices of that generation' (cited in BBC News, 2016j).

The Nazi leader's highest profile in the 2016 referendum came, however, when Boris Johnson, drawing on a Realist interpretation of international order in Europe, claimed that the European Union should be seen as yet another attempt to establish a hegemony over the European continent; ergo the EU shared some commonality with the empires of Napoleon and Hitler. 'The truth is', Johnson argued,

> that the history of the last couple of thousand years has been broadly repeated attempts by various people or institutions – in a Freudian way – to rediscover the lost

childhood of Europe, this golden age of peace and prosperity under the Romans, by trying to unify it. Napoleon, Hitler, various people tried this out, and it ends tragically. The EU is an attempt to do this by different methods. But fundamentally what it is lacking is the eternal problem, which is that there is no underlying loyalty to the idea of Europe. There is no single authority that anybody respects or understands. That is causing this massive democratic void. (Cited in Ross, 2016)

In this historical perspective Brexit became for Johnson 'a chance for the British people to be the heroes of Europe and to act as a voice of moderation and common sense, and to stop something getting … out of control' (cited in Ross, 2016).

Conflating the EU with the Napoleonic Empire and the Third Reich is not unusual amongst Eurosceptics. Just as Cameron's speech at the British Museum on Europe Day 2016 drew selectively on the idealist interpretation of EU's post-war origins as a peace project, Johnson's comments were rooted in British foreign policy traditions dating back to the eighteenth century. In this tradition of *realpolitik* Britain's role in Europe was to restore and maintain the balance of power. This understanding of order is what took Britain to war against Louis XIV, Napoleon, Kaiser Wilhelm II and – although we remember it today as a crusade against Nazism – Hitler's Germany. Musing on the counterfactuals of Churchill's first weeks in office in the crisis days of 1940, Johnson argued that 'If Britain had done a deal in 1940 … then there would have been no liberation of the continent. This country would not have been a haven of resistance, but a gloomy client state of an infernal Nazi EU' (Johnson, 2014: 30).

On one level this deployment of the memory of Hitler could be seen as a tactical move by a figure widely distrusted for his self-serving support for Leave. The reference to the past – and especially wars with Britain's Continental neighbours – could be read as an attempt by the Brexiteers to push the debate on to emotive territory where they felt stronger than those arguing for 'Bremain' with their emphasis on the 'rational' economic woes that would befall the UK outside of the EU. Yet this Eurosceptic worldview ran deep. For Brexiteers, it was impossible to understand Britain's democracy without understanding its English origins from the time of Magna Carta, as we have seen in Chapter 4. It was also impossible to understand British democracy without the flattery of its global emulation and imposition in the nineteenth and twentieth centuries, as we have seen in Chapter 5. Most importantly, it was impossible for Brexiteers not to reflect on how close that form of democracy came to extinction in 1940 when fighting against present-day EU members and their quisling allies.

Thus '1940' represents the defence of British sovereignty *par excellence*. Only the Spanish Armada in 1588 comes close in the national mythology, although we should note that this memory is explicitly English since Scotland was part of the English state's strategic problem in the late sixteenth century. Even the Battle of Trafalgar became something for the press to tease the French with at the announcement of the awarding of the Olympic Games in 2005 (cited in Sumartojo, 2013: 154–155).

Arguing for Brexit in 2016, Defence Secretary Penny Maudant lamented the fact that 'We live in an age of forgetfulness' (forgetting herself the £50 million David Cameron pledged to the First World War Centenary). 'But we ought never to forget what our forefathers taught us: that democracy doesn't just happen' she continued. 'This EU referendum is not about the narrow issues of the recent deal. It's about something much greater' (Mordaunt, 2016):

> In our long island history there have been many times when Britain has not been well-served by alignment with Europe. Rather it has been our country's vision, inspiration and courage that have acted as the catalyst to betterment on the continent. We should be proud of our part in liberating Europe, of guaranteeing its borders and of our involvement in those seismic changes which have extended freedom to all its peoples. (Mordaunt, 2016)

In addition to this goal of liberating Europe once again, Mordaunt was emboldened by unnamed friends abroad. 'When Britain stood alone in 1940 after the defeat at Dunkirk, we were cut off and ridiculed. True leadership sometimes does feel isolating. Yet we have never suffered for it. We are resourceful; we are well connected; our brand is strong in the world' (Mordaunt, 2016).

But it is in '1940' that the conflation between England and its 'wider categories of belonging' are most starkly evident. The framing of this episode in English and British history is entirely British (Hitler's use of the term 'England' notwithstanding). But surprisingly at this moment, Empire is both almost entirely forgotten and assumed to be the same as Britain. Britain only 'stood alone' in 1940 if we omit support from India, Canada, Australia, New Zealand, South Africa and other parts of the Empire, the Lend Lease arrangements with the United States, and the Free French, Poles and Czechs. Again, England gets lost in this British picture with the exception of the small ships of Dunkirk, memory of which built on an inter-war theme of English diminutiveness (Mandler, 2006: 163).

The successful defence of the United Kingdom against Nazi invasion in 1940 was an event of huge importance in world history. Yet it was not a decisive victory in itself; it was not even the 'end of the beginning'. The second aspect of the memory of the Second World War in Anglosphere thinking is of the English-speaking peoples as an agent of liberation from tyranny and militarism in Europe and Asia, first in 1944–45 and eventually at the end of the Cold War in 1989–91. In English-speaking memory, D-Day is remembered as an Anglo-US-Canadian endeavour that began the Liberation of Western Europe. Such a memory was pointedly deployed during the first years of the Iraq invasion when President George W. Bush visited a US cemetery in Normandy during the anniversary of D-Day to underscore US displeasure at the resistance to this policy in 2002–03.

The Iraq War – especially its outbreak – represented a major moment of tension between the Anglosphere and European worldviews. As Daniel Mandel noted when reflecting on New Labour's commemorations for the bicentenary of the Battle of Trafalgar, the Franco-Spanish defeat was 'assiduously played down in deference to the sensitivities of these sturdy allies whose troops are to be found nowhere at Britain's side in Iraq' (Mandel, 2005: 32). Yet for all the Anglo-US cooperation in Iraq, Afghanistan and during the Cold War, there were tensions in the relationship in the twenty-first century even before the Trump presidency. The memory of Anglo-American cooperation needed to actively marginalise a difficult episode in 'Anglosphere' relations: the conflicts of 1775 to 1815. This historical episode could still cause diplomatic tensions. In August 2014, the UK Embassy in Washington was forced to apologise after it tweeted a photo of a cake of the White House surrounded by sparklers at a 200th anniversary of the burning of the White House during the War of 1812. The 'joke' was criticised for poor taste in the English press and in the Twittersphere. This was because, as Carl Cavanagh Hodge argued, the Anglospheric interpretation of the War of 1812 became a tool for 'measuring the meaning of the connections between Americans and "kindred peoples" in the wake of the trauma of 11 September 2001' (Cavanagh Hodge, 2014: 307). Despite this the *Mail Online* could not help noting that 1814 was 'the only time in history that the US capital has been invaded' (McTague, 2014).

Despite these tensions within the Anglosphere, memory of the Second World War and Britain's status as a non-defeated power is foundational to Eurosceptic and Anglosphere thought. John Redwood expressed the centrality of this memory of the Second World War to Brexiteer thought:

> Britain is at peace with its past in a way that many continental countries could never be … We do not have to live down the shame that many French people feel regarding the events of 1940–44. We do not have to live … with the collective guilt that Germany feels about the Holocaust. (Redwood, 2005: 12)

Liam Fox went further during the referendum campaign itself. Writing in *Conservative Woman*, Fox argued that the EU was on 'a downward spiral'. Anticipating Johnson's arguments about EU hegemony in Europe, Fox felt that Britain had a chance not only to save itself, but to save Europe too, framing the referendum as another element in the history of conflict in Europe since 1914: 'there is a real chance that a simple cross on a ballot paper here could precipitate change across an entire continent. The people of this country have the chance to liberate Europe for the third time in a century' (Fox, 2016). The political use of forms of remembrance in England reinforced the notion that the Second World War represented Britain's global apogee. But this apogee was followed by eclipse. Greatness and decline are bound up in the English memory of the Second World War. For Brexiteers, the EU was the institutional expression of Britain's diminished status. Margaret Thatcher may have reversed this national decline in the 1980s, but by then it was too late: Britain was locked into the EU that risked dragging a newly resurgent Britain under. Since accession in

1973, English memory of the war has remained locked in the political constraints determined by Britain's new place in Europe and the world. In this view, Britain won the war but lost the peace. Only leaving the EU could represent a belated escape to victory.

'Dulce et decorum est': England between Commonwealth and neighbourhood

When not campaigning to get the UK out of the EU, Nigel Farage enjoyed fishing, cricket, *Dad's Army*, red wine and participating in First World War battlefield tours (BBC News Politics, 2016a). If it had not been obvious before, this profile would surely have alerted Facebook and Cambridge Analytica that Farage was likely to be a Brexit supporter. Despite Farage's support, collective remembrance of the First World War is also the carrier of an English war memory that aligns most closely with the Euro-myth narrative. (Similarly, French memory of the First World War is more like the English memory of the Second World War – a necessary victory without the complications of defeat or collaboration.) Yet this memory of the Great War does not have the post-1945 redemptive qualities of an anti-totalitarian crusade and remained – despite the efforts of some involved in its Centenary planning and execution – to be strongly associated in the dominant English memory with pointless slaughter. Paul Cummins' and Tom Piper's *Blood Swept Lands and Seas of Red*, consisting of 888,246 ceramic poppies installed at the Tower of London in 2014 and the 2016 ad-vention 'We're here because we're here', commemorating the first infantry attack of the Battle of the Somme that took place just days after the Brexit vote, spoke to local memory and community loss without a grand redemptive narrative. As well as focusing English commemoration around locality and neighbourhood, the Centenary displayed an overall effort to weaken the analogous 'never again' and 'war to end all wars' narratives that might have tied English memory of the Great War to European integration. At a moment of foreign policy reorientation, the political direction behind the Centenary sought to re-establish links with 'traditional allies' in the Commonwealth. By linking memory of the First World War with the Commonwealth, Centenary strategists aligned official memory in the UK with the Commonwealth and occluded England between state-sponsored British history and local community-oriented narratives.

The First World War Centenary that took place between 2014 and 2018 was an especially fruitful moment for analysis because it coincided with a major shift in UK foreign policy and the greatest set of crises ever faced by the European Union. Given that the Centenary was 'state sponsored history' (Wouters and Bevernage, 2018), there was significant international and European cooperation, such as that between the UK, Belgian and Flanders governments concerning the football matches commemorating the Christmas Truce in 2014. There was also a concerted effort to re-remember the 'global' dimensions of the conflict (Strachan, 2010: 3). But 'England' got lost in the official Centenary activities, squeezed between UK-wide and local remembrance. The emphasis on regional and local commemorations was designed to reflect patterns of local recruitment and loss during the Great War. But England's occlusion was also due to devolved structures of authority. Devolved governments such as Scotland and Northern Ireland organised their own commemorative activities in line with community expectations and governing party preferences. England could not do this and the 'national' level remained the purview of the UK Government. Therefore, like the 'ecstatic nationalism' (Skey, 2011: 95) of the 2012 Olympics and its Opening Ceremony, the First World War Centenary continued the official conflation of Britain and England.

This 'official nationalism' revived Britain and England's links with Commonwealth countries. The United Kingdom's First World War Commemorative activities were framed as Commonwealth as well as European projects from the outset. The parliamentary organising committee noted the pluri-national and inter-national dimensions of the commemorations which it said should be cast as 'national events to capture the moment and set the tone. They will have an identi-fiably Commonwealth look and feel, reflecting the historical reality. We have been working with our international partners and with the devolved Administrations to that end' (Hansard, 2013b, 7 November, vol. 570, col. 484). To avoid 'commem-orative fatigue', the UK's commemorative high points were restricted to commem-orating the outbreak of war in 2014, the Battle of Jutland (allowing the Navy some commemorative activity), the 'first day' of the Somme in 2016, and the armistice in 2018. There was official UK participation in other events such as at Gallipoli in 2015 and Vimy Ridge in 2017, but the main organisation of these was left to 'more appropriate' countries, such as Australia, New Zealand and Canada (including Newfoundland).

Nevertheless, contestation about collective remembrance of the English past linked political projects such as Euroscepticism with wider narratives of belonging. However, linking remembrance and a political project was not necessarily straight-forward territory. On Remembrance Sunday 2015, Leave.EU tweeted 'Freedom and democracy. Let's not give up values for which our ancestors paid the ultimate sacrifice. #LeaveEU' (cited in Chorley, 2015). This tweet linking war dead to pre-serving British freedom and liberties from the EU was widely criticised. Yet Brexit seemed to embolden supporters of this view of England and Britain's past. The *Daily Express*' 'crusade' to get Britain out of the EU focused on this intersection between remembrance, belonging and tradition even after the Brexit vote itself. Claiming that the EU was attempting to ban (aspects of) Remembrance Sunday on occupational health and safety grounds, the *Express* contrasted an interpretation of the motives for fighting in the Great War with a contemporary critique of the democratic deficit of the EU noting that 'critics have hit out at the prohibitive law, claiming that soldiers in the First World War fought for the freedom of people across Europe and that the new law flies in the face of their sacrifice' (Efstathiou, 2016); an interpretation of motives that would have been rejected in nationalist Ireland and by the nascent anti-colonial movements within the Empire.

As Christine Cadot has argued, the First World War often came a poor second to its successor as part of the legitimising European narrative (Cadot, 2014: 260). Yet if the 'Euro-myth' was certainly focused on the Second World War, academic attention to the First World War was not unrelated to the process of European integration either. This was not quite in the same way as the Second World War that produced a committed and partisan support amongst academics, but the link was nevertheless there. Jay Winter noted that

> Due to the emergence of trans-national networks in many fields in Europe in the 1970s and 1980s, reinforcing economic and political trends expressed in the Maastricht Treaty of 1992 ... historians' attention turned to the massive shock of European *dis*integration in 1914. (2008: 34)

The First World War centenary occurred not only when the future of the United Kingdom was under threat of profound change via the Scottish referendum on independence in 2014, but also when the process of European integration went into reverse for the first time with the Brexit referendum of 2016 (simultaneously threatening British disintegration given Scotland's strong vote to remain). First World War commemorative activity and associated public history events focusing on the European disintegration of 1914–18 found themselves playing out against a fissiparous political background of threats to British unity and the prospect of European disintegration on its western borders.

The centenary of the First World War came at what initially seemed to be an opportune political moment. With Centenary preparations launched in earnest in October 2012 (later than most European counterparts given the Department of Culture, Media and Sport's understandable absorption with staging the London Olympics earlier that year), the First World War Centenary allowed the Conservative-led Coalition Government to stress British war narratives in the face of Scottish secessionism, as well as emphasise historic (security) links with Anglosphere countries as demands for a referendum on Britain's EU membership grew ahead of the Conservative conference in October 2012.

Before the government was able to use the Centenary as a means of cohering British unity, it had to confront internal ideological divisions over the memory and legacy of the War within England itself. First of all, the government had to move away from a negative memory of the conflict as one of futility; a collective memory that Michael Gove dismissed as the 'Blackadder' view of the First World War, when he was Secretary of State for Education (Jeffries, 2014). This was part of a wider attempt to reform the history curriculum in England that had been outlined when the Conservatives were in opposition and focused around the re-publication of *Our Island Story* as noted in Chapter 4. It was part of an even wider attempt by the right across the Anglosphere to win the 'History' or 'Culture Wars' – an area of only moderate success for the Right despite their victory in the 'Battle of Ideas' over the economy in the 1980s. Relationships between Gove and teachers were not cordial. In such an oppositional relationship the chances of an enlightened and truly sceptical discussion in which different sides of the debate might alter their opinion based on evidence were slim.

The notion of the First World War as a futile conflict conducted by unimaginative and incompetent senior officers was difficult to dislodge not only because of fraught relationships between the Minister and teachers. This view of the Great War was bound up with the work of the later war poets and the inter-war pacifist and disarmament movements. Although it is possible to overstate enthusiasm for war in 1914 and antipathy to in in 1918, there is a discernible shift from the romantic melancholy of Rupert Brooke and John McCrea, to the sardonic pathos of Wilfred Owen. There was an even more marked shift in Rudyard Kipling's movement from the imperial bombast of 1914 to the bitter grief of 'Common Form': 'If any question why we died, / Tell them, because our fathers lied'. Kipling's *Recessional* and his work with the Imperial War Graves Commission did much to shape the language of mourning in post-First World War England, Britain and the Dominions. The poem that most anticipated the 'Blackadder' view of the First World War was Siegfried Sassoon's 'The General' published in 1917 at the height of British agitation for peace given the increasing losses and events in Russia:

> He's a cheery old card, grunted 'Arry to Jack,
> As they slogged up to Arras with rifle and pack.
> But he did for them both with his plan of attack. (Cited in Richards 2014)

Such views were strong within the disarmament and peace movements of 1920s and 1930s and became part of the youth view of the war in the 1960s thanks to the popularity of Richard Attenborough's *Oh What a Lovely War!* (1959/61). These views found satirical expression in the 1980s culminating in Richard Curtis's and Ben Elton's *Blackadder Goes Forth,* first aired on television in 1989 after a decade of 'leftie' satire.

The debate about history was conducted in England for structural administrative reasons. The national curriculum in question pertained in England and to a lesser extent Wales, Holyrood having jurisdiction over education in Scotland. Despite this English structure, commemorative activity was British and local. The attempt to recast the memory of the First World War was predominantly an English debate generated by the Conservatives' antipathy towards a negative narrative of the War. The debates and commemorations were used instead to cohere the United Kingdom at a moment of threat to its unity in 2011–18 and were presented as part of a wider, *British* narrative at a moment when this identity appeared to be weakening given strains created by secessionist movements and Brexit itself. The UK Government needed to use the Centenary as a means to cohere a sense of Britishness under threat from Scottish separatism. It was in the context of the Scottish referendum on independence set for 2014 that David Cameron called for the Centenary to be a 'truly national commemoration' (Cameron, 2012). Without specifying which nation was to be truly represented, it was assumed in the speech that the nation was Britain.

Britain was not the only wider category of belonging operating in the Centenary commemorations. 'Commonwealth' had a double meaning during the Centenary and the lead up to it. First of all, it was used as a way to incorporate 'multiculturalism' into the Centenary so as to include the descendants of immigrants from 'undivided India' into commemorations in which it was claimed everyone was somehow connected via family history. Memory of the First World War was therefore important for the ongoing project of British integration (British Futures, 2014: 23). Secondly, it was also used to re-emphasise links with the settler Dominions that had fought with Britain against countries whose successor states were now part of the EU. The post-accession preferable treatment to erstwhile enemies on arrival at Heathrow irked Commonwealth citizens at an individual level, a sentiment picked up by Conservative MP Julian Brazier. In 2000 Brazier introduced a bill in the House of Commons calling for a third entry channel at UK ports for nationals of states recognising the Queen as head of state, arguing 'When the chips are down, again and again, we have found that shared ties of blood, values and heritage count for more' (Hansard, 2000, 18 January, vol. 342, col. 689).

Commemorative activity around the Commonwealth in terms of what Matthew Graves has called 'memorial diplomacy' (Graves, 2014: 169) was offset by the strong local emphases in acts of remembrance. It was possible for England to get lost in this mix of international, national and local remembrance. This meant that the national framing for official commemorations in England defaulted to a British register, whereas in Scotland from 2011 the SNP Government articulated an alternative national mode of remembrance.

Unlike Ireland, Scottish secessionists could not use the First World War as a means of generating a separatist myth, but they could place a different emphasis on Scottish participation. Unlike the British commemorative calendar that emphasised the outbreak of war, the Battles of Jutland and the Somme and the Armistice, the Scottish calendar focused on the train crash at Quintinshill, the battles of Gallipoli, Loos, Jutland, Arras, the Armistice and the sinking of *HMY Iolaire* off Lewis (Scottish Government, 2014). The choice of Loos (where Rudyard Kipling lost his son Jack) for the major Scottish commemorative activity in 2015 laid down a subtle nationalist challenge to the official British narrative focused on the first day of the Somme, suggesting that Scots had a different set of memories by which to remember loss of life.

The SNP Government made its own claims on the Anglosphere in the ceremony marking the start of the War that followed closely on from the 2014 Commonwealth Games in Glasgow. 'As the curtain falls on 2014 Commonwealth Games', said First

Minster Alex Salmond, 'we acknowledge the countries of the Commonwealth we fought alongside during the Great War … From now until the start of 2019, we want people of all ages from all corners of Scotland, and those with Scottish connections around the world, to ask themselves and each other what can be learned from the Great War' (cited in Scottish Government, 2014).

In Alex Salmond's account, neither Britain nor the United Kingdom was mentioned. In Cameron's speeches on this subject, it was England that was absent. The comparison between Scotland and England during the Centenary of the First World War served to highlight an important point about imagining England as a historical and political community. The difference was between the form and content of such a community. Constitutional change in the United Kingdom had allowed England to come into relief. However, the content of England's imaginaries remained officially 'British', or local and regional. The election of an SNP Government in 2011 and the referendum of 2014 highlighted what devolution created in 1999: that England was a de facto political community without its own means of political representation. English Votes for English Laws was supposed to address this issue within the Westminster framework. But the ideational level followed the structural one. England was obscured between Britain, the United Kingdom and local and regional narratives.

Conclusion

The memory of twentieth century conflict is the 'third pillar' on which Anglosphere thinking rests and a major point of intersection between Englishness and Euroscepticism. It is also a point of difference between the EU's 'never again' narrative and an English worldview. In contrast to the EU's 'never again' narrative, the Anglosphere allowed the Brexiteers a more positive teleology that made leaving the EU seem not only desirable, but also possible.

Memory of the Falkland campaign broke with the 1960s tradition of seeing war as futile; an ideology that bound English memory of conflict to that aligned with legitimising European integration. With '1940' functioning as England's 'finest hour' and D-Day standing in for an Anglo-American-Canadian liberation of Europe, memory of the Second World War operated as a national heuristic, permitting nostalgia for lost sense of community and greatness as well as using the past as a pointer to the future. The First World War was presented as a dangerous lesson in Continental entanglements in which the contribution of the Empire and Commonwealth was crucial for England's survival, but one that contributed to the occlusion of England amongst official (British) and local and regional commemorative events. At best, the EU was portrayed as a solution to the problems of the twentieth century that was holding Britain back at the outset of the twenty-first.

Part III

England's Brexit and the Anglosphere

7

Leap into the known: the Anglosphere, England and the Brexit referendum

---

Thames and Tiber, 2015 and 2018

If two politicians' ideas enjoyed a retrospective and posthumous success as a result of Brexit, it was those of Winston Churchill and Enoch Powell. The fiftieth anniversary of Churchill's funeral took place in January 2015 with a re-enactment of his funereal trip along the Thames. Three years later, Enoch Powell's 'Rivers of Blood' speech was dramatised on BBC radio.

The dominant memory of Churchill remained that of his leadership during Britain's 'finest hour' in 1940, even if critical voices of his pre- and post-war leadership entered the public realm through cinema and Netflix. Always more concerned with grand strategy than the provision of eyeglasses for the myopic, it was Churchill's inter-war characterisation of the United Kingdom's relationship to Europe, the United States and the Commonwealth that appeared to ring true as the UK Government disengaged from the EU and sought new, old allies. In 1931 Churchill argued that Britain was 'in Europe, but not of it' and 'linked but not compromised'. This idea was elaborated into his 'three circles' schema for British foreign policy. Yet it was the idea of the 'English-speaking peoples', whom he historicised and embodied, that linked America and the Commonwealth in his worldview.

The re-enactment of the dipping of the cranes during his funeral procession along the River Thames in 1965 sustained the memory of the cross-class alliance of the War years. But it was another river – the Tiber – that resurfaced into public consciousness in 2018. For all his thinking about the English-speaking peoples there was very little of England in Churchill's worldview. This was the inverse of Enoch Powell. At a speech to the Royal Society of St George in April 1961, Powell reflected in his own way on the need for a new conceptualisation of England. Powell believed that 'we today, at the heart of a vanished empire, amidst the fragments of demolished glory, seem to find, like one of her own oak trees, standing and growing, the sap still rising from her ancient roots to meet the spring, England herself'. But it was his inflammatory prophesy that if not stopped and reversed immigration from the New Commonwealth would lead to conflict that stuck in the collective memory: 'like the Roman before me', he told his audience in Wolverhampton in April 1968, 'I seem to see the Tiber foaming with much blood.'

The re-enactment and broadcast of this speech by the BBC in 2018 elicited a hostile response. The fear was that it legitimised the sentiments expressed; fears enhanced by the rise in hate crimes recorded after the referendum campaign and the xenophobia deployed by the Leave campaign. But the Brexiteers were not Powellites in strict emulation of the Enoch's worldview. Despite his enthusiasm for free trade and his early articulation of a right-wing antipathy to European integration, Powell believed that the Empire was gone and England was on its own. He distrusted, rather than revered, America. These attitudes set him apart from the Brexiteers for whom the United States – once President Obama was gone – served as an exemplar: a vision rather than a reality once President Trump's tariffs started to bite. Whereas Powell openly revered England, the Brexiteers were far more circumspect. Whilst using its animating forces to advance their political project of withdrawal from the EU, England was subsumed in the Brexiteer rhetoric of Britain and the Anglosphere.

This chapter analyses the place of the Anglosphere in the Brexit referendum campaign and the ways in which this English understanding of the Anglosphere was inter-related with English national narratives. It will argue that unlike the last time Britons went to the polls to decide on membership of the European Communities, the idea of the Anglosphere gave Eurosceptics an alternative vision of an international community to the EU. The Anglosphere's core states provided Brexiteers with economic and political models to emulate (and exceed) those of the European Union. Crucially these alternative models resonated powerfully with the wider categories of belonging in English conceptions of nationhood and the past.

By framing the UK's withdrawal from the European Union as a return to the Anglosphere, Brexiteers were able to lessen the sense of rupture associated with Brexit in England (there was little evidence of what this might have implied for other parts of the United Kingdom) and situate a potentially radical departure within narratives of continuity. The Remain campaign's narrative suggested that membership of the European Union was something to be barely tolerated rather than happily endorsed, but that things could only get worse outside of the EU. In contrast, the two Leave campaign narratives were far more optimistic, even if critics claimed they were unrealistic. These narratives suggested that the UK's membership of the European Union was a historic interregnum, situated between its global past and what promised to be a global future once an English understanding of British sovereignty and greatness had been restored. The Brexiteer critique of the present was inspired by a vision of the past that mobilised anti-EU sentiment towards an Anglosphere future.

When seeking to analyse the inter-relationship between English nationalism and the Anglosphere in the Brexit referendum campaign, an obvious place to start is to look for conscious calls for a realignment of UK foreign policy and trade with the Anglosphere by self-consciously English actors. But such open goals are not available to those researching nationalism in England. Explicit mentions of the Anglosphere were made in UKIP's 2015 UK election manifesto. They were also found in the pages of the *Express*, the *Daily Mail*, the *Telegraph* and especially the *Spectator* (the 'party in the media') often articulated by high-profile parliamentarians and senior Conservative party figures. Yet such explicit references to the Anglosphere and its core component states by senior figures were muted after the initial weeks of the campaign.

As we have seen in preceding chapters, the influence of thinking and policies that align with the Anglosphere idea have been advanced in less explicit ways. The Anglosphere idea allowed Brexiteers to suggest a more positive teleology than the Remainers. This aligned with John Hutchinson's analysis of nationalist mobilisation, whereby historical memory 'was used to stimulate revival through invidious comparisons with a decadent present' (Hutchinson: 2005: 53). The narrative arc of this nationalist critique runs that the nation was once great (a vision of the past); there is a problem now that is holding it back (a critique of the present); and that the nation can be great again if it takes a certain course of action (a future goal). Articulations of collective identity are important in this trajectory because as Srdjan Vucetic suggests, political decisions should 'follow the discourses and debates over identity, wherever these might take them' (Vucetic, 2011: 25). Such discourses and debates took Brexiteers to the Anglosphere.

Present critique: globalisation and the Anglosphere

The year 2015 was not a good one for the Anglosphere's supporters. The loss of Tony Abbott and Stephen Harper as Prime Ministers of Australia and Canada respectively was a blow to Anglosphere enthusiasts. These two men had been keen proponents of the Anglosphere idea. One place where the Anglosphere found new tribunes and an unexpected boost, however, was the United Kingdom. The launch of the referendum campaign groups in the aftermath of the Conservatives' General Election victory in 2015 gave urgency to the need to find alternative sources of markets and allies to provide arguments for the debates about Britain's place in the world to come.

In February 2016, former Conservative leadership contender David Davis framed his decision to campaign to leave the EU with an explicit reference to the Anglosphere and Commonwealth:

> This is an opportunity to renew our strong relationships with Commonwealth and Anglosphere countries. These parts of the world are growing faster than Europe. We

share history, culture and language. We have family ties. We even share similar legal systems. The usual barriers to trade are largely absent. The Prime Minister has repeatedly stated that we are a trading nation with global horizons. This is undoubtedly true. So it is time we unshackled ourselves, and began to focus policy on trading with the wider world, rather than just within Europe. (Davis, 2016)

MEP Daniel Hannan was the highest profile exponent of the Anglosphere amongst the official Leave campaign's organising committee. For Hannan, the Anglosphere not only had the short-term advantage of greater economic growth than the EU (mired as it was in the worst set of crises in its history), but it also made more cultural sense. Ahead of the campaign, Hannan wrote that 'the world's leading English-speaking democracies – the US, Canada, Australia and India – are growing handsomely. And these are countries where Britain has strong cultural links. What a contrast with the European Parliament, where we are forever hectored and criticised by people who resent us for having kept our currency and for our commitment to Anglo-Saxon capitalism'. Consequently it was time, Hannan concluded, to return to closer ties with 'our true friends' (Hannan, 2015).

The argument that another referendum on UK membership of the EU was required because 'Europe' had changed dramatically since 1975 had international as well as domestic drivers. It was not just that the EU had changed since 1975, but the world had too. Past and future interlinked closely in this Eurosceptic critique of Britain's present. An image of Britain's expansive global future was contrasted with one of Europe's constraining regional past. The EU was presented as a solution to the twentieth century's problems: 'Vote Leave's core argument is that the EU's institutions remain stuck in the post-1945 era', wrote Allister Heath in the *Telegraph*. 'In those days' he continued, 'bureaucratic centralism was the fashionable answer; 60 years on, the EU's creaking, lumbering structures cannot cope with change involving genetic engineering, cybercrime, driverless cars and digital manufacturing' (Heath, 2015).

The tension between globalisation and European integration in the English imagination has deep roots. As Chris Gifford has argued, 'If the EU attempts to mediate the relationship of European states to globalisation, then in the case of the United Kingdom, globalisation mediates its relationship to the EU ... The United Kingdom should first and foremost be viewed as a global political order, and its trajectory as a "European state" can only be understood in relation to this primary materialisation' (Gifford, 2016: 783). For Brexiteers globalisation provided the context and reason for leaving the EU and underwrote their optimism about the UK's future outside of it. Rallying the Leave.EU supporters after Vote Leave had been named by the Electoral Commission as the official 'Leave' campaign, Arron Banks rallied the 'People's Army' in a temporary alliance with Vote Leave despite the 'stitch up' of the decision. 'It is time to turn our collective guns on the real opponents in this campaign: those who are repeatedly trying to scare the British public into thinking that Britain is too small and insignificant to be an independent nation engaged with the whole world, not just one corner of it' (Banks, 2016). The past operated as a source of inspiration for these nationalists, providing them with a critique of the present inspired by a retelling of the past, which in turn propelled them towards a future political goal.

This dynamic was in evidence before and during the referendum campaign. Referring to Shadow Foreign Secretary Hilary Benn's speech at Chatham House in February 2016, Douglas Murray, writing in the *Spectator*, argued that 'if there is one thing to really object to in Mr Benn's speech it is his warning of the untold risks of Britain leaving the EU':

> According to his ominous, risk-filled warning, 'Stepping into the unknown is very, very unwise.' Except that we wouldn't be stepping into the unknown. We would be stepping into the situation we have been in for most of our history, when we have been an independent, stable and successful country, governed by our own laws. (Murray, 2016)

For both soft Eurosceptics and Brexiteers the past operated as a political destination, as well as a point of conceptual departure, but Brexiteers took this interpretation of the past to its extreme. This portrayal of Britain's European years as a four-decade interregnum in its otherwise global vocation allowed Brexiteers to imagine the United Kingdom outside of Europe, bringing the past and future into alignment with a critique of the present.

Past vision: the three pillars of the English Anglosphere

The Brexiteer critique of the present rested on a vision of the past that was heavily conditioned by the influence of the Anglosphere idea. Michael Gove invoked Anglosphere countries and the radical tradition in British politics as aspirational models for the (unspecified) nation:

> The ability to choose who governs us, and the freedom to change laws we do not like, were secured for us in the past by radicals and liberals who took power from unaccountable elites and placed it in the hands of the people. As a result of their efforts we developed, and exported to nations like the US, India, Canada and Australia a system of democratic self-government which has brought prosperity and peace to millions. (Cited in Ridley, 2016)

Aside from explicit references to the core Anglosphere countries, the Anglosphere idea also helped frame the way that arguments about Brexit were made. The Englishness of this was expressed in the way that the 'three pillars' of the 'English Anglosphere' – representative government, empire and war memory – were invoked in arguments about Brexit from inside and outside of the United Kingdom. Liam Fox outlined all three elements in an article for *Conservative Woman* at the outset of the official campaign period in April. Combining the Thatcherite auto-critique of Britain's ruling class with a view of Britain inspired by its global past, and linking this with the idea of representative democracy as Britain's 'gift to the world', Fox claimed that 'For the Remain camp, Britain is a beaten country; once proud, but now incapable of surviving without the rule of Brussels', and that it was 'left to the Leave campaign to carry the banner of hope, and with it the idea that directly elected British parliamentarians will prove better lawmakers than the anonymous bureaucrats of the European Union' (Fox, 2016). Eliding the notion of Britain as an imperial power, Fox pinned this delegitimising label on the EU itself. 'The European Union has all the hallmarks of a modern empire', argued Fox. Correctly, he pointed out that 'Manuel Barroso, the former President of the European Commission, likes to describe it as such'. Less accurately, he suggested that 'Like an empire, the EU's policies are dictated by an unelected central bureau-cracy, it has a democratically unaccountable leadership, and a powerless parliament bereft of a popular mandate. And like the Continental empires of the early twen-tieth century, it finds itself unable to react or adapt to external pressures in a rapidly changing world' (Fox, 2016). For three of the four empires that Fox presumably had in mind, the 'external pressures' that brought about their collapse included war with the British Empire. But this conscious forgetting of Britain's imperial status allowed Brexiteers to recast the UK from an imperial power to a vassal state of the European Union. It was this historical framing that helped Nigel Farage to 'Dare to dream that the dawn is breaking on an independent United Kingdom' and that 23 June 2016 would 'go down in our history as our independence day!' (cited in Withnall, 2016).

In a campaign notable for its focus on senior figures of the opposing campaigns, other leaders framed their arguments in English Anglosphere terms. In his declar-ation for the Brexit campaign in February 2016 Boris Johnson linked his arguments to claims about representative democracy in the European Union:

> We have given so much to the world, in ideas and culture, but the most valuable British export and the one for which we are most famous is the one that is now increasingly in question: parliamentary democracy – the way the people express their power. (Johnson, 2016a)

Arguments about the European Union's 'democratic deficit' were used by Brexiteers to strengthen claims that a vote for Brexit was a vote for the restitution of democ-racy in Britain. This was not just a concern in England alone. Linking democracy and sovereignty and reflecting this view of Britain's 'gift to the world' back at the UK from an Australian perspective, conservative commentator Matthew Dal Santo wrote that no Australian government would tolerate the intrusions that Brussels daily visits upon Britain's institutions – and neither, it is to be hoped, would the democratic instincts of the Australian people who inherited responsible government, from Westminster in the 1850s, long before it existed in much of Europe. (Dal Santo, 2016)

Reinforcing messages coming back to Britain from the Anglosphere not only helped counter the 'Anglo-scepticism' of established governments that were wary of the dislocation to the international order that Brexit might entail, but reinforced the English narrative about greatness and the historic significance of the United Kingdom and its place in the world. Such co-constitutive narratives resonating back from the Anglosphere were one source of political sustenance for Brexiteers. They also helped discursively create an image of Remainers as lacking belief in Britain and its former (and hence future) greatness. In April 2016 Johnson described Remain colleagues as 'the Gerald Ratners of British politics', because they believed that the EU was 'crap', but that there was no alternative (cited in BBC News, 2016e).

With its emphases on the development and export of representative government throughout the globe and the memory of Empire as an on-balance positive contribution to world history, when combined with the memory of endurance in 1918 and 1940, it was only historic 'losers' who could really take European integration to heart in the English worldview. For this reason, the 'Euro-myth' or 'Nobel narrative' did not resonate in England in the way it did in Germany and other parts of Western Europe. Consequently, the Remain campaign's attempts to harness the 'Euro-myth' during the referendum misfired. This argument was made with suitable modifications for a UK audience by pro-Remain voices. *The Economist* made the 'Euro-myth' argument from a US security perspective when it argued that European integration was a benefit to America because 'it has helped to stop Europeans killing each other and thus reduced the need to send American armies across the Atlantic to fight' (*Economist*, 2016). John Major argued in the *Telegraph* that

In an uncertain world the UK, as part of the EU, is better able to face up to the aggressive policies of hostile nations. We are safer, because the EU has brought together former enemies to face common perils. In the last thousand years of history, no previous generation has been so fortunate. (Major, 2016)

The greatest misfire came after a major speech given at the British Museum on Europe Day, 9 May 2016. David Cameron argued that 'The European Union has helped reconcile countries which were once at each others' throats for decades'. Linking the development of peace in Europe to significant moments in English and British national narrative in a way that was pitched to different levels of historical knowledge, he stated that

> Britain has a fundamental national interest in maintaining common purpose in
> Europe to avoid future conflict between European countries. And that requires British
> leadership, and for Britain to remain a member. The truth is this: what happens in our
> neighbourhood matters to Britain. That was true in 1914, in 1940 and in 1989. Or,
> you could add 1588, 1704 and 1815. And it is just as true in 2016. (Cameron, 2016)

Although the notion of European integration leading to reconciliation between
former warring nations was standard fare at EU institutions and External Action
Service Delegations the world over, Cameron's words were widely misinterpreted
in England as another 'Project Fear' over-claim: that exit from the EU would inevitably lead to 'World War Three'. One month later, Cameron was able to respond
to a parliamentary question from the SNP member for Moray, Angus Robertson.
Robertson, who noted that 'European co-operation emerged from both world
wars as the best way to secure peace', asked 'does the Prime Minister agree that we
should never take peace and security for granted, and that that is a strong reason to
remain in the European Union?' Cameron was resolute in his defence of the Nobel
narrative, but trimmed it for Conservative consumption. 'I want to be clear about
this: the words "world war three" have never passed my lips':

> But can we really take for granted the security and stability we enjoy today, when we
> know that our continent has been racked by so many conflicts in the past? Like all
> Conservatives, I would always give the greatest credit to NATO for keeping the peace,
> but I think that it has always been a Conservative view that the European Union has
> played its role as well. (Hansard, 2016b, 6 June, vol. 611, col. 1184)

But that 'Conservative view' no longer held as strongly as it did in the days of
Macmillan and Heath. An alternative view had set deep roots and one that was explicitly linked to the Anglosphere. Writing in *Conservative Home*, David Davis, still a
backbencher at the outset of the referendum campaign, wrote that 'The European
Union was a noble vision. It was borne out of Europe's history: a history of war, conflict, tyranny and destruction'. But here British and European memories diverged:

> But this history is not our history. Britain has its own proud tradition of fighting tyr-
> anny, of protecting liberty and democracy both at home and abroad. For us, Europe
> has always been about trade. For the continent, it is about so much more. This does
> not mean either side is wrong. But the European Project is not right for us. The Global
> Project is. (Davis, 2016)

Importantly, a 'global project' such as UK exit from the EU required a global
narrative. It was this 'proud tradition of fighting tyranny, of protecting liberty and
democracy both at home and abroad' that meant that memories of the global
conflicts of the twentieth century were an important part of the Anglosphere and
Brexit projects. Older Thatcherite campaigners echoed the anti-German sentiment

that found expression from Cabinet members at the time of German reunification. Bernard Ingham argued that 'A Europe of freely co-operating states, without the drag of EU interference, would strengthen the West and make Germany, as the dominant nation, face up to its responsibilities. The sooner Germany finds the will to control itself the better off we shall all be' (Ingham, 2016).

It was not only in the field of political memory that security played a part in the Brexit campaign, allowing British and Anglosphere military values and networks to be contrasted with European ones. Richard Dearlove was Head of MI6 from 1996 to 2004. In the wake of the 2016 terrorist attacks in Brussels, Dearlove argued that 'Whether one is an enthusiastic European or not, the truth about Brexit from a national security perspective is that the cost to Britain would be low' and that it would bring 'two potentially important security gains: the ability to dump the European Convention on Human Rights ... and, more importantly, greater control over immigration from the European Union' (Dearlove, 2016). Dearlove concluded confidently that despite some disapproval and disappointment in Washington, Brexit would not 'damage our defence and intelligence relationship with the United States, which outweighs anything European by many factors of 10' (Dearlove, 2016). The former Central Intelligence Agency (CIA) Director Michael Hayden reinforced this view. Hayden told Radio 4 that the European Union was 'not a natural contributor to national security to each of the entity states. In fact in some ways [it] gets in the way of the state providing security for its own citizens' (cited in BBC News EU Referendum, 2016a). Phillipe de Backer MEP from the Alliance of Liberals and Democrats for Europe (ALDE) group in the European Parliament disagreed and said that member states must now move on from the 'old concept of sovereignty' towards a 'shared sovereignty where we understand that we are better off when we share information and pool resources' (cited in BBC News EU Referendum, 2016a). But this was not the lesson that Anglosphere supporters had drawn from two world wars and the hostile peace that followed them. For such critics, the lessons of the twentieth century led not to 'more Europe' but to 'more Anglosphere'.

Future ideal: the Anglosphere as exemplar

By the time of the Brexit referendum, the idea that emulating those parts of the Anglosphere that had once emulated Britain itself could restore sovereignty and democracy to the United Kingdom in 2016 had taken root. Yet it was one thing to win over a sufficient number of party members to this view, but it was another to make this a convincing argument in a referendum. The Anglosphere idea was deployed to reassure as much as mobilise potential leave voters in 2016. As noted in Chapter 2, it was not entirely new to contemporary campaigning. It was part of UKIP's foreign policy outlined in its 2015 manifesto that situated Britain as 'not merely a European country but part of a global community, the Anglosphere ... a network of nations that share not merely our language but our common law, democratic traditions and global trading interests' (UKIP, 2015).

The fact that it was only UKIP that endorsed this idea actively and explicitly in 2015 suggested that, like UKIP, the idea of the Anglosphere was found on the margins of British politics (Kamal, 2012). Yet it was one that was rising with the pro-Brexit tide. More frequently the vulnerability of the Anglosphere idea – that it could easily be portrayed as imperial-racist nostalgia – meant that activists were cautious with it in the public realm. Nevertheless, its supporters took the view that the Anglosphere was not an exercise in nostalgia, but a reworking of a much older political tradition for twenty-first-century politics. Extending the argument beyond UKIP amongst grassroots Conservatives, UKIP member Andrew Cadman weighed up some of the alternatives to membership of the EU and noted that 'Sadly, strengthening our ties with the Commonwealth is too easily caricatured as a Colonel Blimp hankering after the past, and the institution is probably too freighted with historical baggage, not least Britain's callous betrayal of its ex-colonies when it joined the EU'. As a result, he concluded that 'A better bet would be a formal Anglosphere club of Commonwealth members, the United States and Ireland' (Cadman, 2015).

Nevertheless, it was easier to speak of individual Anglosphere countries as examples of what an independent UK might be like than to push the idea of the Anglosphere itself. This underpinned Michael Gove's foray into Anglosphere territory as he announced his decision to back the Leave campaign in February 2016. Gove argued that 'Instead of grumbling and complaining about the things we can't change and growing resentful and bitter, we can shape an optimistic, forward-looking and genuinely internationalist alternative to the path the EU is going down'. He concluded that 'Like the Americans who declared their independence and never looked back, we can become an exemplar of what an inclusive, open and innovative democracy can achieve' (cited in Watt, 2016).

Gove's intervention illustrated the way in which Anglosphere countries operated as exemplars in the Brexiteer imagination. Such claims carried an unspoken legitimacy that did not need any explanation or elaboration in the way that aligning England and the United Kingdom with the EU did. But it also illustrated the way that, at the elite level, the Anglosphere was a love that dare not speak its name, because it was seldom referred to explicitly during the referendum campaign. Indeed, there was significant pushback from within the very Anglophone countries that were supposed to form the basis of a post-EU Britain's new world order. Speaking in Munich in February 2016 US Secretary of State John Kerry reminded his audience of US policy towards Britain and Europe since the very beginnings of the process of European integration: 'the United States has a profound interest in … a very strong United Kingdom staying in a strong EU' (cited in BBC News, 2016g).

Leaders of the other three core Anglosphere states reinforced this view during the Brexit referendum campaign. Canadian Prime Minister Justin Trudeau argued from first principles that 'I believe that we're always better when we work as closely as possible together, and separatism or division just doesn't seem to be a productive path for countries' (cited in Tasker, 2016). From a more instrumental point of view, New Zealand's Prime Minister John Key added his country's support for David Cameron's attempt to keep Britain in the EU during a Washington summit in April 2016. Key said: 'If we had the equivalent of Europe on our doorstep … we certainly wouldn't be looking to leave it' (*Otago Daily Times*, 2016). Australian Prime Minister Malcolm Turnbull echoed this international consensus, repeating in May 2016 the Australian Government's position that had been submitted to the UK's 'Balance of Competencies' review three years previously:

> We welcome Britain's strong role in Europe. The EU is an enormous economic and political entity and from our point of view – you might say from our selfish point of view – having a country to whom we have close ties and such strong relationships … is definitely an advantage.' (Cited in BBC News EU Referendum, 2016b)

Such support from international leaders was seized upon by the Remain campaign to suggest that Britain would find itself isolated outside of the EU in a hostile world (a re-run of an argument from 1975). Foreign Secretary Philip Hammond said that international support for the UK to remain underlined 'the simple fact that our Commonwealth partners see Britain as being stronger and more influential as a member of the EU'. From this he concluded that 'it would be dangerous and arrogant to dismiss out of hand the concerns and feelings of some of our closest and oldest allies, partners with whom we share so much history and heritage, and with whom we work so closely on trade, defence and security' (cited in BBC News EU Referendum, 2016b). Endorsing John Kerry's argument in Munich, Britain Stronger in Europe's executive director Will Straw said Kerry's comments reinforced how staying in the EU enhanced Britain's global influence: 'Being in an alliance with 27 other European democracies strengthens our hand when dealing with threats like terrorism and a resurgent Russia … and increases our clout and credibility in Washington' (cited in BBC News, 2016g).

Harsher judgements were reserved for the concept of the Anglosphere itself, which revealed tensions within the policy communities of the core Anglophone states. The Australian Foreign Minister, Julie Bishop, dismissed the idea of the Anglosphere as a 'fantasy' (cited in Cohen, 2016), whereas the former Australian foreign secretary Gareth Evans described the idea as an 'illusion' (Evans, 2016). John Key's endorsement of British membership of the EU came despite tensions over increasing visa restrictions for New Zealand nationals seeking to enter and remain in the UK that took effect on 6 April 2016 resulting in numbers falling from about 18,000 in the year 2000 to 8,500 in 2014.

Given this hostility, explicit appeals to the Anglosphere were muted, despite extensive media coverage that focused on senior figures, amongst whom most of the support for the Anglosphere was to be found. Instead the Anglosphere's most frequent invocations during the referendum were made in the form of its discrete components. These included the adoption of what was called an 'Australian-style points-based immigration system', using the Canada–EU Free Trade Agreement signed in 2015 as a model for the UK's new economic relations with the world and – in a negative sense – the intervention of the US President Barack Obama and the Canadian Governor of the Bank of England, Mark Carney.

The Remain campaign's use of leader endorsements from Anglosphere countries backfired. In a trip to Europe to visit the UK and Germany, President Barack Obama lent the US Government's support to the campaign to keep Britain in the EU. Speaking to his audience in a version of English they could understand, Obama stated clearly that a non-EU United Kingdom would be 'at the back of the queue' (rather than 'line') when it came to negotiating a free-trade agreement with the United States. Prior to this intervention Obama had argued that the UK's EU membership gave the United States 'much greater confidence about the strength of the transatlantic union' (cited in BBC News 2015a).

Such support was not surprising for two main reasons. The first was that close British collaboration with Continental Europe had been a goal of US policy since the Marshall Plan was launched in 1948. The US State Department had always been keen on British involvement in the process of European integration and Obama was not going to change that policy. In this light, the vote to leave the EU was a major defeat for post-war US grand strategy in Europe. The second reason was because the United States was (at that time) negotiating a free-trade agreement with the EU – the Trans-Atlantic Trade and Investment Partnership (TTIP) – and having a new arrival on the scene would only complicate matters. In this sense *The Economist* was able to use the opinions of the Anglosphere's leaders against Brexit. Describing Britain's friends and allies outside of Europe as 'flummoxed', 'Bagehot' editorialised on St George's Day 2016 that

> The other Anglosphere countries (Canada, Australia and New Zealand) are horrified. It matters less to them, but the Indians and the Japanese, who are big investors in Britain, are quietly dismayed. India's prime minister, Narendra Modi, says he sees Britain as 'our entry point into the EU'. Even China hopes Britain will stay in. Only Russia's Vladimir Putin is cheering the Brexiteers. (*Economist*, 2016)

'Bagehot' continued that with so much of the case for Brexit 'built on the idea that a buccaneering Britain would forge wonderful new partnerships with powerful and dynamic countries outside Europe', to ignore the President's intervention would be catastrophic. 'When Britain's oldest and closest partner says, sorry, you won't be nearly so interesting to us in the future if you take this step, that idea crumbles' (*Economist*, 2016).

However, the response to Obama's interventions in 2015 and 2016 revealed some of the tensions within the idea of the Anglosphere and the way in which the pasts of

Anglosphere countries, particularly the American Revolution, could be deployed in support of Brexit. During the referendum debate, the United States was invoked as a model of independence, but Brexiteers also attacked US support for Britain's continuing EU membership as hypocritical. In addition to Michael Gove's use of the the the United States as an exemplar of the energising forces of liberty, Leave.EU carried an exhortation to 'make 23 June our Independence Day' for its website/twitter banner (Leave.EU, 2016). Following Obama's 2015 intervention on the UK's membership of the EU former Environment Secretary Owen Paterson, a leading Brexiteer back-bencher, countered the US President's argument with one about political lessons to be drawn from the Anglosphere's past, turning historical division into an argument for state sovereignty. Paterson noted that two centuries ago the Americans 'fought not to have laws imposed on them so I don't think [Obama's] in a strong position when we want to make our own laws in our own Parliament'. Patterson continued that 'It is massively in America's interest that a strong UK, using all its contacts in the Anglosphere, with Canada, New Zealand and Asia re-galvanises the movement for world free trade that would be massively positive for thousands of people' (cited in BBC News, 2015a).

Important here was the idea that supporting the Anglosphere did not mean adherence to the Washington line, especially when the President of the United States was what his detractors thought was a 'socialist' or a 'dictator' (cited in Blake, 2015). The right of British politics had hitherto been the foremost defender of the 'Special Relationship', previously leaving criticism of that alliance to the left. But in this instance, the pro-Leave Anglosphere enthusiasts took their cue from criticisms voiced by the Tea Party and the 'alt-right'. After Obama had said that Britain would be at the back of the queue for any FTA negotiations, Republican presidential candidates, Ted Cruz and Mark Rubio suggested otherwise. Ted Cruz argued in response as follows:

> Instead of standing with our allies President Obama routinely hurls insults at them. Sadly, it happened in London last Friday, when the President of the United States informed the British people they would be at the "back of the queue" for a US–UK free trade deal if they dared to vote to leave the EU on June 23. This was nothing less than a slap in the face of British self-determination as the president, typically, elevated an international organisation over the rights of a sovereign people. (Cruz, 2016)

Donald Trump was unusually circumspect about Brexit during his presidential campaign. He did, however, endorse the result – or the means of achieving it – after the fact.

Not all criticism of the status quo was directed at Obama. Malcolm Turnbull's endorsement of Remain outlined above did not go unnoticed during the referendum campaign. Turnbull's support for Britain in the EU was criticised by

Brexiteer Andrew Rosindell, a member of the Foreign Affairs Select Committee, who rebutted Turnbull's position by asking the rhetorical questions: 'Come on Malcolm, when are you going to do your political union with Indonesia or Japan? When are you going to have free movement with Asia?' (cited in Cannane, 2016).

Despite this endorsement of Britain's EU membership by the Australian Prime Minister, it was the free movement of people that was the issue over which Australia featured most prominently in the campaign. The Royal Commonwealth Society released a report that appeared to show support amongst Commonwealth citizens for a European Union-style system of free movement between the United Kingdom, Australia, Canada and New Zealand. Seventy per cent of Australians surveyed were in favour of the idea. Support was stronger still amongst Canadians (75 per cent) and New Zealanders (82 per cent) and people under the age of thirty-five, suggesting a general propensity amongst the young for mobility anywhere in the world rather than just the EU alone. The policy proposal was least popular in Britain, but even a majority of 58 per cent of those surveyed supported it. Vox-popped by the Australian Broadcasting Corporation (ABC) about the idea Jo McGregor, a barwoman from London thought 'Well I think if you observe history it seems only fair.' She continued as follows: 'Why should people from Australia or New Zealand have a harder time [working in Britain] than people from Europe? We've got the same Queen, we fought the same wars, we have the same language and similar culture' (cited in Glenday, 2016). On the basis of its report, the Royal Commonwealth Society strongly urged the UK Government

> to address the potential diplomatic blowback, and damage to Britain's soft power and to the economy, that will result if it continues to overlook the skilled workers of the Commonwealth. As the UK gazes on myriad European continental concerns, it must not forget its much wider international make-up of which the Commonwealth proudly plays its part. (Howell and Hewish, 2016)

Boris Johnson had been pushing for a zone of free movement for some years in his capacity as Mayor of London and Honorary Australian of the Year for 2014. Daniel Hannan also called for such an initiative in the days after the vote, a position consistent with his support for the Anglosphere. What the inhabitants of the Antipodes might have thought about 65 million Britons given the sudden opportunity to live and work in Australia and New Zealand was not canvassed. The importance of the idea lay in it as an alternative to the free movement of labour across the EU that would fill skills gaps whilst maintaining social cohesion through a common language.

In another respect, however, Australia played an important part in the British exit from the EU. John Howard, Prime Minister of Australia from 1996 to 2007, publically backed Brexit during the campaign. Reflecting Brexiteer arguments back at the United Kingdom, Howard stated that 'The European project is fundamentally flawed' and 'I think its best days are probably behind it … Britain can't control its borders – it is ridiculous to say it can. If I were British, which I'm not, I'd vote to leave. You have lost your sovereignty' (cited in Smyth, 2016). Howard's term as Prime Minister was best known internationally not only for his deployment of troops in support of the 'Coalition of the Willing' in Iraq but also for his strong and electorally successful link between sovereignty and border control; precisely the issue that was such an important element of the Leave campaign's mass appeal.

The deployment of what was clumsily called an 'Australian-style points-based immigration system' was an important part of the Brexit campaign's alternative to the current immigration system linked with the free movement of people within the European Union. Although the United Kingdom was not part of the Schengen Treaty that eliminated border controls within the other parts of the EU, the damaging link between the free movement of labour and the movement of asylum seekers and refugees had already been made to good effect by UKIP since 2009. This linkage became of critical importance after the EU's 'migration crisis' in the summer and autumn of 2015. As a result of the crisis of political will about the correct response to the humanitarian crisis across the EU, the *Daily Mail* claimed that 'Three-quarters of adults said a rigorous Australian-style points system for people coming to the UK from outside the EU would be a successful method of curbing migration' (Slack, 2015). This issue provided an example of attempted policy and rhetorical transfer ahead of the Brexit referendum. Speaking at the Margaret Thatcher Foundation, former Australian Prime Minister Tony Abbott warned that Angela Merkel and Jean-Claude Juncker's approach to the Syrian refugee crisis was a 'catastrophic error'. Speaking about Australia's Operation Sovereign Borders policy, Abbott told his audience that 'stopping the flow of illegal immigrant boats' was important 'because a country that can't control its borders starts to lose control of itself' (Abbott, 2015).

Thus it was that Australia became an exemplar of what a post-Brexit Britain might be and do: 'my ambition is not a Utopian ideal – it's an Australian reality', Michael Gove told an audience of Vote Leave supporters in April 2016:

> Instead of a European open-door migration policy we could – if a future Government wanted it – have an Australian points-based migration policy. We could emulate that country's admirable record of taking in genuine refugees, giving a welcome to hardworking new citizens and building a successful multi-racial society without giving into people-smugglers, illegal migration or subversion of our borders. (Gove, 2016)

When Vote Leave claimed that they would establish a 'genuine' Australian-style immigration system' (Vote Leave, 2016), they presumably meant an update of the Australian-inspired system that had already been adopted under New Labour. This issue provided common ground for the two 'Leave' campaigns. Senior UKIP MEP Stephen Woolfe called for 'Freedom to introduce an Australian points based system that allows equality of opportunity to all those seeking work from abroad whilst controlling the numbers to helps wages and jobs'. In the disruptive manner associated with the political insurgencies of the mid-2010s, Woolfe merged and complicated the usual association of Commonwealth 'kith and kin' with whiteness:

> Those from the Commonwealth are a kith and kin to Britain. Two and a half million Indians fought in the second world war and millions of Africans, West Indians, Canadians and Australians stood alongside each other to fight a European dictator bent on domination. (Woolfe, 2016)

Australia's immigration policy was often conflated with its border protection policies. The issue of asylum-seeker arrivals by sea had been an intractable, divisive and internationally contentious issue in Australia since John Howard won an election on border protection in 2001. Given the existence of 'dog-whistle' politics on this issue in Australia and the accusations of such tactics having been levelled at the Conservative mayoral election campaign in May 2016, it was as much Australia's 'Operation Sovereign Borders' as its points-based immigration system to which Brexiteers were appealing.

Nor was this an issue of policy alone, but one of resonance too. The Brexiteers were not suggesting that any country's immigration system be adopted, but one with strong historic ties of emigration and immigration to the UK. The historic appeal was picked up by some sceptical of the motives behind adopted Australian practice. The *Guardian* ran an op-ed when this policy was announced, claiming that 'the campaigning value of the Australian reference is obvious enough, though the campaign will deny it. It is a code for friendly white Anglo-Saxon people who speak English' (*Guardian*, 2016). But, as was the case for the Australian anti-immigration politician Pauline Hanson's migration to the UK in 2010, this view showed little understanding of the post-imperial development of demographics in either Australia or Britain (in Hanson's case). In contrast to 1975, Vote Leave Brexiteers were able to make the argument that the Anglosphere was a far more diverse entity than the EU and hence a cosmopolitan perspective should favour the links of a post-EU UK with Anglosphere and Commonwealth countries. Leave.EU supporters and leaders were less concerned with cosmopolitanism. For them, Australia's Operation Sovereign Borders with its policy of refugee boat turn-backs was the model to be emulated.

New Zealand had less visibility in the campaign. The *Sun* likened David Cameron's pre-referendum negotiations with the EU to a Maori *haka* – understood amongst England rugby fans as featuring a lot of posturing but with little of substance. This low profile – in contrast to the period prior to accession in 1973 – linked in with questions of greatness and the status of small nations in the English imaginary. Cameron was at pains to reject Norway and Iceland (the old European Free Trade Area model) as models for a reformed UK–EU relationship. He explicitly rejected these options on a visit to Reykjavik on 28 October 2015 for the

Northern Futures Forum and during subsequent Prime Minister's Questions on 28 October (BBC News, 2015b). In response to a question from Conservative MP Christopher Pincher, the Prime Minister said 'Some people arguing for Britain to leave the European Union, although not all of them, have pointed out a position like that of Norway as a good outcome. I would guard strongly against that. Norway pays as much per head to the EU as we do and takes twice as many migrants per head as we do in this country, but has no seat at the table and no ability to negotiate' (Hansard, 2015b, 28 October, vol. 601, col. 345).

In all of these considerations there was always a feeling that somehow none of these countries were really great enough for Britain to emulate. Emulating Anglosphere countries spoke to the historical ties of Empire and Commonwealth. They were used because it was assumed that their examples resonated more than those of existing European alternatives. In the wake of the 2015 General Election and Brexit, it was clear that one of the few points of commonality shared between politicians in England and Scotland was a desire to be more like Norway. But this commonality was only skin-deep. Scottish nationalists admired Norway's social democratic model, whereas English Eurosceptics tended to admire its access to the Single Market. Iceland – the small nation responsible for England's second surprise exit from Europe within the week commencing 23 June – was also mooted as a model for the United Kingdom to emulate along with Switzerland and even Lichtenstein. Likewise, Switzerland's relationship with the EU was initially rejected as an off-the-peg model for suggested UK–EU relations.

There was, however, one novel relationship between the EU and a third country that was suitably bound by language, culture and history and that was the Free Trade Agreement struck between the EU and Canada in 2015. Canada's reputation went before it. Widely seen as a better if slightly more boring version of the United States, journalist Gabby Hinsliff described Canada in the midst of the referendum campaign as 'like the solid but rather earnest man you realise too late that you actually should have married', but added enviously that in the wake of Justin Trudeau's election in 2015 it was 'still surfing a wave of sunny progressive feeling when the US and much of Europe are increasingly convulsed with rage against either poor migrants or privileged elites, or both' (Hinsliff, 2016: 48).

Brexiteers seized on Canada's understated charms too, although for more transactional reasons. Norman Lamont, Chancellor of the Exchequer at the time of the UK's exit from the European Exchange Rate Mechanism (ERM) in 1992 suggested that the EU–Canada Comprehensive Economic and Trade Agreement (CETA) (or 'Canada+'), which was ratified in 2015, would be a good model for the UK after Brexit. He said a post-Brexit UK would have the same World Trade Organization (WTO) means of trading with the EU as the United States or Australia (BBC News Politics, 2016b). But Canada+ was especially attractive to Brexiteers who, with the small exception of Labour Leave, were all committed free traders. During the campaign it served as an important existing model for the way that a post-EU UK could and should underpin its new economic relationships with the EU and the wider world. Where Canadian intervention was not appreciated amongst Brexiteers was from Mark Carney. Carney was one of a group that the *Spectator* described during less fractious times as 'the new colonials', a group of Canadians, Australians and South Africans who were invigorating public life in Britain (Forsyth, 2013). However, his pro-Remain views as head of the Bank of England were not appreciated by Leave campaigners.

Conclusion

In 2016, there was an alternative to Europe in the Eurosceptic imagination: it was the Anglosphere. In the years leading up to the referendum, Anglosphere countries were presented as Britain's 'true friends' in a changing world, binding nations and political communities with historic ties in the context of a globalisation that had been largely influenced by Anglo-liberal ideas about the correct relationship between states and markets. For Brexiteers, Anglo-liberal globalisation was the context in which the United Kingdom could be imagined outside of the European Union. The past acted as a national heuristic, providing for Brexiteers a critique of the present as well as a vision of the future.

The Anglosphere was implicit rather than explicit for most of the campaign. Instead, three of the four 'core' Anglosphere countries (excluding Britain and its history itself) featured to varying degrees in the referendum campaign. Canada's CETA with the EU was attractive to Brexiteers as a model for a new UK–EU trade relationship based on free trade. Australia's points-based immigration system (and its reputation for hard border protection policies) fed into both Leave campaigns' emphases on immigration and the free movement of labour. Barack Obama's intervention in April 2016 operated in a different way. Rather than being a model for emulation as in the Canadian and Australian examples, the United States, as represented by Obama, became part of the global system of governance that Brexiteers saw – not without reason – arrayed against their initiative to get Britain out of the EU. Here their analysis aligned with the right wing of US politics and provided an unusual instance of the British right criticising American policy. Importantly, the 'three pillars' of the English Anglosphere framed Leave arguments about why leaving the EU made sense historically, politically and economically.

England was also implicit during the referendum campaign. It was rarely invoked explicitly in the elite project that used the Anglosphere as a means to soften the rupture of British withdrawal from the EU. The language of Britain and Britishness obscured England once again, even as a politicised Englishness was mobilised in order to carry the leave vote over the line. Both the Anglosphere and England assumed increased importance after the shock win, as Leave leaders sought to elaborate an alternative to Europe that – despite the rhetoric – they seemed not to have developed deeply before 24 June 2016.

8

Taking back control: global Britain
and Brexit England

Regicide, rump Parliament and independence, 2016

As the United Kingdom recovered from the shock or elation of Brexit and as its political parties tried to deal with the aftermath, the blue and gold stars of the European Union fluttered from a bronze equestrian statue of Charles I, barely 100 metres from Canada House. Perhaps the person who put it there saw it only as a convenient mast during one of the large demonstrations in support of the UK's membership of the EU that snaked their way through central London in July 2016. The combination of the EU and the king beheaded by regicides was striking: both had their sovereignty decisively challenged.

Charles is best known for losing the war with Parliament: a defeat that led him to the scaffold in 1649 and eventually helped to establish Crown-in-Parliament sovereignty. Yet Parliament's position in the wake of the vote was insecure. In the days and weeks following the referendum, pro-EU Londoners demonstrated in Parliament Square. One suggestion was that the pro-Remain MPs at Westminster, who formed a majority before the vote, might choose to ignore the result of the referendum and block Brexit in Parliament. Technically speaking this was possible. The doctrine of parliamentary sovereignty implies that referendums are merely advisory. Brexiteers took to social media to counter this suggestion by turning Berthold Brecht's description of 'democracy' in East Germany against the Remainers: if the People are in conflict with those in power then it is time to dissolve the People and elect a new one.

There is an irony here. Euroscepticism in the UK functioned persistently as an attempt to reassert the sovereignty of Parliament in the face of deepening European integration. Aside from the misinformation used by the Leave campaign, something important happened to the means of representing political opinion in Britain through the campaign for Brexit. Popular sovereignty appeared to challenge parliamentary sovereignty from below. The Executive's attempt to force Brexit through with prerogative powers challenged Parliament from above. Parliament's tenuous hold on its sovereignty was only restored by the intervention of the UK High and Supreme Courts, who ruled that Parliament should have a say on when negotiations to withdraw the UK from the EU should be triggered. For this judgment, three of the High Court judges were branded 'enemies of the people' by the unelected editorial board of the *Daily Mail*.

Yet the powerful statement of popular sovereignty that referendums represent posed as many questions as answers: which 'people' were represented by the vote of 23 June 2016 and whose 'independence' was at stake? The overall vote of 52–48 per cent in favour of leaving the EU was not replicated evenly throughout the UK. The Scottish electorate voted 62–38 per cent to stay. Northern Ireland's vote demonstrated the enduring division between Catholic-Nationalist and Protestant-Loyalist communities, yet delivered an overall vote to remain in the EU of 56–44 per cent. Wales voted to leave by 52–48 per cent, but the vote showed a division between Welsh-speaking Wales and Anglophone Wales. England – with the notable exception of London and other metropolitan centres – voted to leave by 53–47 per cent.

Thus although the vote on 23 June 2016 appeared to resolve one of England's dilemmas – the UK's relationship to the EU – it exacerbated the question of England's relationship to the rest of the UK. For the English, it seemed more important to leave the EU than to keep the UK together. Brexit started to look like a kind of 'normal' nationalism based on independence from a larger polity by recourse to popular sovereignty. The Brexit vote, however, had to be interpreted. Theresa May's Government interpreted it as not only a vote for a 'hard' Brexit, but as a vote for the United Kingdom's unity. May was explicit about the Britishness of this English moment. The UK's Brexit governments, both before and after the general election of 2017, sought to take back control, not just from the EU, but also from the idea of England as a political community that the Brexit issue mobilised. The Brexit referendum may well have been about 'independence' and 'taking back control', but as the UK Government negotiated to leave the EU, it was unclear what sort of control or independence was being won or taken back from whom.

Obscured by the neologism 'Brexit' was a complex interplay of elite projects and popular grievances that combined through the device of a referendum to start the process of the United Kingdom's withdrawal from the European Union. The place of the Anglosphere in the referendum campaign illustrated the way that Brexit could be profitably understood as a nationalist project that sought to realign the United Kingdom's place in the global order framed within powerful English national narratives. These narratives operated to legitimise a significant rupture in the British, European and global order and sought to provide a reassuring sense of continuity (in England). With Brexiteer free traders in the Conservative party and UKIP insisting that Britain's EU past was merely an interregnum in its hitherto global story, allied with popular grievances over immigration that were strongest in the least 'global' parts of England, what can be identified as English nationalism played a major part in reshaping British, European and global politics.

Yet if Brexit was a peculiarly English 'moment', then its aftermath was rhetorically 'British'. It was characterised by efforts – unintended and deliberate – to contain the politicised Englishness that had emerged in the decade before the Brexit referendum. Theresa May's governments concluded the tacit alliance between elite project and popular grievance after June 2016. The politics of Brexit after June 2016 therefore operated on three levels, all of which operated to obscure England at a moment of significant political impact. The first level was to withdraw the United Kingdom from the European Union through inter-state bargaining between the UK and the EU-27, whilst containing the sense of English discontent that had produced the vote to leave. The second was to keep the United Kingdom together whilst withdrawing it from the EU, during which the position of Scotland augmented the delicate situation in Northern Ireland, again to the exclusion of England. The third was to re-engage the Anglosphere as an alternative to membership of the European Union: this time as an urgent and looming priority rather than the musings between the Eurosceptic right of English politics and ideological confreres in other English-speaking countries. The Brexit vote introduced a three-cornered struggle to assert who was ultimately charge in the Westminster system: the Government, Parliament or the People. If it were the People, this raised a further question about which People exactly were being invoked and where the boundaries of political community lay in the United Kingdom. Examining Brexit as an expression of a historically conditioned English nationalism opens up new ways of understanding this momentous political event as well as comprehending this crucial 'moment' in the history of English nationalism.

Containing England: exiting the European Union

If memory politics in Germany was dominated in the post-war era with a self-conscious 'coming to terms with the past' (*vergangenheitsbewältigung*), the result of the referendum vote of June 2016 forced the English to come to terms with the future. Responding to the shock of the Brexit vote in June 2016, Conservative MP and Remain campaigner Grant Schapps sought to adapt to the unfolding reality by reaching back into the past to make some sense of the present. In anticipation of leaving the EU he argued that 'we must resolve to make ourselves the world's greatest trading nation'. Avoiding mention of England itself in the wake of the vote – terms like 'UK', 'nation', 'island' were used instead and Singapore, Vietnam and Taiwan were mentioned more often than any nation of the UK – Schapps opened his argument for what the UK needed to do now with the peroration that 'As an island, we need to rediscover that swashbuckling spirit of the 19th century when we practically owned the concept of free trade. Yes, we may have voted to Leave the EU's political project, but now is not the time to turn inwards' (Schapps, 2016). Schapps need not have feared. If the EU responded to Brexit with the idea of 'more Europe', the answer to this new and urgent political dilemma in England and around the Cabinet table was 'more Britain'. It was certainly not 'little England', despite – and indeed because of – the Englishness of the vote to leave the EU. As an elite project, leaving the EU was predicated on an understanding of globalisation that differed from that tied to regional integration when the Treaty of Maastricht was signed and ratified between 1991 and 1993. Far from being fearful, Brexiteers and Anglosphere enthusiasts – Fox, Davis and Johnson occupied key cabinet positions after 2016 – were keen to restore the United Kingdom to its former, pre-EU sovereignty.

But this political approach carried risk. Leaving the EU meant searching for new markets on the basis of free trade. But more globalisation risked stirring the anti-establishment and resentful nationalism, proclaimed by Brexiteers as a popular revolt, which had played an important part in the Brexit vote. Anna Soubry gave voice to this idea when introducing the Third Reading of the Customs Bill in July 2018. She claimed that government members admitted in private conversations that

> the loss of hundreds of thousands of jobs will be worth it to regain our country's sovereignty – tell that to the people who voted leave in my constituency. Nobody voted to be poorer, and nobody voted leave on the basis that somebody with a gold-plated pension and inherited wealth would take their jobs away from them. (Hansard, 2018, 16 July, vol. 645, col. 83)

Thus the first imperative driving the occlusion of England after the Brexit referendum was occasioned by the perceived need to contain the politicised Englishness that had been mobilised around the issue of EU membership and associated concerns about sovereignty and immigration. English discontent was contained at the very moment when it was used by Brexiteers to justify a major shift in British policy.

As Theresa May explained in an open letter to Donald Tusk when triggering Article 50 of the Lisbon Treaty on 31 March 2017, 'the referendum was a vote to restore, as we see it, our national self-determination' (May, 2017). That restored self-determination was underwritten by a new 'global' role, which rhetorically needed to downplay the EU's own operations as a global actor and agent of globalisation. The European Union was a long-standing and major actor in the World Trade Organization. It had signed free-trade agreements with the Republic of Korea and Canada in the decade before the Brexit vote and had FTAs with Australia, Japan, Singapore and Vietnam pending in 2016 and another ten FTAs under negotiation, mostly with Asian economies (European Commission, 2018). But the Brexiteers had successfully portrayed the EU as 'merely' a regional player during the referendum campaign, as if it had no interest in the world beyond Estonia. The concept of 'Global Britain' that emerged from Theresa May's pro-Anglosphere Cabinet was itself undergirded by a memory of sovereignty predicated on ties with

English-speaking peoples and an interpretation of a 'swashbuckling' past that, as we have seen in preceding chapters, resonated with the rehabilitation of Empire in English narratives.

This emphasis on the past was also evident in Brexiteer interpretations of the 'Special Relationship' with the United States. Soon after the 2016 election, Nigel Farage met President-elect Trump in New York. A UKIP spokesman subsequently confirmed that Farage had asked the President-elect to return the now famous bust of Winston Churchill to the White House Oval Office. Farage was 'especially pleased' by Trump's 'very positive reaction' to the idea, a symbol of a new friendship on the illiberal wing of Anglo-American politics (cited in BBC News, 2016k). Writing in the *Telegraph* about the prospects for a post-EU free-trade agreement between the United Kingdom and the United States, Liam Fox argued that the tentative discussions between British and American officials marked 'the beginning of an exciting new chapter for the UK where, for the first time in over 40 years we will be able to take advantage of the growing markets in the world and determine a trade relationship designed around Britain's national interest' (Fox, 2017). Not only was the memory of a pre-EU British past inscribed into the act of leaving the EU. The initial optimism on the right of English politics was complicated by the election of Donald Trump. Trump's difficult position for the free-trade Brexiteers was confirmed by his equivocation over the merits of an FTA with the UK ahead of his reception at Blenheim Palace (Churchill's birthplace) in July 2018 that strengthened the hand of the pro-hard-Brexit European Research Group.

The memory of a pre-EU national interest was not the only ghost at the banquet. 'Brexit is soaked in the blood of Powellism' editorialised *The Economist* in the wake of the triggering of Article 50 of the Treaty of Lisbon (*Economist*, 2017: 2). Powell's stances on Europe and immigration were clearly recognisable in the politics of Brexit. Even if Powell was concerned with the effect on England of immigration from New Commonwealth countries rather than Europe, the Runnymede Trust found great unease amongst visible minorities about the tone and implications of the politics of Brexit in the months before the referendum, even if older respondents especially were less likely to feel 'European' in any affective way (Khan and Weekes-Bernard, 2015).

One area in which Powell's views differed from those of contemporary supporters of the Anglosphere was his dislike for the United States, which was itself predicated on a fear of racial tensions (Martin Luther King's assassination two weeks before Powell's 'Rivers of Blood' speech had given rise to the type of race riots that Powell prophesied for England). Yet a significant aspect of Powellism that was often overlooked was his commitment to free trade. This return to a more 'Birmingham' style of Conservatism was a crucial element in the Anglosphere-inspired, post-Brexit strategy adopted in the aftermath of the referendum. 'As we leave the European Union', Theresa May told readers in the *Telegraph* after the Conservative annual conference, coincidentally held in Birmingham:

we have the chance to forge a new global role for the UK – to look beyond our continent and towards the economic and diplomatic opportunities in the wider world. I am determined to capitalise on those opportunities, and as we embark on the trade mission to India we will send the message that the UK will be the most passionate, most consistent, and most convincing advocate for free trade. (Cited in Riley-Smith, 2016)

May made this argument when embarking to India with Liam Fox on the first trade mission of her new government. It was not just business that was determining the choice of India as this first destination. Prime Ministerial aides told the *Telegraph* that Theresa May believed that there was a 'unique tie' between Britain and India, and consequently that there was an 'enormous potential to grow' the relationship (cited in Riley-Smith, 2016).

The Prime Minister was not alone in her optimistic assessment of this past-oriented future for Britain. A reinvigoration of the Commonwealth was notable after July 2016. Speaking before the Commonwealth trade summit that took place in London in March 2017 ahead of the Commonwealth Heads of Government Meeting the following year, Lord Marland, a former Conservative trade representative who proposed the summit in his capacity as chairman of the Commonwealth Enterprise and Investment Council, noted that 'We will have more than 30 Commonwealth trade ministers under the same roof for the first time ever', allowing Britain to 'initiate a Commonwealth trade accord which will endorse the benefits of free trade' (cited in Shipman, 2017). Again this was not just the international language of trade and business driving this renewed direction in British policy. Marland told *The Times* that there were huge opportunities available for Britain in the Commonwealth. 'Everyone in the Commonwealth speaks English and it is underpinned by the UK rule of law. We enjoy a lot of cultural links like sport as well' (cited in Shipman, 2017). These historic links would – it was hoped – translate readily into mutually beneficial trading and diplomatic arrangements.

As the UK Government began the process of negotiating its way out of the EU, the second pillar of the English Anglosphere – war memory – was never far from the surface. As noted above in Chapter 2, nationalism provides a way of seeing the world that helps to frame the way in which actors interpret evidence and behave towards others. Brexit negotiations provided evidence of this framing. In January 2017, Boris Johnson caused outrage amongst EU politicians when he urged the French president not to 'administer punishment beatings' on Britain for choosing to escape the EU 'rather in the manner of some World War Two movie' (cited in Landale, 2017). This genre of film was not without influence amongst senior British politicians. The BBCs James Landale claimed that David Cameron had, at the time of writing, seen *The Guns of Navarone* more than seventeen times and he knew one former Conservative cabinet minister who could quote extensively from *Where*

Eagles Dare (cited in Landale, 2017). These cinematic expressions of English war memory pitted the English view of the past against the EU memory of the past. One EU diplomat explained the outrage to the BBC:

> You Brits don't understand us when we talk about European values. To us they are important because they are not Nazi values, they are not Vichy values, they are not fascist values, not the values of the Greek junta. They are the values of a different Europe. So for that clown to compare us to the Nazis, well, that hurts and will not be forgotten. (Cited in Landale, 2017)

Even pro-EU arguments displayed this tendency to view UK–EU relations through a historic lens focused on the Second World War. Michael Heseltine articulated both a pro-EU and an anti-German position when he argued that the Brexit vote had lost Britain the post-war peace. 'Hitler was democratically elected in Germany', he noted to *The House Magazine* in March 2017. 'He unleashed the most horrendous war. This country played a unique role in securing his defeat. So Germany lost the war. We've just handed them the opportunity to win the peace' (cited in Macrory, 2017). Inverting progressive fears of the encroachment of neo-fascism, Nigel Farage claimed that the transition period for leaving the UK would result in 'Vichy Britain' (cited in Withers, 2018a). Memory of a more recent conflict – and a crucial one in the Thatcherite tradition – resurfaced when former Conservative leader Michael Howard suggested by analogy that the UK Government might go to war with Spain (a NATO ally) over the rights of Gibraltarians to remain under British rule, despite their overwhelming 96 per cent vote to remain in the EU (cited in Watts, 2017).

Brexit did strange things to allegiances in British politics: a phenomenon that was fully revealed at the June 2017 General Election. A new, cross-party ideological cleavage opened up in the wake of the Brexit vote. Raphael Behr characterised the state of affairs well for the *Guardian* in 2016:

> Pro-Europeanism became a proxy for the fusion of economic and social liberalism that had been a dominant philosophy of the political mainstream for a generation, although its proponents were scattered across partisan boundaries. These centrists were the ruling class of an unrecognised state – call it Remainia – whose people were divided between the Conservatives, Labour and Lib Dems; like a tribe whose homeland has been partitioned by some insouciant Victorian cartographer. (Behr, 2016)

Despite the disappointing and equivocal Conservative performance in the general election of June 2017, analysing 'Remainia' through the lens of English nationalism posed more problems for the centre-left than the centre-right. Theresa May's Conservatism was well grounded in the Tory traditions of provincial England.

Labour's support, in contrast, appeared split on questions of national identity between professional urbanites and smaller town, working-class whites (Mann and Fenton, 2017: 120). Attempts to articulate a consistent position on Englishness had foundered under Ed Miliband and were only advanced from the margins of the party, even after Labour's consistently poor showing in England where it last won a majority of votes in 2001. Englishness was equally difficult terrain for Jeremy Corbyn, whose radicalism inclined him away from identification with any form of nationalism or identity politics (other than Palestine). Nevertheless, Corbyn was forced to make some concessions to the growing idea that Labour needed to respond directly to the growth of a politicised Englishness mobilised by the issue of Brexit. On St George's Day during the 2017 election campaign Labour announced the idea of national public holidays for England, Scotland, Wales and Northern Ireland. Corbyn said 'the four nations that make up our great country have rarely been more divided due to the damaging and divisive policies of this Conservative Government. But where Theresa May divides, Labour will unite our four nations' by providing time 'for workers to spend time with their families, in their communities and with their friends' (Press Association, 2017). By so doing, individuals and communities would sustain their life-world with the opportunity to 'celebrate the national cultures of our proud nations' as a happy and optional by-product of this anti-system day off (Press Association, 2017).

Social divisions, starkly revealed in the aftermath of the Grenfell Tower fire of June 2017, were not the only divisions needing to be contained and managed during Brexit, as Corbyn's sotto voce recognition of the national dimension of British politics showed. In fact, this nationalist dimension to Brexit was a crucial concern in the future of the United Kingdom even if Scotland and especially Northern Ireland occupied the political attention as negotiations to leave the EU progressed. The English question was merged with a social one, which itself got subsumed in the enthusiasm for free trade pushed by the Brexiteers who suggested cure for the UK's economic dilemma risked exacerbating the initial malaise.

Obscuring England: maintaining the Union

Despite the referendum ostensibly being about the UK's membership of the European Union, the fundamental priority of the Brexit project was to keep the United Kingdom united. Theresa May made it clear that this was her top priority in her first speech outside Downing Street, having just accepted the Queen's offer to form a new government. This was despite – or in fact because – the possible effects of Brexit on Northern Ireland and Scotland, which had played little role in English deliberations during the referendum campaign. Acknowledging that social divisions also played an important part in the outcome of the referendum, May noted that Cameron had led 'a one-nation government', and – establishing continuity within the leadership – she reassured the party and country that it was 'in that spirit that

I also plan to lead'. Importantly, this 'one nation' approach addressed the politics of nationalism within the UK before the issue of leaving the EU was even raised. 'Not everybody knows this', the new Prime Minister explained, 'but the full title of my party is the Conservative and Unionist Party, and that word "unionist" is very important to me':

> It means we believe in the Union: the precious, precious bond between England, Scotland, Wales and Northern Ireland. But it means something else that is just as important; it means we believe in a union not just between the nations of the United Kingdom but between all of our citizens, every one of us, whoever we are and wherever we're from ... As we leave the European Union, we will forge a bold new positive role for ourselves in the world, and we will make Britain a country that works not for a privileged few, but for every one of us. That will be the mission of the government I lead, and together we will build a better Britain. (May, 2016)

Ultimately May's 'better Britain', rooted in the English Tory tradition, had little place for England as a discrete political community. This occlusion was clearer when compared with the growing place of England in David Cameron's politics prior to 2016. May's assertion of a 'precious' Union (with its connotations of fragility) was part of a line that had been developed under Cameron in response to the push for Scottish independence: Cameron sought to cautiously nurture England whereas 'May's 'Global Britain' subsumed it. In what had become a regular billing as a St George's Day Address, Cameron inverted the usual framing of England as domestic and bucolic and highlighted what one might call 'global England' in 2014:

> Our counties and cities are known the world over: in America, where Newcastle Brown Ale is the most imported ale; in China, where the most popular international football team is from London: Arsenal; in Australia, where they go mad for a Cornish cuisine – the humble pasty; in South Korea, where Yorkshire-set Downton Abbey is a TV favourite. And across the globe where the best-selling band is from Liverpool, the Beatles. (Cameron, 2014d)

But this 'global England' remained within the frame of an ignored nationality that was invoked in order to counter separatism in Scotland. 'St George has been England's patron saint since 1350', Cameron's statement claimed, 'but for too long, his feast day – England's national day – has been overlooked' (Cameron, 2014d). Cameron's Englishness was in the unionist-nationalist mould. 'This St George's Day, I want us to reflect on one of England's greatest achievements: its role in the world's greatest family of nations – the United Kingdom':

> In just five months, the people of Scotland will go to the polls and decide whether they want to remain a part of this global success story. So let's prove that we can be proud of

our individual nations and be committed to our union of nations. Because no matter how great we are alone, we will always be greater together. (Cameron, 2014d)

The major political events of 2014–16 that followed Cameron's message on St George's Day 2014 – the elections to the European Parliament; the Scottish referendum; the general election of 2015 and the Brexit referendum – pushed the politics of nationalism and the place of England in the Union up the political agenda. The Conservatives attempted to deal with this through the introduction of English Votes for English Laws (EVEL) in October 2015, as we have seen. The Scottish and Northern Irish elections in May 2016 saw 41 per cent of Northern Irish voters vote for parties in favour of unification (Sinn Fein or the Social Democratic and Labour Party) and returned a minority SNP Government to Holyrood. This increase in salience for (Scottish) secessionism and reunification in Northern Ireland hardly featured in the English referendum campaign.

The 'absence' of this emergent England was notable in May's rhetoric and government after 2016. The political problems caused by the fact of Brexit and the majorities to remain in the EU in Scotland, Northern Ireland and Gibraltar pushed nationalist and unionist politics up the political agenda for these nations and had the effect of decreasing the salience of England's constitutional position even as Brexit politicised Englishness. In March 2018, one year after the triggering of Article 50 of the Lisbon Treaty, the Prime Minister pledged to defend the integrity of the UK that, as it prepared to exit the EU, she described once again as a 'precious union' of four nations that was 'at heart one people' (cited in BBC News Scotland, 2017b). Yet an LBC-YouGov poll conducted on 21–22 March 2018 (YouGov, 2018) provided further evidence of the variance between this official unionism and a politicised Englishness. A majority of those polled in England, Scotland and Wales (36 per cent) thought it more important to leave EU than to keep Northern Ireland in the UK (29 per cent). This finding was even starker when disaggregated: 71 per cent leave voters felt that leaving the EU was more important than retaining Northern Ireland in the UK (12 per cent). Again English attitudes, indeed the existence of England itself, had to be inferred from the pollster's questions. The LBC headline that it was 'Brits' who wanted to abandon Northern Ireland on their way out of the EU if that is what it took, obscured the Englishness of this poll result (LBC, 2018), which can be inferred from the results in Scotland. For Scots, the results were notably different different at 28 per cent for maintaining the UK in its present form as opposed to 21 per cent for abandoning Ulster (YouGov-LBC, 2018).

The differentiated vote across the UK – particularly Scotland's resounding vote to remain in the EU – dramatically reversed the West Lothian Question, and revived arguments about the 'democratic deficit' that had sustained the democratic argument for change ahead of devolution in the 1990s. England's vote to leave the EU starkly posed the question once again about why English votes should affect policy in Scotland, especially for such a fundamental matter as (Scotland's) membership of the EU. This differentiated vote also raised questions about the legitimacy of referendums and the political community whose will such devices were supposed to express. The problem with referendums as a decisive expression of the popular will is that it is not clear how long the 'will of the People' lasts even if 'the People' can be determined in a pluri-national polity in the first instance. After the failure of the push for independence, the SNP reserved the right to call another referendum if Scotland's 'material conditions' changed. Brexit appeared to change those conditions decisively, not least because an important argument sustaining the Scottish vote to stay in the UK in 2014 was predicated on support for the UK remaining in the EU. The prospect of a second referendum on independence in Scotland diverted attention back on to Scottish secessionism as the political 'question' that needed to be addressed most urgently.

But Scottish sovereignty was not the only sovereignty that had been challenged by the Brexit vote; it was no longer clear who or what was the ultimate authority in the UK as a result of the referendum. This was a particular problem for what Arthur Aughey referred to as the 'fifth nation' (Aughey, 2010b: 265) of the United Kingdom: Westminster. Referendums sit uneasily in the British political tradition, posing a challenge to the notion of Parliament as the ultimate sovereign in the UK. There are other challengers to this idea of parliamentary sovereignty – general elections, devolved parliaments and assemblies, the European Union, the European Court of Human Rights, NATO, the UN, the IMF – but the referendum to end the EU's sovereignty over the UK suggested that 'the People' were the ultimate sovereign and that its vote (for despite the manifold divisions within this collectivity, 'the British people' were always conceived of in the singular) should be respected whatever interpretation was made of that vote by political actors.

Both 'the People' and the UK executive posed challenges for the sovereignty of Parliament in the early months following the Brexit referendum. Defending and invoking parliamentary sovereignty in the immediate wake of the Brexit referendum Labour MP for Tottenham David Lammy urged Remainers to 'Wake up. We do not have to do this. We can stop this madness and bring this nightmare to an end through a vote in Parliament':

> Our sovereign Parliament needs to now vote on whether we should exit the EU. The referendum was an advisory, non-binding referendum. The Leave campaign's platform has already unraveled and some people wish they hadn't voted to Leave. Parliament now needs to decide whether we should go forward with Brexit, and there should be a vote in Parliament next week. Let us not destroy our economy on the basis of lies and the hubris of Boris Johnson. (Cited in *New Statesman*, 2016)

Although Lammy's argument about the non-binding nature of a referendum was constitutionally sound, treating the referendum as merely an advisory vote was politically inflammatory. Theresa May's government was initially not inclined to involve Parliament in the process of leaving the EU, instead seeking to do so via Royal Prerogative. The UK Government sought to appropriate and enact this expression of the General Will when negotiating the UK's withdrawal from the EU, masking the difficulty in interpreting the vote – for 'hard' or 'soft' forms of disassociation – with the mantra that 'Brexit means Brexit'. Initially, the attempt to withdraw the UK from the EU was via Crown prerogative, which is the mechanism by which the executive – on behalf of the Crown – can take action such as declaring war without the consent of Parliament.

Yet the balance between the powers of the Crown and Parliament was of long provenance and was fundamental to the British system of government. What was novel in 2016 was a right-populist challenge to the representative mechanisms of British politics, whereas before conservatives had defined themselves in the system's defence. The Supreme Court eventually restored a measure of parliamentary sovereignty by ruling in January 2017 that Parliament should play its part in triggering Article 50 of the Lisbon Treaty, not before the (unelected) *Daily Mail*, in language reminiscent of Jacobins and Bolsheviks, labelled three High Court judges 'enemies of the people' for their interpretation of Parliament's rights (Slack, 2016). Despite its frequent claims about upholding democracy, the *Daily Mail*'s actions fitted Jan-Werner Müller's definition of populists whose invocation of 'the People' was a 'moralized form of anti-pluralism' designed to silence dissent and was therefore *anti*-democratic (Müller, 2017: 20). The High and Supreme Court rulings of 2016–17 not only upheld, but, in fact, reasserted the notion of parliamentary sovereignty, by ensuring that Westminster had a 'meaningful vote' on the final Brexit agreement and by also denying the devolved legislatures a vote on the same.

The executive's efforts to 'take back control' not only from the EU, but also from Westminster and the devolved administrations, did not run smoothly. In April 2017, Theresa May sought a Parliament that reflected the post-Brexit 'People' by calling an election. The strategy, which was designed to deliver a large majority to the Conservatives in order to strengthen the government's hand during Brexit negotiations, failed. But in one important way it succeeded: England faded from political view in the most 'British' election since 1992, in which the distinctiveness of politics in England, Scotland and Wales blurred. The SNP vote fell from its (unsustainable) high in 2015. Ulster Unionism, represented by the Democratic Unionist Party (DUP), found itself in a strong position at Westminster despite there being no working government at Stormont. England emerged more politically divided than before Brexit, but along new cleavages brought about by Brexit. Ultimately, the politics surrounding the UK's membership of the EU from 2014 to 2017 added an extra dimension to Arthur Aughey's 'ironies of inversion' (Aughey, 2016: 353). England's decisive moment in British and European politics ended in the occlusion of England as a political community. The Brexit issue not only mobilised English nationalism, but also brought England into political being – only for it to be subsumed quickly thereafter in a reaction to its major political manifestation.

Unlike David Cameron's governments from 2014 to 2016, there was little explicit recognition given to England's constitutional status within the Union or to the politics of nationalism in England, even though the ramifications of the English vote to leave the EU – or at least the government and political parties' interpretation of that vote – entered implicitly into political calculations as the UK began the process of withdrawal. This was a response to the statecraft dilemma surrounding the place of England in the Union that had been apparent to Conservatives for a decade or more (English, Hayton and Kenny, 2009). It also marked an attempt to end the 'threadbare defence of increasingly compromised central authority' that Alan Convery perceived to be a hallmark of the previous government (Convery, 2014: 26). It was one that one that sought to contain England within the Unionist tradition.

The General Election campaign of 2017 provided further evidence of this Brexit-related occlusion of England. Although most Conservative campaigning took place in the 'Brexit heartlands' of the English North-West and Midlands, campaigning in Scotland revealed a clearer expression of the Unionism that underpinned Brexit. Theresa May told a gathering of supporters in Eurosceptic Aberdeenshire that she wanted to build a more united nation by 'standing up against the separatists who want to break up our country'. This stand against separatism was part of a combined Brexit strategy to keep the United Kingdom united:

> My message to the people of Scotland is clear – every vote for me and my team will strengthen my hand in the Brexit negotiations. That will strengthen the Union, strengthen the economy and the UK and Scotland together will flourish, because if Scotland is flourishing the rest of the United Kingdom is flourishing too. (Cited in BBC News Scotland, 2017a)

This revived Unionism paid dividends for the Scottish Conservatives who won thirteen Westminster seats in 2017 to become the second largest party in Scotland at the expense of a Labour party still recovering from its near collapse after the (Scottish) independence referendum three years previously.

But there remained important differences between the revived Scottish 'unionist nationalism' under Ruth Davidson and the UK Government's more 'English' version of this commitment to the Union expressed in the language of Britishness. Indeed, the Conservative 'English' version of unionism of the 2010s was increasingly defined against Scottish separatism. Campaigning in Bolton on 19 April 2017, building on fears of a Labour–SNP coalition that had been deployed in 2015, May illustrated the way in which Brexit was framed as an implicitly English project. 'There's a very clear choice at this election', she said, 'It is a choice between strong and stable leadership under the Conservatives or weak and unstable coalition of chaos led by Jeremy Corbyn ... with Nicola Sturgeon's Scottish nationalists. They are very clear they want to do everything they can to frustrate our Brexit negotiations' (cited in Sparrow, 2017)

The Conservatives did indeed increase their UK-wide vote share from 37 per cent to 42 per cent (46 per cent in England), but lost their overall majority at Westminster. UKIP were a victim of their own success in the effort to get the UK out of the EU and saw their number of votes fall from 3,881,099 in 2015 to 594,068 in 2017. The outcome of the 2017 election was a confidence and supply agreement between the Conservatives and the DUP; a re-energised Labour Party led by Jeremy Corbyn; and a deflated SNP whose plans for a second independence referendum had to be tailored carefully to the new dispensation in Scotland and at Westminster. Nevertheless, questions of which peoples and what institutions were sovereign and where that sovereignty lay, sustained nationalist politics' elevated place on the political agenda, but subsumed England within the government's Unionist project.

Merging England: re-engaging the Anglosphere

Deployments of political traditions in the face of the major dilemma facing the UK and England within it as a result of the 2016 referendum force us to examine English nationalism 'from the outside in'. As shown in Chapter 5, one persistent trope of the Remain campaign was that any vote to leave the EU was an act of inward-looking parochialism. This 'Little England' criticism was levelled at Brexiteers again after the referendum itself and as negotiations played out. Speaking to the Australian Broadcasting Corporation (ABC) on the day that Article 50 of the Lisbon Treaty was triggered by the UK Government, David Lammy explained to his Australian audience that 'Britain had a huge identity crisis ... after it lost most of its empire':

> We rediscovered our mojo if you like when we entered the European Union. We're now posing to give that up. We will become little England and I think the sort of Britain that you're looking at in the future is something like we were in the 1970s, when we were described as the sick man of Europe. There are lots of reasons to worry about the complete breakup of the United Kingdom and there are many of us who do not want to live in little England. (Cited in ABC, 2017)

Aside from the commonplace conflation of England and Britain, this accusation also conflated an interpretation of the vote as an expression of nationalist-populist resentment, with the motives behind Brexit as an elite project. For pro-Brexit parliamentarians along with their funders and fellow travellers, such as Arron Banks, the goal of Brexit was far from national introversion. Given their reliance on free trade and the framework of globalisation that underpinned their vision of the UK outside of the EU, these Brexiteers were more often 'hyper-globalists' rather than 'parochial' protectionist nationalists.

Accordingly the international manifestation of the consequences of England's vote to leave the EU was a prescription for more globalisation rather than less, as might have been inferred from the basis of support in the less well-off parts of England. Although there were some links between England and the global in constructions of Englishness (the English Premier League being the most globalised of English consumer exports), England was usually portrayed as domestic and local. When it came to the world stage (again with the exception of sport, especially football) England's political guise was 'Britain' and all the historic connections that went with it. Those historic ties had been helping to shape the United Kingdom's foreign policy reorientation since the Coalition Government assumed power in 2010. In the policy vacuum that opened up after 24 June 2016, the Anglosphere had an off-the-peg appeal for a government that needed to find friends and partners quickly. But this was not its sole attraction. It also sat very well with the persistent theme in English nationalism that conflated England and Britain and tied it (or them) to other parts of the world. In this way, English nationalism contained within it the seeds of its own occlusion: the device of a referendum gave expression to a political England and a politicised Englishness, which Brexiteers and reconciled Remainers used to advance a global reorientation of the United Kingdom in the language of Britishness. Brexit may well have been 'made in England' (Henderson et al., 2017), but the finished product was 'Global Britain'.

The official courting of bilateral relations with Anglosphere states, such as Boris Johnson's promotion of Australia or Narendra Modi's visit to Britain in November 2015, fed into the idea amongst Brexiteers that the Anglosphere was an actually existing alternative to the EU. Instances of 'policy transfer', such as UKIP's adoption of Australia's immigration and asylum seeker policies, as well as transfer of ideas and personnel between networks, think tanks and 'ginger groups' across the English-speaking world also helped create a sense of the Anglosphere as a living community. Even calls for a more 'global' role for the UK more generally, seeking engagement with 'emerging economies' such as China and Indonesia, formed an important context for the articulation of Anglosphere ideas, resting heavily on an understanding of neo-liberal economics that Anglospherists claimed as their own contribution to the betterment of humankind.

The Anglosphere certainly appealed to Brexiteers. YouGov polling (that did not differentiate between the nationalities of those surveyed) found that Anglosphere countries rated highly in terms of leave voters' priorities for post-Brexit free-trade deals. Surprisingly, Australia was given top priority by Leave voters in September 2016 for a new FTA (YouGov, 2016), despite the 16,912 kilometres separating London from Melbourne, which complicated the trade in goods. Even if this flew in the face of the highly regional basis of global trade, it could be explained through the prism of Aughey's 'fantasy echo' (Aughey, 2007: 11), whereby, in this case, the imperial dimension of English nationhood helped shape visions of the UK's future place in the world order. Such 'fantasy echoes' help explain the idea floated during the 2017 General Election – and quickly dropped – of re-establishing the Board of Trade for a post-EU UK.

It was true, however, that there were signs that the Anglosphere was open for business, reinforcing – in England – an 'imperial' interpretation of Englishness and British policy; even if it was not seen in this way from Canberra, where it was viewed as a political windfall, reopening markets that had been impeded by the UK's accession to the EEC (Murray and Matera, 2018: 217). The Australian Government was therefore especially keen for a free-trade agreement once the UK left the EU. It even provided a team of trade deal negotiators to the UK to help it leave the EU and re-establish itself as an independent global trader thereafter. Canada too signalled its willingness for a Canada–UK free-trade agreement, as did the National Party Government of New Zealand before it lost office in 2017.

But not all views and attitudes coming from the Anglosphere were positive, as was the case during the referendum campaign, in what we might term post-Brexit 'Anglo-scepticism'. Former Australian Treasurer Wayne Swan elaborated this 'Anglo-scepticism':

> There are many in British politics who make the passionate and articulate case that a strong alliance with the Commonwealth, and with the English-speaking countries in particular, could be a viable alternative to the EU. I cherish and value the Commonwealth of Nations. It allows countries with a shared history to retain a link and to work together in pursuit of goals like greater democracy and ending extreme poverty. But the Commonwealth cannot be a replacement for the European Union. Turning the Commonwealth into a free trade area with harmonised regulations and a common trade policy is not on the agenda. (Swan, 2016)

Writing specifically about the Anglosphere alternative to the European Union in *The National Interest* during the referendum campaign, Matthew Pennekamp correctly noted that 'the two massive bookends on which the stability of such an organ would doubtless have to rest, the United States and India, are in any case disinclined toward such a plan' (Pennekamp, 2016).

Furthermore, the scepticism cut both ways. However important to bilateral trade, FTAs with Australia and New Zealand would not replicate the economic strength of the Single Market and therein lay the tension between hard and soft Brexiteers. Speaking to the British Chambers of Commerce's annual conference in February 2017, former Chancellor and Remainer George Osborne described withdrawing from the Single Market as 'the biggest single act of protectionism in the history of United Kingdom' and noted that 'no amount of trade deals with New Zealand are going to replace the amount of trade we do with our European neighbours' (cited in Merrick, 2017). Even the prospect of an FTA with New Zealand dimmed when it took a left-protectionist turn with the formation of a Labour-led coalition under Jacinda Adern later that year. Such ideas and developments led Sir Martin Donnelly, who left his role as permanent secretary to the Department of International Trade in 2017, to tell BBC Radio 4's *Today* programme that the policy of pursuing FTAs to compensate for membership of the Single Market was equivalent to 'giving up a three-course meal, which is the depth and intensity of our trade relationships across the European Union and partners now, for the promise of a packet of crisps in the future' (cited in Withers, 2018b).

Anglo-American relations became more complicated with the election of Donald Trump in 2016. Celebrating the end of the Obama presidency, Nigel Farage told Fox News that Obama was 'an American president who loathed Britain', but that Trump was an Anglophile, who 'understands and recognises what our two great nations have done together between us' (cited in BBC News, 2016i). In the heady days of Donald Trump's election, the UK Government quickly quashed a suggestion that Farage might be the UK's next ambassador to the United States. Building on existing transnational Euroscepticism, the Trump Administration was dismissive towards the EU, which the president ultimately described as a 'foe' in July 2018. Despite its protectionist rhetoric, it (or rather Trump) initially welcomed the idea of increased trade with the UK (Khan, 2017), although such rhetorical support seemed capricious and ill considered by the time of his official visit to the UK in 2018. Yet relations were strained on other matters such as anti-Muslim 're-tweets', the abortive state visit invitation made by the Prime Minister, rather than the Queen, during Theresa May's visit to Washington in January 2017 as well as attitudes towards Putin's Russia and differences over the Paris climate change agreement and the Iran nuclear deal. For all his incoherence, the US President was fundamentally unlikely to do the UK any special favours as was illustrated by his tariffs on steel from which Canada and Australia were exempted, but not the UK. This reinforced the asymmetrical nature of the 'Special Relationship': if the UK has one 'special relationship', then the United States has many and the UK was not high on that list. 'Trump is an American nationalist', concluded Andrew Gamble 'with no interest in constructing a new world order with nostalgic imperialists' (Gamble, 2017).

Thus it was not difficult to find counterposing views to those of Davis, May and Fox on the nature of the 'special relationship' between Britain and India, where the notion of *Britannia Unchained* was disquieting. Shashi Tharoor, an Indian National Congress MP, Chair of the Parliamentary Standing Committee on External Affairs in 2017 and author of *Inglorious Empire,* articulated a different memory of the British Empire in India that was unreceptive to 'Global Britain' (Tharoor, 2017). None of this deterred May's Government from making India its first destination for a Trade Mission in November 2016. The Mission was not a success, however, for two reasons relating to the English element of the Brexit vote and the distorted view of the past framing the Brexiteer actions. The first was that the post-imperial ties so prized by the Brexiteers did not match the economic realities of India's trade with the UK and the rest of the EU. 'Given the important Indian diaspora living in the UK and the common past', noted a group of non-British MEPs, 'the UK tends to attach particular importance to its economic relations to India, however, trading ties are more important with other EU member states'. As a trading partner for India, Germany was the top EU country, ranked sixth, whereas the UK ranked only in eighteenth place (cited in Boffey, 2017).

The second reason was the interpretation of Brexit as a xenophobic vote delivered by the white English working class. This echo of England inhibited the trade mission because the Indian Government wanted greater access to the UK for its skilled workers. Having made a reduction of immigrants a key part of pre- and post-Brexit policy, the UK Government could not accept the idea of explaining to supposedly xenophobic Brexit voters how the free movement of EU labour was to be replaced by more immigration from the 'New Commonwealth'. In the wake of the 'Windrush Affair' of 2018, Brexiteers were keen to point out that it was not immigration per se to which the British public objected, but its uncontrolled nature under EU principles for the free movement of labour. Yet such fondness for less restrictive immigration from Commonwealth and Anglophone countries was still to be tested. By pursuing renewed relationship with the Anglosphere, the UK Government's 'Global Britain' obscured Brexit's England by merging it within a rhetoric of Anglosphere-inflected Britishness.

Conclusion

During the summer of 2018, England became globally visible through the national team's progression to the semi-finals of the FIFA World Cup. This progress occasioned display of self-consciously English ecstatic nationalism, and encouraged debate about the nature of Englishness quite different to those that had characterised the referendum debate about membership of the EU. England manager, Gareth Southgate suggested that England's run could help heal divisions in the national community caused by and about Brexit (cited in Cook, 2018). Yet this cultural salience was not matched politically.

In each of the three political moves that played out after the Brexit referendum, England was an 'absent presence' shaping government decisions which had the effect of obscuring England. This was true in the case of the statecraft required to maintain the United Kingdom in the face of secessionist challenges within the UK, whilst the UK itself withdrew from the EU, as well as the struggle for sovereignty within the UK itself. Thus despite its decisive contribution to the decision to leave the European Union, England was subsumed by Britain once again: this time in the guise of 'Global Britain'. This occlusion was created first of all by the UK Government seeking withdrawal from the EU as a unitary actor; secondly by a Unionist Government in Westminster, seeking to keep the United Kingdom together as the strains of withdrawing from the EU became clearer; and thirdly by the projection of 'Global Britain' and the emphasis on renewed ties with the Anglosphere in a post-Brexit UK.

Although the 2017 general election was the most 'British' in terms of its two-party vote since 1992, the issues that drove support for UKIP had not gone away, despite the dramatic loss of votes that party suffered compared to its perform-ance two years earlier. The English question receded compared to those posed by Scotland and Northern Ireland as the UK Government sought to 'take back control' from competing sources of sovereignty across and within the UK. But it never went away entirely and ended being hidden in plain view. 'Global Britain' was thus a very English sort of Britain that had been revived by the politics of withdrawing from the European Union and that spoke British with an English accent.

9

Interregnum and restoration: Brexit as English nationalism

Brexit was a significant moment of political Englishness, with consequences for the rest of the United Kingdom, the European Union and beyond. This book developed existing arguments about the links between English nationalism and Euroscepticism by showing how understandings of the 'wider categories of belonging' that inform political Englishness shaped responses to the dilemma posed by the United Kingdom's membership of the European Union. When viewed in this light, with Brexit seen as a protracted event that pre- and post-dated the 2016 referendum, we can see that England's wider categories of belonging operated not only as a point of ideational departure for addressing a political dilemma, but suggested a political destination too.

By examining the links between English nationalism, Brexit and the Anglosphere, we can start to offer an explanation of Brexit that pushes us beyond accounts that give greatest causal force to a protest by those 'left behind' from the benefits of globalisation. This is not to say that we should discount such an explanation of the material deprivations and subsequent political de-alignments and re-alignments that led to the referendum in 2016 and the outcome of the vote itself. But such an explanation only explains the 'negative' vote to leave and not the 'aspirational' vote to go somewhere else. In other words, overemphasising the 'left behind' explanation might explain what people were voting against, but is less helpful in seeking to understand what they might have been voting for and which frames helped inform such a decision.

Of course, we cannot infer the motives of voters from what the advocates of a particular policy – in this case leaving the European Union – were asking them to vote for, especially when some evidence for leaving was presented in a duplicitous manner. Nevertheless, the range of policy alternatives offered to the electorate was remarkably consistent with what we can call (at the risk of anachronism) 'the Anglosphere tradition'. This was a tradition that aligned with powerful narratives of English nationalism conditioned by the need to defend and legitimise British sovereignty. It also offered Brexiteers a positive alternative to membership of the European Union and ultimately permitted them to deploy a more 'positive' message during the referendum campaign itself.

This book has called for a greater consideration of the role of nationalism and 'identity' in explanations of Brexit. It used the politics of Brexit to illuminate a deeper understanding of contemporary English nationalism that privileged an 'outside in' perspective. Identity matters in politics and international relations. It helps individuals and groups make sense of the world around them and shape their ideas and actions accordingly. Amongst those who felt that the UK's membership of the EU was problematic, the self-reinforcing narratives within English nationalism, Euroscepticism and the Anglosphere held the promise of resolving the dilemmas created once England emerged as a de facto political community during and after the 1990s. England's national dilemmas were generated first by its relationship to the European Union, and then to the rest of the United Kingdom following devolution. The UK's famous awkwardness with European integration was, by the 2010s, a product of England's awkward relationship with the UK. By problematising the constitutional relationships within the United Kingdom, these dilemmas entailed by extension a reworking of England's relations with the rest of the world. This reworking had to be conducted through the United Kingdom and hence dragged Scotland, Northern Ireland and Gibraltar out of the EU in England's wake.

The fact that this dilemma could be resolved – not without great political contentions – within the frames of English political tradition significantly softened the rupture associated with Brexit for those pushing for the UK's withdrawal. Despite the historic magnitude of England's decision to leave the European Union and the effects of this on the rest of the UK, the Englishness of this moment made it seem like a 'leap into the known'. Brexit could be portrayed as reclamation of British sovereignty in the face of decades of European integration. By necessity as much as choice it came with a reassertion of the Atlantic and Commonwealth 'circles' of Churchill's political cosmology. It was an English restoration after a European interregnum articulated in the language of Anglosphere Britishness.

Yet isolating and identifying the Englishness of this event is not an easy task. This is owing to the merged nature of political Englishness itself. England is a nation that had various polities through which its collective identities and political traditions have been shaped and through which its collective problems are addressed: the United Kingdom, the British Empire and the European Union. English nationalism is not as immediately identifiable as Scottish nationalism, for example, because there is an absence of an explicitly secessionist political party pushing for independence. English distinctiveness was blurred over time through historic contact with other parts of the world. What we would otherwise understand as its secessionist expressions (the Euro-rejectionism of the Brexiteers) were historically conditioned by a defence of polities larger than England itself.

The political difficulty of identifying English nationalism is mirrored by a methodological difficulty: how should a sub-state, yet dominant, nationalism such as England's, which lacks direct institutional representation on the nation-state model, be researched? It is in this light that definitions of English nationalism become crucial for comprehending Brexit. Switching from Britishness to Englishness as a category of analysis opened up the possibility of new conceptual terrain to understand the political dilemmas playing out in the 2010s. Allied to this was the idea that Englishness had to be approached from 'the outside in' as Krishan Kumar argued. In other words, when examining English nationalism it is important to be aware of the 'wider categories of belonging' that have historically conditioned – and continue to inform – notions of political nationhood in England. Marrying this insight to Bevir and Rhodes' 'traditions and dilemmas' approach to collective problem solving opened up space to understand the political ideologies that informed and animated what we can call English national*ism* (as opposed to nationhood) as well as the imperatives that drive it and shape the imaginaries of those who cleave to its dominant worldview. In this light, English nationalism was and remains conditioned by a *defence of British sovereignty*; such an imperative instinctively positions it against European integration and inclines it towards relations with the English-speaking peoples who go in today's parlance under the name of the 'Anglosphere'.

Examining the points of intersection between a narrative of English nationalism and how this linked England to the rest of the world helps in comprehending Brexit as a moment of English nationalism. In this light Brexit is more explicable than from accounts that imply that people were voting against their own interests. Identity matters, but identity itself is not a sufficient explanation. Its persuasive narratives need to be unpacked and linked to other narratives to build up a picture of a broadly coherent worldview. These transnational, Anglosphere links were sustained in the Brexit era by commemorative politics and debates about the teaching of history in schools – issues that had risen in political salience and gained sustained official support in the first decade of the twenty-first century. The most obvious of these commemorative interpretations of the past in the Brexit era was the Centenary of the First World War, but this popularisation of history was not confined to war memory. Memory of England's constitutional development and the debates about the British Empire also informed public life in the years and months before and after the Brexit referendum.

The English worldview that underpinned Brexit rested on three 'pillars' that linked English nationalism with Euroscepticism and the Anglosphere. This linkage made leaving the European Union seem desirable *and* possible. The first of these was a narrative concerning England's part in the development and extension of representative democracy. This narrative, which was derived from English Whig histories, underpinned Eurosceptic and Anglosphere worldviews. In this narrative, exemplified in the centenary re-publication *Our Island Story*, England was understood as the fount of representative democracy, an event linked back to Magna Carta in 1215 and even beyond to Anglo-Saxon forms of government. This argument was popularised by newly professional academic historians in the nineteenth and early twentieth centuries. This was a pivotal moment in the development of nationalism in general and one the helped inform subsequent English national consciousness when England's institutions were being developed in its overseas dominions. The endurance of the British state and its form of representative government in the face of existential threats in the first half of the twentieth century, gave it a providential air. But Imperial and Nazi Germany were not seen as the only threats to the endurance of this system. The Soviet threat forced the United Kingdom and the United States into a permanent post-war alliance and shored up ideas of Anglophone exceptionalism. This exceptionalism ultimately weakened the commitment of the English to that other anti-Soviet bulwark, European integration. The idea that the British system of representative democracy enshrined in the concept of parliamentary sovereignty might be incompatible with membership of the European Communities was first raised in the 1960s and 1970s. It was nurtured in the period of Conservative opposition between 1997 and 2010. It returned with full force after 2010, allied to the waning output legitimacy of the EU, and it eventually forced a referendum on the UK electorate when the party management of this issue proved too complicated for the Conservative leadership. The irony was that in defending parliamentary sovereignty by recourse to a referendum its supporters actually threatened to usurp Westminster as the ultimate sovereign in the United Kingdom by invoking popular sovereignty in its defence.

The second of these pillars was memory of Empire, a concept that had been rehabilitated since the end of Empire itself in the 1960s. Although there were important lineages, one of the elements that distinguished English nationalism in the Brexit era from its Powellite forerunner was the positive memory of the British Empire infusing English imaginaries of a post-EU UK. Despite this, the Anglosphere must not be dismissed simply as 'Empire 2.0' or an outlet for swashbuckling inclinations amongst English free traders. Although the memory of Empire was problematic as far as relations with the United States and Ireland were concerned, it was an important hinge that linked English nationalists with pasts and futures outside of the EU. It seemingly provided friends and allies to replace the diplomatic and trading ties with the EU weakened by the UK's disengagement from Europe, thereby appearing to solve a dilemma of its own creation. It did this in two ways: first by reconnecting England with its wider categories of belonging; and secondly by linking the English political imaginary to what we might call the broad, sunlit uplands of yesteryear. In this way, it created a positive narrative trajectory that helped imagine the United Kingdom outside of the European Union. Memory of Empire operated as a national heuristic, encouraging voters not to be 'Little Englanders' but to be 'greater Britons' once again.

Allied to this memory of Empire was the third pillar linking English nationalism, Euroscepticism and the Anglosphere: war memory, especially that of twentieth-century conflict. Although never reaching the intensity of the 1990s, war memory put England on a different trajectory to its EU counterparts. The Franco German narrative of 'never again' (the twentieth century understood as a catastrophe followed by renaissance) contrasted with the English narrative of the 'finest hour' (the twentieth century understood as an apogee followed by decline). This war memory aligned with Anglosphere notions of an English-speaking defence of liberty against totalitarianism and tyranny during the twentieth century. It was a major source of inspiration for the view that the world was a safer and better place when the English-speaking peoples acted in concert and were not divided by regional polities like the European Union. It was this perspective that allowed Brexiteers to appear sympathetic towards the EU's 'Nobel narrative', but also claim that this history was not 'our' history. Thus a vote for Brexit could be portrayed as a way to liberate Europe for a third time in a century even if the basis for comparing the EU to German domination of Europe or the operation of Soviet Communism was hardly well developed.

The 'our' in 'our history' leads us back to the blurred boundaries of English nationalism. The nation in common was often unspecified, but when it was referred to in England it often went by the name of Britain. This blurring was a historical product of the development of English nationalism within the British state and at the height of the British Empire. The expansion of British sovereignty required changing, yet seemingly constant, discursive means of legitimising the operation of that sovereignty over parts of the world far beyond England itself.

Yet this historic blurring had more contemporary drivers too. The Brexit vote itself was the result of an elite project sustained by popular grievances, a contingent cross-class and cross-party alliance that gave the vote its 'national' feel, even whilst it created new sources of political division. The Brexiteer project of seceding from the EU and realigning the UK with Anglosphere countries reached a particular intensity once the Conservatives were in government after 2010. This elite project, favourably disposed to free trade, was implicitly allied with popular grievances that were drivers of a newly politicised Englishness that found its greatest expression amongst the least educated of that nation and those most exposed to the negative effects of the political economy of a globalising United Kingdom.

Thus, although the elite rhetoric of Brexit was British, the animating force was English. The numerical preponderance of the English within the United Kingdom ensured that the UK-wide referendum was dominated by English concerns even if England itself rarely featured explicitly in the campaign rhetoric. English grievances coalesced around three main issues: devolution; resistance to and resentment towards European integration; and immigration, although the latter two categories merged after the eastern enlargement of the European Union in 2004–07. The issue of this linkage was made and exploited with particular effect by the UK Independence Party and helps to explain its electoral success in EP elections from 2009 and particularly in 2014. UKIP provided a good illustration of the blurred rhetoric of English nationalism. Although UKIP was avowedly seeking to defend the UK's sovereignty from what it saw as encroaching forms of European integration, the party's rhetoric was British, although its support was predominantly English. This contrasted with the growth in support for an explicit Scottish secessionism in the 'Brexit era' from 2010 to 2017 and provided a very different register to address national dilemmas north of the Tweed.

If Brexit should be considered as an 'English moment', an extended political event beginning with the election of 2010 and playing out during the UK's withdrawal from the EU, it raises the question of what happened to England after the vote. More pointedly it is worth asking, was the 'English moment' over once the referendum was won? The fate of UKIP in 2017 – a victim of its own success – suggested that the party that came closest to representing the 'resentful' English electorate was no longer needed in British politics. In the year between the Brexit referendum and the General Election of 2017, there was a concerted political effort to realign English nationalism to the political projects and causes that characterised its historical development. This was attempted by subsuming it in Unionist and Anglosphere projects. After 2016, Brexit was characterised by a three-level game. Theresa May's Government sought to simultaneously maintain the unity of the United Kingdom, take the UK out of the EU and realign the UK with Anglosphere countries to soften the rupture associated with secession from the EU. England was occluded once again.

The outcome of the 2017 General Election was characterised by irony. That which was supposed to deliver strong and stable government ended up greatly weakening and destabilising the incumbent's position. A loss for the Labour Party was nevertheless met with jubilation from opposition supporters. But the irony for England as a political community began before the election itself. England – a political community that had become a visible majority in the decade before Brexit – was subsumed not by progressives who were wary of its political expression during the surge in support for populist parties and policies in the second decade of the twenty-first century, but by those politicians who courted it in order to leave the EU. What was frequently described as a 'resurgent' English nationalism was subsumed in the unfolding political projects to which it had been historically conditioned to support: defence of British sovereignty and relations with the English-speaking peoples of the world. English nationalism helped engender the latest version of 'global Britain' as a pro-Union, Anglosphere-inclined government interpreted the Brexit vote in a way that spoke to the harshest expressions of Euroscepticism and framed its political project in language and actions designed to create a reassuring continuity in times of a major rupture. But the reliance on free trade, together with a hyper-globalist ideology stemming from hardened Brexiteers, risked reproducing the material conditions that had sustained the resentful part of the Brexit vote in the first place. Thus it was too soon for an elegy for England. England was not dead; it was just resting. Nevertheless, the politics of Brexit after 2016 were notable for an attempt to 'take back control' and put England back in its British box.

Analysing Brexit through the lens of English nationalism and its links with the Anglosphere allows us to open up mid-range explanations for the UK's withdrawal from the EU. It also allows us to analyse a case study of the operationalisation of

English nationalism. Arguments about sovereignty were where English nationalism and Euroscepticism most closely aligned. But an older animating tradition of the English-speaking peoples re-emerged to provide an alternative to membership of the European Union for Brexiteers. Importantly, this alternative aligned with traditions of thought and previous policies structuring an English worldview. Euroscepticism was the most formed-up and coherent expression of English nationalism in the years straddling the turn of the twenty-first century. When refracted through the mobilising device of a referendum, its historic alliance with the re-emergent Anglosphere ideology allowed it to find political expression at a most decisive historic moment. The contingent alliance between an elite project to leave the EU and a politicised English identity shifted Englishness from a mood, to a movement, and ultimately to a moment.

It may well be that this particular 'English moment' has passed. Brexiteers implied that England's bounds had been set – in the words of 'Land of Hope and Glory' – 'wider still and wider'. Having realised the principal goal of this version of England's historic trajectory, a politicised Englishness may find itself contained within a United Kingdom outside of the EU. But at the time of writing, the process had not yet played itself out. Other Englands were in the process of being created through political contestation and cultural expression. Some of these Englands were supportive of the European Union, some of the United Kingdom and some of neither. To modify Dean Acheson's famous appraisal of Britain's position in the early 1960s, through the politics of Brexit, England had lost Europe without yet finding a role.

References

Abbott, Tony. 1995. *The Minimal Monarchy and Why It Still Makes Sense for Australia*. Kent Town, SA: Wakefield Press.

Abbott, Tony. 2015. 'Transcript: Tony Abbott's controversial speech at the Margaret Thatcher Lecture', *Sydney Morning Herald*, 28 October 2015: www.smh.com.au/federal-politics/political-news/transcript-tony-abbotts-controversial-speech-at-the-margaret-thatcher-lecture-20151028-gkkg6p.html#ixzz3swUz7oo5, accessed 30 November 2015.

Abjorensen, Norman. 2009. 'The history wars', in Kim Huynh and Jim George (eds.), *The Culture Wars. Australian and American Politics in the 21st Century*. South Yarra, VIC: Palgrave Macmillan.

Anderson, Benedict. 1991. *Imagined Communities. Reflections on the Origins and Spread of Nationalism*. London: Verso.

Anthem4England. 2017. 'Welcome': anthem4england.co.uk, accessed 14 April 2017.

Ascherson, Neal. 2016. 'England prepares to leave the world', *London Review of Books*, 38, 22: 7–10: www.lrb.co.uk/v38/n22/neal-ascherson/england-prepares-to-leave-the-world, accessed 21 November 2016.

Aughey, Arthur. 2007. *The Politics of Englishness*. Manchester: Manchester University Press.

Aughey, Arthur. 2010a. 'Anxiety and injustice: the anatomy of contemporary English nationalism', *Nations and Nationalism*, 16, 3: 506–524.

Aughey, Arthur. 2010b. 'Fifth nation: the United Kingdom between definite and indefinite articles', *British Politics*, 5, 3: 265–285.

Aughey, Arthur. 2013. 'Review: *English Nationalism and Euroscepticism*', *Scottish Affairs*, 2013, 1: 115–118.

Aughey, Arthur. 2016. '"Never reflective because so obviously a fact": institutions and identity in English political thought', *Political Studies Review*, 16, 3: 349–358.

Aughey, Arthur. 2018. 'England and Britain in historical perspective', in Michael Kenny, Iain McLean and Akash Paun (eds.), *Governing England: English Institutions and Identity in a Changing United Kingdom*. London: British Academy/Oxford University Press.

Australian Broadcasting Corporation. 2017. 'As Theresa May triggers Article 50, what next for Britain's future?' *Lateline*, 29 March 2017: www.abc.net.au/lateline/as-theresa-may-triggers-article-50,-what-next-for/8399016, accessed 5 February 2018.

Bale, Tim. 2010. *The Conservative Party from Thatcher to Cameron*. Cambridge: Polity Press.

Balfour, Arthur. 1936 [1867]. 'Introduction', in Walter Bagehot, 1936 [1867], *The English Constitution*. London: Oxford University Press.

Banks, Arron. 2016. 'Judicial review: Statement from @Arron_Banks, Chairman of Leave. EU', 14 April 2016: bit.ly/1S9nTh8 #LeaveEU.

Barroso, José Manuel. 2007. 'We are all new Europeans now'. Speech at the Lithuanian Parliament, 29 March 2007: europa.eu/rapid/press-release_SPEECH-07–211_en.htm, accessed 4 April 2018.

Baxendale, Helen and Wellings, Ben. In press. 'Underwriting Brexit: the European Union in the Anglosphere imagination', in Ben Wellings and Andrew Mycock (eds.), *The Anglosphere: Continuity, Dissonance and Location*. London: British Academy/Oxford University Press.

BBC News. 2014. 'Cameron tells UKIP voters only Tories can deliver', 8 May 2014: www.bbc. com/news/uk-politics-27333322, accessed 9 May 2014.

BBC News. 2015a. 'Obama urges UK to stay in European Union' BBC News, 24 July 2015: www.bbc.com/news/uk-politics-33647154, accessed 14 February 2016.

BBC News. 2015b. 'David Cameron attacks Eurosceptic case ahead of summit', 28 October 2015: www.bbc.com/news/uk-politics-34654797, accessed 20 July 2018.

BBC News. 2016a. 'MPs back calls for English national anthem', 13 January 2016: www.bbc. com/news/uk-england-derbyshire-35296296, accessed 14 January 2016.

BBC News. 2016b. 'Brexit would make Britain like Guernsey, says French minister', 18 June: www.bbc.com/news/uk-politics-eu-referendum-36567469, accessed 19 June 2016.

BBC News. 2016c. 'EU referendum: leaving EU a stride into the light – Duncan Smith', 28 February 2016: www.bbc.com/news/uk-politics-35681525, accessed 29 February 2016.

BBC News. 2016d. 'Osborne says EU referendum "fight for UK's soul"', 8 June 2016: www.bbc.com/news/uk-politics-eu-referendum-36484357, accessed 6 May 2017.

BBC News. 2016e. 'EU referendum: Boris Johnson accuses Barack Obama of "hypocrisy"', 15 April 2016: www.bbc.com/news/uk-politics-eu-referendum-36057947, accessed 16 April 2016.

BBC News. 2016f. 'The dark depths of hatred for Hillary Clinton', 12 October 2016: www. bbc.com/news/magazine-36992955, accessed 13 October 2016.

BBC News. 2016g. 'EU referendum: US wants "strong UK in strong EU"', 13 February 2016: www.bbc.com/news/uk-politics-eu-referendum-35569134, accessed 14 February 2016.

BBC News. 2016h. 'UK stronger in EU, says New Zealand PM', 1 April 2016: www.bbc.com/ news/uk-politics-eu-referendum-35943388, accessed 2 April 2016.

BBC News. 2016i. 'Boris Johnson to skip EU special meeting on Trump win', 12 November 2016: www.bbc.com/news/uk-politics-37963046, accessed 13 November 2016.

BBC News. 2016j. 'Jo Cox: Man jailed for "terrorist" murder of MP', 23 November 2016: www.bbc.com/news/uk-38079594, accessed 24 November 2016.

BBC News. 2016k. 'Farage: "Real opportunity" for UK business with Donald Trump', 13 November 2016: www.bbc.com/news/uk-politics-37965089, accessed 14 November 2016.

BBC News EU Referendum. 2016a. 'Ex-CIA Director: EU "gets in way" of security services', BBC News EU Referendum, 25 March 2016: www.bbc.co.uk/news/uk-politics-eu-referendum-35898255, accessed 25 March 2016.

BBC News EU Referendum. 2016b. 'EU referendum: Australia would welcome In vote, says PM Turnbull', 1 May 2016: www.bbc.com/news/uk-politics-eu-referendum-36183444, accessed 2 May 2016.

BBC News Europe. 2013. 'David Cameron speech: UK and the EU', www.bbc.co.uk/news/uk-politics-21160684, accessed 24 January 2013.

BBC News Politics. 2014. 'UKIP gains first elected MP with Clacton win', www.bbc.com/news/uk-politics-29549414, accessed 10 October 2014.

BBC News Politics. 2015a. 'New "veto" announced for English MPs', BBC News Politics, 2 July 2015: www.bbc.com/news/uk-politics-33351688, accessed 25 June 2018.

BBC News Politics. 2015b. 'English votes plan "act of vandalism" warns Miliband, BBC News Politics', 7 July 2015: www.bbc.com/news/uk-politics-33415474, accessed 25 June 2018.

BBC News Politics. 2016a. 'The Nigel Farage story', BBC News, 4 July 2016: www.bbc.co.uk/news/uk-politics-36701855, accessed 4 July 2016.

BBC News Politics. 2016b. 'The daily politics: Norman Lamont on leaving the EU', 26 January 2016: www.bbc.com/news/uk-politics-35410796, accessed 27 January 2016.

BBC News Politics. 2017. 'Brexit: UK must not be EU "colony" after Brexit', BBC News Politics, 16 December 2017: www.bbc.com/news/uk-politics-42375059, accessed 16 December 2017.

BBC News Scotland. 2017a. 'General Election 2017: May urges Scots to "strengthen Union"', BBC News Scotland: www.bbc.com/news/uk-scotland-scotland-politics-39750467, accessed 30 April 2017.

BBC News Scotland. 2017b. 'PM Theresa May makes case of "our precious union"', BBC News Scotland, 3 March 2017: www.bbc.co.uk/news/uk-scotland-scotland-politics-39151250, accessed 16 July 2018.

Behr, Rafael. 2015. 'Marmite nation: is the idea of Britishness broken beyond repair?' *Guardian*, 8 July 2015, 31.

Behr, Raphael. 2016. 'How remain failed: the inside story of a doomed campaign', *Guardian*, 5 July 2016: www.theguardian.com/politics/2016/jul/05/how-remain-failed-inside-story-doomed-campaign, accessed 5 July 2016.

Bell, Duncan. 2007. *The Idea of Greater Britain: Empire and the Future of World Order, 1860–1900*. Princeton, NJ: Princeton University Press.

Bell, Duncan. 2017. 'The Anglosphere: new enthusiasm for an old dream', *Prospect*, 17 January 2017: www.prospectmagazine.co.uk/magazine/anglosphere-old-dream-brexit-role-in-the-world, accessed 24 May 2018.

Bennett, James. 2004. *The Anglosphere Challenge: Why the English-Speaking Nations Will Lead the Way in the Twenty-First Century*. Lanham, MD: Rowman and Littlefield.

Bentley, Michael. 2005. *Modernizing England's Past: English Historiography in the Age of Modernism, 1870–1970*. Cambridge: Cambridge University Press.

Berryman, Jim. 2015. 'Civilisation: a concept and its uses in Australian public discourse', *Australian Journal of Politics and History*, 61, 4: 591–605.

Bevir, Mark and Rhodes, Rod. 2003. *Interpreting British Governance*. Abingdon: Routledge.

Bevir, Mark and Rhodes, Rod. 2006. *Governance Stories*. Abingdon: Routledge.

Bevir, Mark; Daddow, Oliver and Hall, Ian. 2013. 'Introduction: interpreting British foreign policy', *British Journal of Politics and International Relations*, 15, 2: 163–174.

Bevir, Mark; Daddow, Oliver and Schnapper, Pauline. 2015. 'Interpreting British European policy', *Journal of Common Market Studies*, 53, 1: 1–17.

Billig, Michael. 1995. *Banal Nationalism*. London: Sage.

Black, Jeremy. 2018. *English Nationalism: A Short History*. London: Hurst.

Blair, Tony. 1999. 'Doctrine of the international community'. Speech given at the Economic Club, Chicago, IL, 24 April 1999: webarchive.nationalarchives.gov.uk/+/www.number10.gov.uk/Page1297, accessed 24 April 2018.

Blake, Aaron. 2015. 'The Obama presidency from socialist to dictator', *Washington Post*: www.washingtonpost.com/news/the-fix/wp/2015/01/20/the-obama-presidency-from-socialist-to-dictator/?noredirect=on&utm_term=.6626d10838d1, accessed 2 May 2018.

Boffey, Daniel. 2017. 'Brexit could help EU strike free trade deal with India, MEPs believe', *Guardian*, 23 February 2017: www.theguardian.com/politics/2017/feb/23/brexit-could-help-eu-strike-free-trade-deal-india-meps, accessed 26 February 2017.

Brack, Natalie and Startin, Nicholas. 2015. 'Introduction: Euroscepticism, from the margins to the mainstream', *International Political Sciences Review*, 36, 3: 239–249.

Breuilly, John. 2001. 'The State and Nationalism', in John Hutchinson and Monsterrat Guibernau (eds.), *Understanding Nationalism*. Cambridge: Polity Press.

British Futures. 2014. *Do Mention the War: Will 1914 Matter in 2014?* London: British Futures.

Brocklehurst, Helen. 2015. 'Educating Britain? Political literacy and the construction of national history', *Journal of Common Market Studies*, 53, 1: 52–70.

Bryant, Arthur. 1944. *The Years of Endurance, 1793–1802*. London: A. L. Rowse.

Burleigh, Michael. 2013. *Small Wars, Faraway Places: The Genesis of the Modern World, 1945–65*. London: Pan.

Cadman, Andrew. 2015. 'Let's quit the EU and join a new club based on the Anglosphere', *The Conservative Woman*, 28 May 2015: www.conservativewoman.co.uk/andrew-cadman-lets-quit-the-eu-and-join-a-new-club-based-on-the-anglosphere/, accessed 16 March 2016.

Cadot, Christine. 2014. 'Wars afterwards: the repression of the Great War in European collective memory', in Shanti Sumartojo and Ben Wellings (eds.), *Nation, Memory and Commemoration: Mobilizing the Past in Europe, Australia and New Zealand*. Bern: Peter Lang.

Cadwalladr, Carole; Graham-Harrison, Emma and Townsend, Mark. 2018. 'Revealed: Brexit insider claims Vote Leave team may have breached spending limits', *Guardian*, 24 March 2018: www.theguardian.com/politics/2018/mar/24/brexit-whistleblower-cambridge-analytica-beleave-vote-leave-shahmir-sanni, accessed 28 May 2018.

Cameron, David. 2011. 'Speech at the Munich Security Conference', 5 February 2011: www.gov.uk/government/speeches/pms-speech-at-munich-security-conference, accessed 15 December 2015.

Cameron, David. 2012. 'Speech at the Imperial War Museum', 11 October 2012: www.gov.uk/government/speeches/speech-at-imperial-war-museum-on-first-world-war-centenary-plans, accessed 20 July 2018.

Cameron, David. 2014a. 'The importance of Scotland to the UK.' Speech at the Lea Valley Velodrome, 7 February 2014: www.gov.uk//speeches/the-importance-of-scotland-to-the-uk-david-camerons-speech, accessed 21 April 2017.

Cameron, David. 2014b. 'British values aren't optional, they're vital' *Mail Online*, 15 June 2014: www.dailymail.co.uk/debate/article-2658171/DAVID-CAMERON-British-values-arent-optional-theyre-vital-Thats-I-promote-EVERY-school-As-row-rages-Trojan-Horse-takeover-classrooms-Prime-Minister-delivers-uncompromising-pledge.html, accessed 21 April 2017.

Cameron, David. 2014c. 'Australian Parliament: David Cameron's speech', 14 November 2014: www.gov.uk/government/speeches/australian-parliament-david-camerons-speech, accessed 1 May 2017.

Cameron. David. 2014d. 'St George's Day 2014: David Cameron's message', *UK Government*, 23 April 2014: www.gov.uk/government/news/st-georges-day-2014-david-camerons-message, accessed 7 May 2014.

Cameron, David. 2014e. 'Scottish Independence Referendum: statement by the Prime Minister', 19 September 2014: www.gov.uk/government/news/scottish-independence-referendum-statement-by-the-prime-minister, accessed 21 February 2019.

Cameron, David. 2016. 'PM speech on the UK's strength and security in the EU: 9 May 2016': www.gov.uk/government/speeches/pm-speech-on-the-uks-strength-and-security-in-the-eu-9-may-2016, accessed 8 July 2016.

Cannadine, David. 2003. *In Churchill's Shadow. Confronting the Past in Modern Britain.* Oxford: Oxford University Press.

Cannane, Steve. 2016. 'Brexit: Tory MP slams Turnbull for saying he would welcome the UK remaining in the EU', ABC News, 25 May 2016: www.abc.net.au/news/2016–05–26/tory-mp-takes-aim-at-turnbull-over-brexit/7446946, accessed 4 July 2016.

Carswell, Douglas. 2016. 'Beware the "expert consensus"', Douglas Carswell's Blog, 6 June 2016: talkcarswell.com/home/beware-the-expert-consensus/3070, accessed 4 July 2016.

Cavanagh Hodge, Carl. 2014. 'Weaving national narratives: 1812 and the Atlantic community', *Journal of Transatlantic Studies*, 12, 3: 304–323.

Chorley, Matt. 2015. 'Disgusting! Leave.EU campaign slammed for claiming that staying in the EU threatens the freedoms won by the war dead', *Mail Online*, 9 November 2015: www.dailymail.co.uk/news/article-3309180/Disgusting-Leave-EU-campaign-slammed-claiming-staying-EU-threatens-freedoms-won-war-dead.html, accessed 2 December 2016.

Christinidis, Georgia. 2015. '*Our Island Story*: renegotiating national history', *Journal for the Study of British Cultures*, 22, 2: 209–225.

Churchill, Winston. 1956. *A History of the English-speaking Peoples,* Vol. I: *The Birth of Britain.* London: Cassell.

Clark, Laura. 2009. 'Children to learn about blogging and climate change as Government reforms relegate history in curriculum', *Daily Mail*, 20 November 2009: www.dailymail.co.uk/news/article-1229241/Prince-Charles-mounts-fight-save-traditional-subjects-primary-schools-government-plans-new-themed-lessons.html, accessed 27 January 2015.

Cohen, Nick. 2015. 'Tories' EU mania will bring chaos', *Guardian Weekly*, 10 April 2015, 21.

Cohen, Nick. 2016. 'It's a Eurosceptic fantasy that the Anglosphere wants Brexit', *Spectator*, 12 April 2016: blogs.spectator.co.uk/2016/04/its-a-eurosceptic-fantasy-that-the-anglosphere-wants-brexit/, accessed 2 May 2018.

Colley, Linda. 1992. *Britons. Forging the Nation, 1707–1837.* London: Pimlico.

Colley, Linda. 2014. *Acts of Union and Disunion: What Has Held the UK Together – and What Is Dividing It?* London: Profile Books.

Condor, Susan and Abell, Jackie. 2006. 'Romantic Scotland, tragic England, ambivalent Britain: constructions of "the Empire" in post-devolution national accounting', *Nations and Nationalism*, 12, 3: 453–472.

Condor, Susan. 2010. 'Devolution and national identity: the rules of English (dis)enagagement', *Nations and Nationalism*, 16, 3: 525–543.

Congdon, Tim. 1992. 'Home is where our language is', *Spectator*, 5 September 1992.

Conquest, Robert. 2005. *Dragons of Expectation: Reality and Delusion in the Course of History.* New York: W. W. Norton.

ConservativeHome. 2012. 'An English anthem would give us pride without prejudice', 22 April 2012: www.conservativehome.com/thecolumnists/2012/07/exclusive-jerusalem-is-david-camerons-choice-as-englands-national-anthem.html, accessed 14 January 2016.

Convery, Alan. 2014. 'Devolution and the limits of Tory statecraft: the Conservative Party in coalition in Scotland and Wales', *Parliamentary Affairs*, 67, 1: 25–44.

Cook, George. 2018. *Express.co.uk*, 11 July 2018: 'Gareth Southgate says football can "heal divisions from Brexit" as squad approach final', *Express.co.uk*, 11 July 2018: www.express.co.uk/news/uk/986994/Football-heal-Brexit-divisions-Gareth-Southgate-World-Cup-final, accessed 17 July 2018.

Cowburn, Ashley. 2016. 'Boris Johnson accused of "dog whistle racism" over controversial Barack Obama Kenya remarks', *Independent*, 23 April 2016: www.independent.co.uk/news/uk/politics/boris-johnson-barack-obama-kenya-remarks-accused-dog-whistle-racism-john-mcdonnell-labour-a6996286.html, accessed 26 April 2016.

Cruz, Ted. 2016. 'Britain will be at the front of the queue for a US trade deal', *The Times*, 27 April 2016: www.thetimes.co.uk/article/britain-will-be-at-the-front-of-the-queue-for-a-us-trade-deal-vpg93g25r, accessed 28 April 2016.

Curtice, Sir John. 2018. 'How do the English want to be governed?', in Michael Kenny, Iain McLean and Akash Paun (eds.), *Governing England: English Institutions and Identity in a Changing United Kingdom*. London: British Academy/Oxford University Press.

Daddow, Oliver. 2006. 'Euroscepticism and the culture of the discipline of history', *Review of International Studies*, 32, 2: 309–328.

Daddow, Oliver. 2011. *New Labour and the European Union: Blair and Brown's Logic of History*. Manchester: Manchester University Press.

Daddow, Oliver. 2018. 'Brexit and British exceptionalism: the impossible challenge for remainers', LSE Blogs – Brexit: blogs.lse.ac.uk/brexit/2018/04/10/brexit-and-british-exceptionalism-the-impossible-challenge-for-remainers/#comment-36040, accessed 11 April 2018.

Daigneault, Pierre-Marc and Béland, Daniel. 2015. 'Taking explanation seriously in political science', *Political Studies Review*, 13, 3: 384–392.

Daily Mail. 2016. 'Daily Mail comment: who will speak for England?', 3 February 2016: www.dailymail.co.uk/debate/article-3430870/DAILY-MAIL-COMMENT-speak-England.html, accessed 19 February 2016.

Daily Telegraph. 2016. 'Aussie Navy has its own shade of grey', 26 March 2016.

Dal Santo, Matthew. 2016. 'Britain's history almost demands a Brexit happen', *ABC The Drum*, 1 March 2016: www.abc.net.au/news/2016-03-01/dal-santo-britain's-history-almost-demands-a-brexit-happen/7209620, accessed 17 April 2016.

Davis, David. 2016. 'Britain would be better off out of the EU – and here's why', *Conservative Home*, 4 February 2016: www.conservativehome.com/platform/2016/02/david-davis-britain-would-be-better-off-out-of-the-eu-and-heres-why.html, accessed 16 March 2016.

Dearlove, Richard. 2016. 'Brexit would not damage UK security', *Prospect*, 23 March 2016: www.prospectmagazine.co.uk/opinions/brexit-would-not-damage-uk-security, accessed 24 March 2016.

Delingpole, James. 2016. 'Independence day created greatest empire the world will ever know: the Anglosphere', *Breitbart*, 2 July 2016: www.breitbart.com/big-government/2016/07/02/independence-day-created-the-greatest-empire-the-world-will-ever-know-the-anglosphere/, accessed 21 April 2017.

Dewey, Robert. 2009. *British National Identity and Opposition to the Membership of Europe, 1961–63. The Anti-marketeers*. Manchester: Manchester University Press.

Dilke, Charles. 1869. *Greater Britain: A Record of Travel in the English Speaking Countries during 1866 and 1867*. London: Macmillan.

Dittmer, Jason. 2015. 'Everyday diplomacy: UK-USA intelligence cooperation and geopolitical assemblages', *Annals of the Association of American Geographers*, 105, 3: 604–619.

Economist. 2016. 'More special in Europe', *The Economist*, 23 April 2016: www.economist.com/news/britain/21697251-britains-eu-referendum-nears-barack-obama-joins-remain-campaign-more-special-europe?frsc=dg%7Cd, accessed 28 April 2016.

Economist. 2017. 'The shadow of Enoch Powell looms ever-larger over Britain', *The Economist*, 6 April 2017, 2–4.

Edensor, Tim. 2002. *National Identity, Popular Culture and Everyday Life*. Oxford: Berg.

Edensor, Tim and Sumartojo Shanti. 2018. 'Geographies of everyday nationhood: Experiencing multiculturalism in Melbourne', *Nations and Nationalism*, 24, 3: 553–578.

Efstathiou, Zoe. 2016. 'Outrage as new EU health and safety law wipes out century long Armistice Day tradition', *Express*, 10 November 2016: www.express.co.uk/news/uk/730719/eu-brussels-armistice-day-health-and-safety-poppy-world-war-one-law-remembrance, accessed 12 November 2016.

Eilstrup-Sangiovani, Mette (ed.). 2006. *Debates on European Integration: A Reader*. Basingstoke: Palgrave Macmillan.

Elkins, Caroline. 2005. *Britain's Gulag: The Brutal End of Empire in Kenya*. London: Jonathan Cape.

English, Richard; Hayton, Richard and Kenny, Michael. 2009. 'Englishness and the Union in contemporary Conservative thought', *Government and Opposition*, 44, 4: 343–365.

EU Observer. 2016. 'Post-Brexit UK more racist and homophobic', 13 October 2016: euobserver.com/tickers/135494, accessed 16 October 2016.

European Commission. 2018. 'Negotiations and agreements': ec.europa.eu/trade/policy/countries-and-regions/negotiations-and-agreements/, accessed 9 May 2018.

European Council, 2001. 'Laeken Declaration': www.consilium.europa.eu/media/20950/68827.pdf, accessed 20 July 2018.

European Council. 2007. 'Berlin Declaration': europa.eu/50/docs/berlin_declaration_en.pdf, accessed 20 July 2018.

European Union. 2016. 'Schuman Declaration – 9 May 2016': europa.eu/european-union/about-eu/symbols/europe-day/schuman-declaration_en, accessed 21 November 2016.

European Union. 2017. '60 years of the Rome Treaties': europa.eu/european-union/eu60_en, accessed 9 April 2018.

European Union. 2018. 'The Schuman Declaration – 9 May 1950': europa.eu/european-union/about-eu/symbols/europe-day/schuman-declaration_en, accessed 29 June 2018.

Evans, Gareth. 2016. 'The Anglosphere illusion', *Project Syndicate*, 18 February 2016: www.project-syndicate.org/commentary/uk-little-global-influence-after-brexit-by-gareth-evans-2016–02?barrier=accessreg, accessed 2 May 2018.

Evans, Geoffrey and Mellon, Jonathan. 2016. 'Working class votes and Conservative losses: solving the UKIP puzzle', *Parliamentary Affairs* 69, 2: 464–479.

Evans, Richard. 2012. '1066 and all that', *New Statesman*, 23 January 2012: www.newstatesman.com/education/2012/01/british-history-schools, accessed 16 April 2018.

Express, 2010. 'Get Britain out of Europe'. www.express.co.uk/web/europecrusade, accessed 13 March 2019.

Ferguson, Niall. 2003. *Empire. How Britain Made the Modern World*. London: Penguin Books.

Finlayson, Alan. 2017. 'Interpretation and social explanation', *Political Studies Review*, 15, 2: 210–221.

Fitzgibbon, John; Leruth, Benjamin and Startin, Nick (eds.). 2017. *Euroscepticism as a Transnational and Pan-European Phenomenon: The Emergence of a New Sphere of Opposition*. Abingdon: Routledge.

Flinders, Matthew. 2018. 'The (anti-)politics of Brexit', in Patrick Diamond, Peter Nedergaard and Ben Rosamond (eds.), *The Routledge Handbook of the Politics of Brexit*. Abingdon: Routledge.

Foot, Paul. 1969. *The Rise of Enoch Powell*. London: Penguin Books.

Ford, Robert and Goodwin, Matthew. 2014. *Revolt on the Right: Explaining Support for the Radical Right in Britain*. Abingdon: Routledge.

Forsyth, James. 2013. 'The New Colonials can raise our sights beyond the Channel', *The Spectator*, 18 July 2013, blogs.spectator.co.uk/coffeehouse/2013/07/the-new-colonials-can-raise-our-sights-beyond-the-channel/, accessed 25 February 2019.

Fox, Liam. 2016. 'Fox on Friday: Brexit can liberate Europe for a third time in 100 hundred years', *Conservative Woman*, 22 April 2016: www.conservativewoman.co.uk/fox-on-friday-brexit-can-liberate-europe-for-the-third-time-in-100-years/, accessed 28 April 2016.

Fox, Liam. 2017. 'US talks are just the start of exciting new free-trade era', *Telegraph*, 18 June 2017: www.telegraph.co.uk/news/2017/06/18/us-talks-just-start-exciting-new-free-trade-era/, accessed 19 June 2017.

Fox, Liam. 2018. 'Speech: Global economic outlook: trade, growth and the Commonwealth', 16 April 2018: www.gov.uk/government/speeches/global-economic-outlook-trade-growth-and-the-commonwealth, accessed 19 July 2018.

Frost, David. 2016. 'Don't panic, here's how Brexit can make Britain can be a great trading nation', *Telegraph*, 30 June 2016: www.telegraph.co.uk/news/2016/06/30/dont-panic-heres-how-brexit-can-make-britain-can-be-a-great, accessed 2 July 2016.

Froude, James. 1886. *Oceana. England and her Colonies*. London: Longman, Green.

Gamble, Andrew. 2003. *Between Europe and America: The Future of British Politics*. Basingstoke: Palgrave.

Gamble, Andrew. 2016. 'The Conservatives and the Union: the "new English Toryism" and the origins of Anglo-Britishness', *Political Studies Review*, 16, 3: 359–367.

Gamble, Andrew. 2017. 'British politics after Brexit', *Political Insight*, April 2017.

Gellner, Ernest. 1983. *Nations and Nationalism*. London: Blackwell.

George, Stephen. 1998. *An Awkward Partner: Britain in the European Community*. Oxford: Oxford University Press.

Gifford, Chris. 2014. *The Making of Eurosceptic Britain*, 2nd edn. Farnham: Ashgate.

Gifford, Chris. 2015. 'Nationalism, populism and Anglo-British Euroscepticism', *British Politics*, 10, 3: 362–366.

Gifford, Chris. 2016. 'The United Kingdom's Eurosceptic political economy', *British Journal of Politics and International Relations*, 18, 4: 779–794.

Gillis, John R. 1994. 'Memory and identity: the history of a relationship', in John R. Gillis (ed.), *Commemorations: the Politics of National Identity*. Princeton, NJ: Princeton University Press.

Gilroy, Paul. 2004. *After Empire: Melancholia or Convivial Culture?* Abingdon: Routledge.

Glenday, James. 2016. 'Australia, Canada, NZ and UK support EU-style free movement, new poll says', ABC News, 13 March 2016: www.abc.net.au/news/2016–03–13/australia-canada-nz-support-eu-style-free-movement-poll-says/7242634, accessed 13 March 2016.

Gove, Michael. 2009. 'Speech to the Royal Society of Arts', 30 June 2009.

Gove, Michael. 2016. 'The facts of life say leave: why Britain and Europe will be better off after we vote leave', *Huffington Post*, 19 April 2016: www.huffingtonpost.co.uk/michael-gove/michael-gove-vote-leave_b_9728548.html, accessed 17 April 2018.

Gover, Daniel and Kenny, Michael. 2016. *Finding the Good in EVEL: An Evaluation of 'English Votes for English Laws' in the House of Commons*. London: Centre on Constitutional Change.

Grant, Susan-Mary. 2005. 'Raising the dead: war, memory and American national identity', *Nations and Nationalism*, 11, 4: 509–529.

Graves, Matthew. 2014. 'Memorial diplomacy in Franco-Australian relations', in Shanti Sumartojo and Ben Wellings (eds.), *Nation, Memory and Commemoration: Mobilizing the Past in Europe, Australia and New Zealand*. Bern: Peter Lang.

Greenfeld, Liah. 1992. *Nationalism: Five Roads to Modernity*. Cambridge, MA: Harvard University Press.

Guardian. 2016. 'The Guardian view on the EU debate: it's about much more than migration', *Guardian*, 2 June 2016: www.theguardian.com/commentisfree/2016/jun/01/the-guardian-view-on-the-eu-debate-its-about-much-more-than-migration, accessed 2 June 2016.

Gulmanelli, Stefano. 2014. 'John Howard and the "Anglospherist" reshaping of Australia', *Australian Journal of Political Science*, 49, 4: 581–595.

HAEU. 1931. PAN/EU 000007, 'Letter from Count Richard Coudenhove-Kalergi to Leo Amery', 6 November 1931.

HAEU. 1951. JMDS/70, 'Declaration of Mr. Walter Hallstein', 19 March 1951.

Hague, William. 2013. 'Fourth John Howard lecture. Speech at the Menzies Research Centre, Sydney, January 2013': www.menziesrc.org/fourth-howard-lecture-william-hague, accessed 1 October 2018.

Hague, William. 2015. 'Why I will be voting to stay in Europe', *Telegraph*, 22 December 2015: www.telegraph.co.uk/news/newstopics/eureferendum/12064244/Why-I-will-be-voting-to-stay-in-Europe.html, accessed 11 January 2016.

Hannan, Daniel. 2011. 'Parliament finally debates In/Out referendum: BBC sees only "Tory splits"', *Telegraph*, 18 October 2011: blogs.telegraph.co.uk/news/danielhannan/100111867/the-house-of-commons-will-finally-divide-on-whether-to-give-us-an-inout-referendum-whats-the-betting-that-the-bbc-report-it-wholly-as-a-tory-splits-story/, accessed 30 November 2011.

Hannan, Daniel. 2013. *Inventing Freedom: How the English-speaking Peoples Made the Modern World*. London: HarperCollins.

Hannan, Daniel. 2015. 'Forget the EU, let's take on the world with our TRUE friends', *Daily Mail*, www.dailymail.co.uk/news/article-2922715/Forget-EU-let-s-world-TRUE-friends-Greek-elections-threaten-shatter-Europe-DANIEL-HANNAN-says-Britain-s-destiny-lies-booming-Commonwealth.html, accessed 6 October 2015.

Hansard. 2000. 18 January, vol. 342, col. 689. London: HMSO.

Hansard. 2011. 24 October, vol. 534, part 1, col. 48. London: HMSO.

Hansard. 2013a. 5 July, vol. 565, col. 1202. London: HMSO.

Hansard. 2013b. 7 November, vol. 570, col. 484. London: HMSO.

Hansard. 2014a. 4 June, vol. 582, col. 15. London: HMSO.

Hansard. 2014b. 4 June, vol. 582, col. 24. London: HMSO.

Hansard. 2015a. 22 October, vol. 600, col. 1119. London: HMSO.

Hansard. 2015b. 28 October, vol. 601, col. 345. London: HMSO.

Hansard. 2016a. 13 January, vol. 604, col. 866. London: HMSO.

Hansard. 2016b. 6 June, vol. 611, col. 1184. London: HMSO.

Hansard. 2018. 16 July, vol. 645, col. 83. London: HMSO.

Hardt, Michael and Negri, Antonio. 2000. *Empire*. Cambridge MA: Harvard University Press.

Hastings, Adrian. 1997. *The Construction of Nationhood. Ethnicity, Religion and Nationalism*. Cambridge: Cambridge University Press.

Hayton, Richard. 2012. *Reconstructing Conservatism: The Conservative Party in Opposition, 1997–2010*. Manchester: Manchester University Press.

Hayton, Richard. 2016. 'The UK Independence Party and the politics of Englishness', *Political Studies Review*, 16, 3: 400–410.

Hayton, Richard. 2018. 'Brexit and the Conservative Party', in Patrick Diamond, Peter Nedergaard and Ben Rosamond (eds.), *The Routledge Handbook of the Politics of Brexit*. Abingdon: Routledge.

Hearn, Jonathan. 2006. *Rethinking Nationalism: A Critical Introduction*. Basingstoke: Palgrave Macmillan.

Heath, Allister. 2015. 'Europhiles think history is on their side – they could be in for a shock', *Telegraph*, 11 November 2015, www.telegraph.co.uk/news/newstopics/eureferendum/11989773/Allister-Heath-Europhiles-think-history-is-on-their-side-they-could-be-in-for-a-shock.html, accessed 14 November 2015.

Heffer, Simon. 1998. *Like the Roman: The Life of Enoch Powell*. London: Weidenfeld & Nicolson.

Henderson, Ailsa; Jeffery, Charlie; Scully, Roger; Wincott, Daniel and Wyn Jones, Richard. 2017. 'How Brexit was made in England', *British Journal of Politics and International Relations* 19, 4: 631–646.

Hennig, Benjamin and Dorling, Danny. 2016. 'In focus: the EU Referendum'. *Political Insight*, September 2016, 20–21.

Henry, Julie. 2011. 'Prince Charles's elite teachers will bring back Chaucer and the Crusades', 6 November 2011, www.telegraph.co.uk/news/uknews/prince-charles/8872095/Prince-Charless-elite-teachers-will-bring-back-Chaucer-and-the-Crusades.html, accessed 27 January 2015.

Heppell, Timothy. 2014. *The Tories: From Winston Churchill to David Cameron*. London: Bloomsbury, 133.

Herbert, Nick. 2016. 'The EU must know we're prepared to quit', *Telegraph*, 16 January 2016: www.telegraph.co.uk/news/newstopics/eureferendum/12103757/The-EU-must-know-were-prepared-to-quit.html, accessed 19 January 2016.

Hinsliff, Gabby. 2016. 'As Trudeaumania torches the internet, it's time to realise that there is indeed a vision of what a progressive Britain could be. And it's called Canada', *Guardian Weekly*, 194, 18, 8–14 April 2016: 48.

Hix, Simon. 2010. *What's Wrong with the European Union and How to Fix It*. Cambridge: Polity Press.

Hochschild, Adam. 1999. *King Leopold's Ghost: A Story of Greed, Terror and Heroism in Colonial Africa*. London: Pan Books.

Hoey, Kate. 2015. 'Why leaving the EU is a left wing move', *Independent*, 9 October 2015: www.independent.co.uk/voices/labour-mp-kate-hoey-why-leaving-the-eu-is-a-left-wing-move-a6687936.html, accessed 22 October 2015.

Holmes, Brenton. 2013. 'Tracking the push for an Australian republic', www.aph.gov.au/About_Parliament/Parliamentary_Departments/Parliamentary_Library/pubs/BN/2012–2013/AustralianRepublic, accessed 18 April 2018.

Hooghe, Leisbet and Marks, Gary. 2009. 'A post-functionalist theory of European integration: from permissive consensus to constraining dissensus', *British Journal of Political Science*, 39, 1: 1–23.

House of Lords Constitution Committee. 2016. *The Union and Devolution*, H. L. Papers 149. London: HMSO.

Hunt, Tristram. 2016. 'The lion and the unicorn: socialism and England in the 21st century. Public lecture for the Centre for English Identity and Politics'. University of Winchester, 4 February 2016.

Hutchinson, John. 2005. *Nations as Zones of Conflict*. London: Sage.

Huynh, Kim. 2016. 'Us and them: national identity and the question of belonging', in Jim George and Kim Huynh (eds.), *The Culture Wars: American and Australian Politics in the Twenty-first Century*. South Yarra: Palgrave Macmillan Australia.

Ichijo, Atsuko; Fox, John; Aughey, Arthur; McCrone, David and Bechofer, Frank. 2017. 'Debate on *Understanding National Identity* by David McCrone and Frank Bechofer', *Nations and Nationalism*, 23, 3: 441–462.

Ingham, Bernard. 2016. 'One foot in the grave if Britain doesn't vote to leave the EU', *Yorkshire Post*, 27 January 2016: www.yorkshirepost.co.uk/news/opinion/bernard-ingham-one-foot-in-the-grave-if-britain-doesn-t-vote-to-leave-eu-1-7698291#ixzz3yVF5aADw, accessed 28 January 2016.

ITV News. 2016. 'Cameron urges voters to not go for "Little England" option', ITV News, 7 June 2016: www.itv.com/news/update/2016–06–07/cameron-urges-voters-to-not-go-for-little-england-option/, accessed 6 May 2017.

James, Paul. 1996. *Nation Formation: Towards a Theory of Abstract Community*. London: Sage.

Jeffery, Charlie and Wincott, Daniel. 2010. 'The challenge of territorial politics: beyond methodological nationalism', in Colin Hay (ed.), *New Directions in Political Science: Responding to the Challenges of an Interdependent World*. Basingstoke: Palgrave Macmillan.

Jeffery, Charlie; Henderson, Ailsa; Scully, Roger and Wyn Jones, Richard. 2016. 'England's dissatisfactions and the Conservative dilemma', *Political Studies Review*, 16, 3: 335–348.

Jeffries, Stuart. 2014. 'Blackadder: your country needs you', *Guardian*, 7 January 2014: www.theguardian.com/world/2014/jan/06/blackadder-michael-gove-historians-first-world-war, accessed 1 October 2014.

Johnson, Boris. 2013. 'The Aussies are just like us, so let's stop kicking them out', *Telegraph*, www.telegraph.co.uk/news/politics/10265619/The-Aussies-are-just-like-us-so-lets-stop-kicking-them-out.html, accessed 20 July 2018.

Johnson, Boris. 2014. *The Churchill Factor: How One Man Made History*. London: Hodder & Stoughton.

Johnson, Boris. 2016a. 'There is only one way to get the change we want – vote to leave the EU', *Telegraph*, 21 February 2016: www.telegraph.co.uk/news/newstopics/eureferendum/12167643/Boris-Johnson-there-is-only-one-way-to-get-the-change-we-want-vote-to-leave-the-EU.html, accessed 22 February 2016.

Johnson, Boris. 2016b. 'Please vote leave on Thursday, because we'll never get this chance again', *Telegraph*, 19 June 2016: www.telegraph.co.uk/news/2016/06/19/please-vote-leave-on-thursday-because-well-never-get-this-chance/, accessed 21 June 2016.

Kaiser, Wolfram. 2010. 'From isolation to centrality: contemporary history meets European Studies', in Kaiser Wolfram and Varsori Antonio (eds.), *European Union History, Themes and Debates*. Basingstoke: Palgrave Macmillan.

Kamal, Ahmed. 2012. 'Forget Europe, it's time for the Commonwealth', *Telegraph*, 11 February 2012: www.telegraph.co.uk/finance/comment/kamal-ahmed/9076348/Forget-Europe-its-time-for-the-Commonwealth.html, accessed 2 May 2018.

Kenny, Michael. 2012. 'The political theory of recognition: the case of the "white working class"', *British Journal of Politics and International Relations*, 14, 1: 19–38.

Kenny, Michael. 2014. *The Politics of English Nationhood*. Oxford: Oxford University Press.

Kenny, Michael. 2016. 'The "politicisation" of Englishness: towards a framework for political analysis', *Political Studies Review*, 14, 3: 325–334.

Kenny, Michael; Kumar, Krishan; Aughey, Arthur and Wellings, Ben. 2016. 'Symposium on Michael Kenny's *The Politics of English Nationhood*', *British Politics*, 11, 3: 348–370.

Kenny, Michael and Pearce, Nick. 2018. *Shadows of Empire: The Anglosphere in British Politics*. Cambridge: Polity Press.

Khan, Mehreen. 2017. 'Boris Johnson welcomes Trump's promise on UK-UK trade deal', *Financial Times*, 16 January 2017: www.ft.com/content/67e394da-ef43-30e4-a0d5-dec01046c5fc, accessed 18 July 2018.

Khan, Omar and Weekes-Bernard, Debbie. 2015. *This is Still About Us: Why Ethnic Minorities See Immigration Differently*. London: Runnymede Trust.

Knight, Sam. 2016. 'The man who brought you Brexit', *Guardian*, 29 September 2016: www.theguardian.com/politics/2016/sep/29/daniel-hannan-the-man-who-brought-you-brexit, accessed 19 January 2018.

Kohn, Hans. 2008 [1944]. *The Idea of Nationalism: a Study in Its Origins and History*. New Brunswick, NJ: Transaction.

Kumar, Krishan. 2003. *The Making of English National Identity*. Cambridge: Cambridge University Press, 34.

Kumar, Krishan. 2006. 'Empire and English nationalism', *Nations and Nationalism*, 12, 1: 1–13.

Kumar, Krishan. 2015. *The Idea of Englishness: English Culture, National Identity and Social Thought*. Abingdon: Routledge.

Kwarteng, Kwasi; Patel, Priti; Raab, Dominic; Skidmore, Chris and Truss, Elizabeth. 2012. *Britannia Unchained: Global Lessons for Growth and Prosperity.* Basingstoke: Palgrave Macmillan.

Landale, James. 2017. 'Brexit memo to Boris Johnson: don't mention the war', BBC News, 18 January 2017: www.bbc.com/news/world-europe-38670349, accessed 19 January 2017.

Laughland, John. 2008. 'Why the "Anglosphere" is no alternative for the EU,' *The Brussels Journal*, 1 February 2008: www.brusselsjournal.com/node/2821, accessed 22 March 2011.

Lawson, Nigel. 2016. 'The EU exists only to become a superstate: Britain has no place in it', *Telegraph*, 2 May 2016: www.telegraph.co.uk/news/2016/05/02/the-eu-exists-only-to-become-a-superstate-britain-has-no-place-i/, accessed 5 May 2016.

LBC. 2018. 'Brits would rather leave the EU than keep Northern Ireland: LBC poll', 28 March 2018: www.lbc.co.uk/hot-topics/brexit/brits-would-rather-leave-eu-than-keep-n-ireland/, accessed 16 July 2018.

Leach, Robert. 2002. *Political Ideology in Britain*. Basingstoke: Palgrave.

Leave.EU. 2016. 'Make 23 June our Independence Day', n.d.

Leconte, Cécile. 2010. *Understanding Euroscepticism*. Basingstoke: Palgrave Macmillan.

Leconte, Cécile. 2015. 'From pathology to mainstream phenomenon: reviewing the Euroscepticism debate in research and theory', *International Political Science Review*, 36, 3: 250–263.

Legrand, Tim. 2016. 'Elite, exclusive and elusive: transgovernmental policy networks and iterative policy transfer in the Anglosphere', *Policy Studies*, 37, 5: 440–445.

Leonard, Mark. 2015. 'What would a UK outside the EU look like?' *Guardian*, 5 October 2015: www.theguardian.com/commentisfree/2015/oct/05/brussels-eurosceptics-british-voter-out-lobby, accessed 2 July 2016.

Lequesne, Christian. 2018. 'Brexit and future of EU theory', in Patrick Diamond, Peter Nedergaard and Ben Rosmand (eds.), *The Routledge Handbook of the Politics of Brexit*. Abingdon: Routledge.

Levy, Daniel; Pensky, Max and Torpey, John. 2003. *Old Europe, New Europe, Core Europe*. London: Verso.

Liberal Democratic Voice. 2015. 'Nick Clegg's Speech to Conference, 21 September 2015': www.libdemvoice.org/in-full-nick-cleggs-speech-to-conference-47589.html, accessed 22 September 2015.

Lidington, David. 2010. 'Written ministerial statement on European Union Bill, 13 September 2010': www.fco.gov.uk/en/news/latest-news/?view=PressS&id=22851533, accessed 30 November 2011.

Liew, Jonathan. 2016. 'Sir Ian Botham ready to thrive in time of great uncertainty and hit the EU for six', *Telegraph*, 31 May 2016: www.telegraph.co.uk/cricket/2016/05/31/sir-ian-botham-ready-to-hit-the-eu-for-six/, accessed 1 June 2016.

Lloyd, John. 2000. 'The right prepares for cultural war', *New Statesman*, 27 November 2000: www.newstatesman.com/200011270012, accessed 29 March 2011.

Lord Ashcroft Polls. 2016. 'How the United Kingdom voted on Thursday … and why', 24 June 2016: lordashcroftpolls.com/2016/06/how-the-united-kingdom-voted-and-why/, accessed 29 June 2018.

Lord Howell and Hewish, Tim. 2016. 'Restricting skilled worker visas will hit the economy and harm UK-Commonwealth relations', 21 January 2016: www.cityam.com/232814/restricting-skilled-worker-visas-will-hit-the-economy-and-harm-uk-commonwealth-relations, accessed 13 March 2016.

Loveridge, Steven. 2015. 'The "other" on the other side of the ditch? The conception of New Zealand's disassociation from Australia', *Journal of Imperial and Commonwealth History*, 44, 1: 70–94.

Lynch, Philip. 2015. 'Conservative modernisation and European integration: from silence to salience and schism', *British Politics*, 10, 2: 185–203.

Lynch, Philip and Whitaker, Richard. 2013. 'Rivalry on the Right: the Conservatives, the UK Independence Party (UKIP) and the EU issue', *British Politics*, 8, 3: 285–312.

Macrory, Sam. 2017. 'Lord Heseltine: "Germany lost the war. Brexit hands them the chance to win the peace"', *The House Magazine*, 23 March 2017: www.politicshome.com/news/uk/house/house-magazine/84510/lord-heseltine-"germany-lost-war-brexit-hands-them-chance-win, accessed 25 March 2017.

Magna Carta Trust. 2015. 'Events: a global event to which the whole world is invited', http://magnacarta800th.com/events/, accessed 29 April 2017.

Mair, Peter. 2013. *Ruling the Void: the Hollowing of Western Democracy*. London: Verso.

Major, John. 1993 'Australia and Britain: a relationship which matters'. Speech by the Prime Minister, the Right Honourable John Major MP to the Britain-Australia Society, 21 January 1993, in M. Kooyman and P. Beckingham (eds.), *Australia and Britain: The Evolving Relationship*. Melbourne, VIC: Monash ANZ Centre for International Briefing.

Major, John. 2014. 'John Major's Berlin speech: the full text', 13 November 2014, www.telegraph.co.uk/news/worldnews/europe/eu/11229927/John-Majors-Berlin-Speech-the-full-text.html, accessed 19 January 2015.

Major, John. 2016. 'Voting to leave will poison Europe and divide West', *Telegraph*, 20 March 2016: www.telegraph.co.uk/news/newstopics/eureferendum/12199111/John-Major-Voting-to-leave-will-poison-Europe-and-divide-West.html, accessed 21 March 2016.

Malouf, David. 2003. *Made in England: Australia's British Inheritance (Quarterly Essay 12)*. Melbourne, VIC: Black.

Mandel, Daniel. 2005. 'The secret history of the Anglosphere', *IPA Review*, December 2005: 31–32.

Mandler, Peter. 2006. *The English National Character: The History of an Idea from Edmund Burke to Tony Blair*. New Haven, CT: Yale University Press.

Mann, Robin and Fenton, Steve. 2017. *Nation, Class and Resentment: The Politics of National Identity in England, Scotland and Wales*. Basingstoke: Palgrave.

Manners, Ian and Murray, Philomena. 2016. 'The end of a noble narrative? European integration narratives after the Noble Peace Prize', *Journal of Common Market Studies*, 54, 1: 185–202.

Marquand, David. 2017. 'Britain's problem is not with Europe, but with England', *Guardian*, 19 December 2017: www.theguardian.com/commentisfree/2017/dec/19/britain-problem-not-europe-england-brexit-englishness, accessed 8 January 2018.

Marshall, Henrietta. 2005 [1905]. *Our Island Story: A History of Britain for Boys and Girls from the Romans to Queen Victoria*. London: Civitas.

Marshall, Peter. 2013. 'Forty years on: Britain in the EU', *Round Table*, 102, 1: 15–28.

Mason, Rowena. 2014. 'Emily Thornberry Resigns from shadow cabinet over Rochester tweet', *Guardian*, 2014: www.theguardian.com/politics/2014/nov/20/emily-thornberry-resigns-rochester-tweet-labour-shadow-cabinet, accessed 18 April 2017.

Mass-Observation Archive (University of Sussex). 1982. Special Directive 1982, EEC Membership – Report on Material.

May, Theresa. 2016. 'Statement from the new Prime Minister Theresa May, 13 July 2016': www.gov.uk/government/speeches/statement-from-the-new-prime-minister-theresa-may, accessed 18 September 2016.

May, Theresa. 2017. 'Prime Minister's letter to Donald Tusk triggering Article 50', 29 March 2017: www.gov.uk/government/publications/prime-ministers-letter-to-donald-tusk-triggering-article-50, accessed 17 July 2018.

Mazower, Mark. 2014. *Governing the World: The History of an Idea*. London: Penguin.

McCauley, James. 2014. 'Divergent memories: remembering and forgetting the Great War in loyalist and nationalist Ireland', in Shanti Sumartojo, and Ben Wellings (eds.), *Nation, Memory and Great War Commemoration. Mobilizing the Past in Europe, Australia and New Zealand*. Oxford: Peter Lang.

McCormick, John. 2014. *Understanding the European Union: A Concise Introduction*. Basingstoke: Palgrave.

McCrone, David. 1998. *Sociology of Nationalism: Tomorrow's Ancestors*. London: Routledge.

McGowan, L. and Phinnemore, D. 2017. 'The UK: membership in crisis', in Desmond Dinan, Neill Nugent and William Paterson (eds.), *The European Union in Crisis*. Basingstoke: Palgrave Macmillan.

McKenna, Mark. 2018. *Moment of Truth: History and Australia's Future* (*Quarterly Essay*, 69). Carlton, VIC: Black.

McTague, Tom. 2014. 'British Embassy in Washington sparks fury after holding a party to "commemorate" 200th anniversary of the burning of the White House', *Mail Online*, 25 August 2014: www.dailymail.co.uk/news/article-2733672/British-Embassy-Washington-sparks-fury-holding-party-commemorate-200th-anniversary-burning-White-House.html, accessed 21 November 2016.

Merrick, Rob. 2017. 'Brexit: David Davis urges Cabinet to draw up back-up plans for UK leaving EU without fresh trade deal', *Independent*, 28 February 2017: www.independent.co.uk/news/uk/politics/brexit-latest-news-david-davis-cabinet-back-up-plan-uk-leave-eu-trade-deal-wto-a7603911.html, accessed 2 March 2017.

Miliband, Edward. 2012. 'Full transcript: Ed Miliband's speech on Englishness', *The Staggers*, 7 June 2012: www.newstatesman.com/blogs/politics/2012/06/full-transcript-ed-milibands-speech-englishness, accessed 13 January 2016.

Milward, David. 2017. 'Donald Trump returns Winston Churchill's bust to the Oval Office', *Telegraph*, www.telegraph.co.uk/news/2017/01/21/donald-trump-returns-winston-churchills-bust-oval-office/, accessed 8 June 2017.

Mordaunt, Penny. 2016. 'The spirit of Dunkirk will see us thrive outside the EU', *Telegraph*, 25 February 2016: www.telegraph.co.uk/news/newstopics/eureferendum/12173650/The-spirit-of-Dunkirk-will-see-us-thrive-outside-the-EU.html, accessed 26 February 2016.

Morton, Graeme. 1996. 'Scottish rights and centralisation in the mid-nineteenth century', *Nations and Nationalism*, 2, 2: 257–279.

Mudde, Cas. 2004. 'The populist Zeitgeist', *Government and Opposition*, 39, 3: 541–463.

Mudde, Cas. 2012. 'The comparative study of party-based Euroscepticism: the Sussex versus the North Carolina School', *East European Politics*, 28, 2: 193–202.

Mulholland, Greg. 2012. Early Day Motion 2992, 'English National Anthem', 23 April 2012.

Müller, Jan-Werner. 2017. *What Is Populism?* London: Penguin.

Mungai, Michael. 2012. 'Barack Obama and the sins of the father', *Huffington Post*, 25 September 2012: www.huffingtonpost.com/michael-mungai/barack-obama-and-the-sins_b_1911590.html, accessed 13 October 2016.

Murray, Douglas. 2016. 'Leaving the EU isn't an "unknown"; it's a return to the known', *Spectator*, 11 February 2016: blogs.spectator.co.uk/2016/02/leaving-the-eu-isnt-an-unknown-its-a-return-to-the-status-quo/, accessed 19 April 2016.

Murray, Philomena and Matera, Margherita. 2018. 'Australia's engagement with the European Union: partnership choices and critical friends', *Australian Journal of International Affairs*, 72, 3: 208–224.

Murray-Evans, Peg. 2018. 'Brexit and the Commonwealth: fantasy meets reality', in Patrick Diamond, Peter Nedergaard and Ben Rosamond (eds.), *The Routledge Handbook of the Politics of Brexit*. Abingdon: Routledge.

Mycock, Andrew. 2016. 'The party politics of the "New English Regionalism"', *Political Studies Review*, 16, 3: 388–399.

Mycock, Andrew and Hayton, Richard. 2014. 'The party politics of Englishness', *British Journal of Politics and International Relations*, 16, 2: 251–272.

Mycock, Andrew and Wellings, Ben. 2017. 'The Anglosphere: past, present and future', *Review of the British Academy*, 31, Autumn 2017, 42–45.

Nairn, Tom. 1993 [1988]. *The Enchanted Glass: Britain and Its Monarchy*. London: Vintage.

Nairn, Tom. 1998. *Faces of Nationalism: Janus Revisited*. London: Verso.

Nairn, Tom. 2001. *After Britain: New Labour and the Return of Scotland*. London: Granta Books.

Nairn, Tom. 2002. *Pariah. Misfortunes of the British Kingdom*. London: Verso.

Nairn, Tom. 2003 [1977]. *The Break-up of Britain: Crisis and Neo-nationalism*. Altona, VIC: Common Ground, 285.

National Archives (UK), CAB195/15, Cabinet Secretaries' notebooks, Suez Canal, 28 November 1956.

Nedergaard, Peter and Friis Eriksen, Maja. 2018. 'Brexit and British exceptionalism', in Patrick Diamond, Peter Nedergaard and Ben Rosamond (eds.), *The Routledge Handbook of the Politics of Brexit*. Abingdon: Routledge.

New Statesman, 2016. 'David Lammy calls for parliament to overturn the EU referendum result', *New Statesman* 25 June 2016: www.newstatesman.com/politics/elections/2016/06/david-lammy-calls-parliament-overturn-eu-referendum-result, accessed 3 July 2016.

Newman, Gerald. 1987. *The Rise of English Nationalism: a Cultural History, 1740–1830*. London: Weidenfeld & Nicolson.

Norwegian Nobel Committee. 2012. 'The Nobel Peace Prize for 2012 – Press Release', 12 October 2012: www.nobelprize.org/nobel_prizes/peace/laureates/2012/press.html, accessed 20 July 2018.

O'Toole, Fintan. 2016. 'Brexit is being driven by English nationalism. And it will end in self-rule', *Guardian*, 19 June 2016: www.theguardian.com/commentisfree/2016/jun/18/england-eu-referendum-brexit, accessed 22 June 2017.

Oppermann, Kai. 2018. 'Referendums: derailing integration', in Benjamin Leruth, Nicholas Startin and Simon Usherwood (eds.), *The Routledge Handbook of Euroscepticism*. Abingdon: Routledge.

Otago Daily Times. 2016. 'EU stronger with Britain – Key', 1 April 2016: www.odt.co.nz/news/politics/378192/eu-stronger-britain-key, accessed 3 April 2016.

Özkırımlı, Umut. 2005. *Contemporary Debates on Nationalism: A Critical Introduction*. Basingstoke: Palgrave.

Park, Alison; Bryson, Caroline and Curtice, John (eds.). 2014. British Social Attitudes: The 31st Report. London: NatCen Social Research.

Parris, Matthew. 2017. 'Empire 2.0 is a dangerous post-Brexit fantasy', *The Australian*, 25 March 2017: www.theaustralian.com.au/news/world/the-times/empire-20-is-a-dangerous-postbrexit-fantasy/news-story/c9b0b14c901285fd0c320cad388a6628, accessed 17 July 2017.

Parsons, Craig. 2003. *A Certain Idea of Europe*. Ithaca, NY: Cornell University Press.

Pennekamp. Matthew. 2016. 'Brexit's doomed alternative to the EU: an Anglosphere alliance is more romantic than practical', *The National Interest*, 11 April 2016: nationalinterest.org/feature/brexits-doomed-alternative-the-eu-15730, accessed 30 January 2018.

Pimlott, Ben. 1997. *The Queen: A Biography of Elizabeth II*. London: HarperCollins.

Press Association. 2017. 'Labour plans four new bank holidays – one for each UK patron saint', www.theguardian.com/politics/2017/apr/22/labour-plan-four-new-bank-holidays-for-each-uk-patron-saint, accessed 24 April 2017.

Priestland, David. 2013. 'Michael Gove's disdain for experts is typical of the laissez-faire ideologies', *Guardian*, 19 April 2013: www.theguardian.com/commentisfree/2013/apr/18/michael-gove-disdain-experts-typical-ideologues, accessed 14 November 2014.

Ravenhill, John and Huebner, Jefferson. 2019. 'The political economy of the Anglosphere: geography trumps history', in Ben Wellings and Andrew Mycock (eds.), *The Anglosphere: Continuity, Dissonance and Location, Proceedings of the British Academy*. Oxford: Oxford University Press.

Red Shift. 2015. *Looking for a New England: Ten Shifts Labour Needs to Make to Win a Majority in England*. www.redshiftlabour.co.uk, accessed 18 April 2018.

Redwood, John. 2005. *Superpower Struggles: Mighty America, Faltering Europe and Rising Asia*. Basingstoke: Palgrave.

Richards, Anthony. 2014. 'Sardonic humour: "The General" by Siegfried Sassoon', *Telegraph*, 3 May 2014: www.telegraph.co.uk/history/world-war-one/inside-first-world-war/part-nine/10803454/siegfried-sassoon-the-general.html, accessed 3 October 2018.

Ridley, Louise. 2016. 'EU Referendum: Michael Gove confirms he will support "out" vote after "difficult decision"', *Huffington Post*, 20 February 2016: www.huffingtonpost.co.uk/2016/02/20/michael-gove-eu-referendum_n_9281154.html, accessed 16 March 2016.

Riley-Smith, Ben. 2016. 'Theresa May to visit India in first trade mission since taking office', *Telegraph*, 16 October 2016: www.telegraph.co.uk/news/2016/10/15/theresa-may-to-visit-india-in-first-trade-mission-since-taking-o/, accessed 18 October 2016.

Robinson, Emily. 2016. 'Radical nostalgia, progressive patriotism and Labour's "English Problem"', *Political Studies Review*, 16, 3: 378–387.

Rose, Richard. 1965. *Politics in England*. London: Faber & Faber.

Ross, Tim. 2016. 'Boris Johnson interview: we can be the "heroes of Europe" by voting to leave', *Telegraph*, 14 May 2016: www.telegraph.co.uk/news/2016/05/14/boris-johnson-interview-we-can-be-the-heroes-of-europe-by-voting/, accessed 8 May 2018.

Ryan, Matthew. 2017. 'Using case studies in political science: reflections on Keith Dowding's *The Philosophy and Methods of Political Science*', *Political Studies Review*, 15, 2: 210–216.

Schama, Simon. 2003. *A History of Britain 3: 1776–2000, The Fate of Empire*, London: BBC Worldwide.

Schapps, Grant. 2016. 'Four things Britain must do now', *Huffington Post United Kingdom*, 30 June 2016: www.huffingtonpost.co.uk/grant-shapps/brexit-uk-economy_b_10747900.html, accessed 1 June 2017.

Schnapper, Pauline. 2015. 'The Labour Party and Europe from Brown to Miliband: back to the future?' *Journal of Common Market Studies*, 53, 1: 157–173.

Schrag Sternberg, Claudia. 2013. *The Struggle for EU Legitimacy: Public Contestation, 1950–2005*. Basingstoke: Palgrave Macmillan.

Schulz-Forberg, Hagen and Stråth, Bo. 2010. *The Political History of European Integration: The Hypocrisy of Democracy Through Market*. Abingdon: Oxford.

Scottish Government. 2014. 'FM: journey of commemoration starts today', news.gov.scot/news/fm-journey-of-commemoration-starts-today, accessed 10 April 2018.

Seeley, John Robert. 1971 [1883]. *The Expansion of England*. Chicago, IL: University of Chicago Press.

Sheridan, Greg. 2015. 'Tony Abbott loyal to a fault: why Philip was knighted', *The Australian*, 16 September 2015: www.theaustralian.com.au/opinion/columnists/greg-sheridan/tony-abbott-loyal-to-a-fault-why-philip-was-knighted/news-story/9ded7c1a05079ede801ed993825ef013, accessed 21 April 2017.

Shipman, Tim. 2017. 'Britain to host Commonwealth trade summit', *The Times*, 26 February 2017: www.thetimes.co.uk/edition/news/britain-to-host-trade-summit-625f0tptr, accessed 27 February 2017.

Skey, Michael. 2011. *National Belonging and Everyday Life: The Significance of Nationhood in an Uncertain World*. Basingstoke: Palgrave Macmillan.

Skey, Michael and Antonsich, Marco (eds.). 2017. *Everyday Nationhood: Theorizing Culture, Identity and Belonging After Banal Nationalism*. Basingstoke: Palgrave.

Slack, James. 2015. 'Voters tell Cameron he must curb welfare and end free movement to cut migration numbers and keep Britain in the EU', *Daily Mail Australia*: www.dailymail.co.uk/news/article-3361668/HERE-S-cut-migration-Mr-Cameron-Voters-demand-welfare-curbs-end-free-movement-PM-faces-pressure-make-negotiations-ambitious.html, accessed 17 December 2015.

Slack, James. 2016. 'Enemies of the people: fury over "out of touch" judges who have "declared war on democracy" by defying 17.4m Brexit voters and who could trigger a constitutional crisis', *Daily Mail*, 3 November 2016: www.dailymail.co.uk/news/article-3903436/Enemies-people-Fury-touch-judges-defied-17–4m-Brexit-voters-trigger-constitutional-crisis.html, accessed 17 July 2017.

Smith, Anthony. 2006. ' "Set in the Silver Sea": English national identity and European integration', *Nations and Nationalism*, 12, 3: 433–452.

Smith, Anthony. 2014. 'The rites of nations: elites, masses and the re-enactment of the "national past" ', in Rachel Tsang and Eric Taylor Woods (eds.), *The Cultural Politics of Nationalism and Nation Building: Ritual and Performance in the Forging of Nations*. Abingdon: Routledge.

Smyth, Jamie. 2016. 'Former Australian premier John Howard backs Britain to leave EU', *Financial Times*, 7 April 2016: www.ft.com/cms/s/0/0abe0092-fbee-11e5–8f41-df5bda8beb40.html, accessed 4 July 2016.

Sparrow, Andrew. 2017. 'General election 2017: MPs vote in favour of 8 June poll by margin of 509 – as it happened': www.theguardian.com/politics/live/2017/apr/19/election-2017-theresa-may-mps-early-vote-politics-live, accessed 20 April 2017.

Spiering, Menno. 2004. 'British Euroscepticism' in Robert Harmsen and Menno Spiering (eds.), *Euroscepticism: Party Politics, National Identity and European Integration*. Amsterdam: Rodopi, 127–149.

Stadler, Peter. 1999. 'War and peace', in *The Culture of European History in the 21st Century*. Berlin: Nicolai.

Strachan, Hew. 2010. 'The First World War as a global war', *First World War Studies*, 1, 1: 3–14.

Sumartojo, Shanti. 2013. *Trafalgar Square and the Narration of Britishness, 1900–2012*. Bern: Peter Lang.

Swan, Wayne. 2016. 'Why Australia wants Britain to stay in the EU', *Telegraph*, 12 February 2016:www.telegraph.co.uk/news/newstopics/eureferendum/12154630/Why-Australia-wants-Britain-to-stay-in-the-EU.html, accessed 17 April 2016.

Szczerbiak, Aleks and Taggart, Paul. 2008a (eds.), *Opposing Europe: The Comparative Party Politics of Euroscepticism*, Vol. 1: *Case Studies and Country Surveys*. Oxford: Oxford University Press.

Szczerbiak, Aleks and Taggart, Paul (eds.). 2008b. *Opposing Europe: The Comparative Party Politics of Euroscepticism*, Vol. 2: *Comparative and Theoretical Perspectives*. Oxford: Oxford University Press.

Szczerbiak, Aleks and Taggart, Paul. 2018. 'Contemporary research on Euroscepticism: the state of the art', in Ben Leruth, Nicholas Startin and Simon Usherwood (eds.), *The Routledge Handbook of Euroscepticism*. Abingdon: Routledge.

Tasker, John Paul. 2016. 'Justin Trudeau steps into "Brexit" debate, says Britain should stay in EU', *CBC News*, 19 May 2016: www.cbc.ca/news/politics/trudeau-brexit-eu-1.3590404, accessed 3 July 2016.

Taylor, Paul. 2008. *The End of European Integration: Anti-Europeanism Explained*. Abingdon: Routledge.

Telegraph. 2011. 'Gordon Brown presented £10,000 worth of gifts to Barack Obama', 19 January 2011: www.telegraph.co.uk/news/worldnews/barackobama/8269788/Gordon-Brown-presented-10000-worth-of-gifts-to-Barack-Obama.html, accessed 27 September 2018.

Tharoor, Shashi. 2017. *Inglorious Empire: What the British Did to India*. London: Penguin.

Thatcher, Margaret. 1982. 'Speech to the Conservative Party rally, Cheltenham July 1982', Margaret Thatcher Foundation, www.margaretthatcher.org/document/104989, accessed 1 October 2018.

Toombs, Robert. 2014. *The English and Their History*. London: Penguin.

Tooze, Adam. 2014. *The Deluge: The First World War and the Remaking of the World Order, 1916–31*. London: Penguin.

Tournier-Sol, Karine. 2015. 'Reworking the Euroscepticism and conservative traditions into a populist narrative: UKIP's winning formula?', *Journal of Common Market Studies*, 53, 1: 140–156.

Toye, Richard et al. 2013. 'History teaching, Disney and Michael Gove', 14 May 2013: www.thetimes.co.uk/article/history-teaching-disney-and-michael-gove-h6hckrgr3z2, accessed 23 April 2017.

Trenz, Hans-Jörg. 2018. 'Euroscepticism as EU polity contestation', in Benjamin Leruth, Nicholas Startin and Simon Usherwood (eds.), *The Routledge Handbook of Euroscepticism*. Abingdon: Routledge.

Trenz, Hans-Jörg and de Wilde, Pieter. 2012. 'Denouncing European integration: Euroscepticism as polity contestation', *European Journal of Social Theory*, 15, 4: 537–554.

UK Government. 2016. *The Best of Both Worlds: The United Kingdom's Special Status in a Reformed European Union*. London: HMSO.

UK Independence Party. 2015. *Believe in Britain. UKIP Manifesto 2015*: www.ukip.org/manifesto2015, accessed 1 December 2015.

US House of Representatives. 1975. 'Concurrent Resolution 458', 23 October 1975.

US Senate. 1991. 'Joint Resolution, 150: A joint resolution to designate June 15, 1991 as "Magna Carta Day"', 150, 1991.

US Senate. 1997. 'Resolution 155: A resolution designating April 6 of each year as "National Tartan Day" to recognise the outstanding achievements and contributions made by Scottish Americans to the United States.'

Usherwood, Simon and Startin, Nick. 2013. 'Euroscepticism as a persistent phenomenon', *Journal of Common Market Studies*, 51, 1: 1–16.

van Ingelgom, Virginie. 2014. *Integrating Indifference: A Comparative, Qualitative and Quantitative Approach to the Legitimacy of European Integration*. Colchester: ECPR Press.

Varsari, Antonio. 2010. 'From normative impetus to professionalization: origins and operations of research networks', in W. Kaiser and A. Varsori (eds.), *European Union History: Themes and Debates*. Basingstoke: Palgrave Macmillan.

Vasilopoulou, Sofia. 2013. 'Continuity and change in the study of Euroscepticism: plus ça change?' *Journal of Common Market Studies*, 51, 3: 153–168.

Vasilopoulou, Sofia. 2018. 'Theory, concepts and research design in the study of Euroscepticism', in Benjamin Leruth, Nicholas Startin and Simon Usherwood (eds.), *The Routledge Handbook of Euroscepticism*. Abingdon: Routledge.

Vines, Emma. 2015. 'A common appeal: Anglo-British nationalism and opposition to Europe, 1970–75', *Australian Journal of Politics and History*, 61, 4: 530–545.

Vitor Tossini, J. 2017. 'The five eyes: the intelligence alliance of the Anglosphere', *UK Defence Journal*, 14 November 2017: www.google.com.au/search?q=five+eys+intelligence+sharing+network&oq=five+eys+intelligence+sharing+network&aqs=chrome..69i57j0l5.6342j0j7&sourceid=chrome&ie=UTF-8, accessed 28 May 2018.

Vote Leave. 2016. 'Restoring public trust in immigration policy – a points-based non-discriminatory immigration system. Statement by Michael Gove, Boris Johnson, Priti Patel, and Gisela Stuart', 1 June 2016: www.voteleavetakecontrol.org/restoring_public_trust_in_immigration_policy_a_points_based_non_discriminatory_immigration_system, accessed 2 June 2016.

Vucetic, Srdjan. 2011. *The Anglosphere: A Genealogy of a Racialized Identity in International Relations*. Stanford, CA: Stanford University Press.

Vucetic, Srdjan. 2012. 'The search for liberal Anglo-America: from racial supremacy to multicultural politics', in Peter Katzenstein (ed.), *Anglo-America and its Discontents. Civilizational Identities Beyond East and West*. Abingdon: Routledge.

Ward, Paul. 2013. 'Michael Gove: look at the evidence, not the facts – a historian's response to the Education Secretary's attack on the Historical Association', 15 May 2013: http://blogs.hud.ac.uk/academics/blog/2013/05/15/michael-gove-look-at-the-evidence-not-the-facts-a-historian-s-riposte-to-the-Education-Secretary-s-attack-on-the-Historical-Association, accessed 23 January 2015.

Ward, Stuart. 2001. *Australia and the British Embrace: The Demise of the Imperial Ideal.* Melbourne, VIC: Melbourne University Press.

Warner, Jeremy. 2015. 'Is Europe to blame for Britain's shameful record on trade?', *Telegraph*, 12 November 2015: www.telegraph.co.uk/finance/economics/11992159/Is-Europe-to-blame-for-Britains-shameful-record-on-trade.html, accessed 14 November 2015.

Watt, Nicholas. 2013. 'David Cameron defends lack of apology for British massacre at Amritsar', *Guardian*, 20 February 2013: www.theguardian.com/politics/2013/feb/20/david-cameron-amritsar-massacre-india, accessed 26 April 2018.

Watt, Nicholas. 2016. 'Michael Gove and five other cabinet members break ranks with the PM over EU', *Guardian*, 21 February 2016: www.theguardian.com/politics/2016/feb/20/michael-gove-and-five-other-cabinet-members-break-ranks-with-pm-over-eu, accessed 23 February 2016.

Watts, Jo. 2017. 'Downing Street defends ex-Tory Leader Michael Howard's claim UK would go to war with Spain over Gibraltar', *Independent*, 3 April 2017: www.independent.co.uk/news/uk/politics/downing-street-michael-howard-gibraltar-war-spain-uk-territory-brexit-eu-theresa-may-a7664246.html, accessed 30 January 2018.

Wellings, Ben. 2002. 'Empire-nation: national and imperial discourses in England', *Nations and Nationalism*, 8, 1: 95–109.

Wellings, Ben. 2010. 'Losing the peace: Euroscepticism and the foundations of contemporary English nationalism', *Nations and Nationalism*, 16, 3: 488–505.

Wellings, Ben. 2012. *English Nationalism and Euroscepticism: Losing the Peace.* Bern: Peter Lang.

Wellings, Ben. 2013. 'Enoch Powell: the lonesome leader', *Humanities Research*, 2013, 1: 45–60.

Wellings, Ben. 2015. 'Beyond awkwardness: England, Europe and the end of integration', in Karine Tournier-Sol and Chris Gifford (eds.), *The UK Challenge to the European Union: The Persistence of Euroscepticism.* Basingstoke: Palgrave.

Wellings, Ben and Baxendale, Helen. 2015. 'Euroscepticism and the Anglosphere: traditions and dilemmas in contemporary English nationalism', *Journal of Common Market Studies*, 53, 1: 123–139.

Wellings, Ben and Kenny, Michael. 2018. 'Nairn's England and the progressive dilemma: reappraising Tom Nairn on English nationalism', *Nations and Nationalism*. https://doi.org/10.1111/nana.12479.

Wellings, Ben and Power, Ben. 2016. 'Euro-myth: nationalism, war and the legitimacy of the European Union', *National Identities*, 18, 2: 157–177.

Wellings, Ben and Vines, Emma. 2016. 'Populism and sovereignty: the *EU Act* and the in-out referendum', *Parliamentary Affairs*, 69, 2: 309–326.

Wellings, Ben; Graves, Matthew and Sumartojo, Shanti. 2018. 'Commemorating race and empire in the First World War centenary', in Ben Wellings and Shanti Sumartojo (eds.),

Commemorating Race and Empire in the First World War Centenary. Liverpool and Aix-en-Provence: Liverpool University Press/Presse Universitaire de Provence.

Winter, Jay. 2008. 'On regarding the pain of others', in *The Collections of the Historial of the Great War*. Paris: Somogy, 34.

Winter, Jay and Sivan, Emmanuel. 1999. *War and Remembrance in the Twentieth Century*. Cambridge: Cambridge University Press.

Withers, Matt. 2018a. ' "Repulsive" Farage compares Brexit transition period to Vichy France', *The New European*, 7 February 2018: www.theneweuropean.co.uk/top-stories/nigel-farage-vichy-france-1–5385819, accessed 9 May 2018.

Withers, Matt. 2018b. 'Britain leaving the European customs union to strike free trade deals with countries outside the EU is "giving up a three-course meal for the promise of a packet of crisps", a top ex-civil servant has said', *The New European*, 27 February 2018: www.theneweuropean.co.uk/top-stories/brexit-britain-bag-crisps-1–5410978, accessed 7 May 2018.

Withnall, A. 2016. 'EU referendum: Nigel Farage's 4am victory speech – text in full', *Independent*, 24 June 2016: www.independent.co.uk/news/uk/politics/eu-referendum-nigel-farage-4am-victory-speech-the-text-in-full-a7099156.html, accessed 3 July 2017.

Woolfe, Steven. 2016. 'Reaching out: the referendum challenge'. Speech given at British Futures, 26 January 2016: www.britishfuture.org/articles/reaching-out-eu-referendum/, accessed 27 January 2016.

Wouters, Nico and Bevernage, Berber (eds.). 2018. *The Palgrave Handbook of State-sponsored History since 1945*. Basingstoke: Palgrave.

Wright, Oliver. 2016. 'Ken Livingston suspended by Labour as Party's row over anti-Semitism grows', *Independent*, 28 April 2016: www.independent.co.uk/news/uk/politics/ken-livingstone-suspended-labour-party-hitler-supported-zionism-antisemitism-comments-a7005121.html, accessed 9 April 2018.

Wyn Jones, Richard; Lodge, Guy; Henderson, Ailsa and Wincott, Daniel. 2012. *The Dog that Finally Barked: England as an Emerging Political Community*. London: Institute for Public Policy Research.

Wyn Jones, Richard; Lodge, Guy; Jeffery, Charlie; Gottfried, G.; Scully, Roger and Henderson, Ailsa. 2013. *England and Its Two Unions: Anatomy of a Nation and its Discontents*. London: Institute for Public Policy Research.

YouGov. 2011. 'British history: pride or shame?': cdn.yougov.com/cumulus_uploads/document/qgwqyzen5q/YG-Archives-BritainsHistory-061211.pdf, accessed 2 July 2018.

YouGov. 2014. 'The British Empire is "something to be proud of"': yougov.co.uk/news/2014/07/26/britain-proud-its-empire/, accessed 12 July 2018.

YouGov. 2016. 'Which countries should we focus on for our trade deals?' 17 September 2016: yougov.co.uk/news/2016/09/17/which-countries-should-uk-prioritise-post-brexit-t/, accessed 17 July 2018.

YouGov. 2018. 'YouGov-LBC Survey Results', d25d2506sfb94s.cloudfront.net/cumulus_uploads/document/bhy62x09m0/LBC_Results_180322_w.pdf, accessed 16 July 2018.

Index